GCSE Kit: English

Chris Webster

Hodder & Stoughton
A MEMBER OF THE HODDER HEADLINE GROUP

Acknowlewdgements

The author and publishers would like to thank the following for:

Copyright text:
p. 119 © Cevil Lee Han Tiong, 'Geomany.Net:Chinese Astrology and Horoscope' (1996) www.lovesigns.net; pp. 126–7 © Angela Levin, *Daily Mail*, 12 July 2002; pp. 128–9 © *Daily Express*; pp. 145–6 © *Chicago Sun-Times Inc.*; pp. 156–7 © Tim Dirks; p. 160 'Teenager In Love' by Doc Pomus and Mort Shuman © 1962 by Rumbalero Music Inc. All rights administered by Unichappell Music, Inc. All Rights Reserved. Lyric reproduced by kind permission of Carlin Music Corp., London NW1 8BD; p. 160 'Will You Love Me Tomorrow' Words and Music by Gerry Goffin and Carole King © 1960 Screen Gems-EMI Music Inc, USA. Screen Gems-EMI Music Ltd, London WC2H 0QY. Reproduced by permission of International Music Publications Ltd. All Rights reserved; p. 161 'He's a Rebel' © Words and Music by Gene Pitney © 1962 (renewed) January Music Corp, USA. Warner/Chappell Music Ltd, London W6 8BS. Reproduced by permission of International Music Publications Ltd. All Rights Reserved; p. 162 'Leader of the Pack' Words and Music by George Morton, Ellie Greenwich and Jeff Barry © 1964 Tender Tunes Music Co Inc, USA. EMI Music Publishing Ltd, London WC2H 0QY. Reproduced by permission of International Music Publications Ltd. All Rights Reserved; pp. 170–1 © Helen Ingham; pp. 190–1 © *Daily Mirror*, 12 July 2002; pp. 192–3 © Jason Bennetto, *Independent*, 12 July 2002.

Copyright photographs:
p. 126 © Tim Graham/CORBIS; p. 127 © Murray Saunders; pp. 129, 146 and 156 © The Ronald Grant Archive; p. 160 © Bettmann/CORBIS; p. 172 © Panzani; p. 174 © Alfa Romeo GB; p. 175 © BMW (GB); p. 176 © SEAT UK; p. 177 www.mgmagnette.com; p. 190 © Liverpool Echo; p. 191 © Spindrift; p. 193 © Amit Lennon.

Copyright artwork:
All artwork © Pat Murray, except: p. 78 © Philip Page and p. 178 © Mark Turner (Beehive Illustrations).

Every effort has been made to trace copyright holders of material reproduced in this book. Any rights not acknowledged here will be acknowleged in subsequent printings if notice is given to the publisher.

Orders: please contact Bookpoint Ltd, 130 Milton Park, Abingdon, Oxon OX14 4SB. Telephone: (44) 01235 827720. Fax: (44) 01235 400454. Lines are open from 9.00 am to 6.00 pm, Monday to Saturday, with a 24-hour message answering service. You can also order through our website: www.hodderheadline.co.uk

British Library Cataloguing in Publication Data
A catalogue record for this title is available from the British Library

ISBN 0 340 85937 7

First Published 2003
Impression number   10 9 8 7 6 5 4 3 2 1
Year   2009 2008 2007 2006 2005 2004 2003

Copyright © 2003 Chris Webster

Cover image by Mark Preston (The Organisation).
Typeset by Fakenham Photosetting, Fakenham, Norfolk.
Printed in Great Britain for Hodder & Stoughton Educational, a division of Hodder Headline, 338 Euston Road, London NW1 3BH by Hobbs the Printers, Totton, Hampshire.

CONTENTS

INTRODUCTION

The new GCSE specifications for English were greeted with relief by some – because there was minimal change, and disappointment by others – because an opportunity to develop National Literacy Strategy strategies at GCSE level was missed. In fact, they probably offer the best of both worlds, carrying over the good practice from the previous syllabuses, yet allowing the freedom for teachers to introduce National Literacy Strategy-style teaching methods to the extent that seems appropriate. Whatever approach an English department uses, it would be a pity to miss the opportunity provided by the new specifications to review departmental practices and teaching methods to address developments such as:

■ the rapid development of ICT
■ the increasing importance of media
■ the role of English in the wider curriculum
■ the National Literacy Strategy in Key Stage 3.

This book offers a complete course for GCSE English (with the exception of work related to the anthologies) and at the same time tries to address the developments listed above. By far the most important of these developments is the National Literacy Strategy. Even though the new specifications have more in common with the old syllabuses than the National Literacy Strategy Framework, the students themselves will have been taught English through the National Literacy Strategy, many of them since primary school. Some of the key features of National Literacy Strategy methodology are:

A Specific Lesson Structure

Because of the broad scope of GCSE courses, particularly the wide range of set texts, it has not been possible to provide detailed lesson plans for each unit like those in the *Key Stage 3 English Kits*. Lessons in the Key Stage 3 English kits were based on the National Literacy Strategy model, and this can be equally effective at GCSE. The basic lesson structure is as follows:

■ *Starter Activity* – a short introductory whole-class activity of 10 to 15 minutes which focuses on one of the skills to be used later in the lesson. For example, a viewing of *Metropolis* could begin with a session based on Toolkit Resource 16, 'Film Techniques'.
■ *Introduction* – this is generally a teacher-led session; for example, giving instructions for the individual or group work tasks which follow.
■ *Development* – this is when students work on a range of tasks as individuals or in groups. For example, after a viewing of *Metropolis*, making notes on Resource 83, 'Christian References'.
■ *Plenary* – this is a whole-class session in which the main aim of the lesson is reinforced by students discussing and reporting back and the teacher summing up the main points of the lesson.

It would be unrealistic to apply this model to every lesson. For example, it would be impossible in a typical 70-minute lesson to do all the above on *Metropolis* and still have time to see a worthwhile portion of the film. I would therefore omit the development in lessons when I had a starter activity, and in a subsequent lesson omit the starter activity and spend the time on development. The only session I would always wish to include would be the plenary.

Balanced Emphasis on Word, Sentence and Text-Level Skills

With the huge emphasis on texts at GCSE, it is impossible to do justice to that balance in this book. However, the Toolkit Resources address some of the basic skills required and these can be used as starter activities where appropriate.

Guided Writing

This technique can be used with groups of pupils (usually less able) or even the whole class. Each section of a writing frame, template or similar resource is discussed with the group, a section at a time, followed by writing. This gives students support as they write, rather than advice before and after a long period of writing.

Whole-Class, Group and Individual Work

Balance between these is an important principle of National Literacy Strategy methodology. One way to organise groups is to divide the class into 'home' groups of four, as this allows easy subdivision for pair work. Students can reform into different groups for different purposes, as appropriate, e.g. 'jigsaw groups'. Groups of different levels of ability should use the resources in different ways, as follows:

- *Groups of higher-tier students*
  These students use the resources as a guide only and sometimes work without them, use alternative higher-tier resources (where provided) and always attempt higher-tier questions and tasks where indicated.
- *Groups of 'in-between' students (i.e. could be foundation or higher tier depending how they develop)*
  These students use the resources as explained in the teacher's notes. This usually entails following the prompts closely or making notes on the resource sheets before writing a final draft. These students should sometimes attempt foundation-tier tasks and sometimes higher-tier tasks as seems appropriate to the teacher.
- *Groups of foundation-tier students*
  These students should make particularly thorough use of Toolkit Resources, and will sometimes find it helpful to write their responses directly into the resource sheet boxes (enlarge sheets to A3 to ensure there is sufficient space). They will sometimes need to be supported by guided writing and should always do foundation-tier tasks unless a clear improvement is noted.

Writing Frames and Templates

Many of the resources in the book are writing frames or templates. The principle behind them is that they provide 'props' to support learning. The extent to which they are used and how they are used will depend on the ability of the students, but whatever their ability the idea is that the props should be withdrawn as they are internalised, so that – by the end of the course – the students do not need, for example, Toolkit Resource 11, 'Literary Essay Template', because the template is in their heads – along with a lot of experience of adapting the template for different purposes.

Linked website

This book has a linked website, which may be found at www.english-kit-hodder.co.uk. The website contains information on all of the GCSE Kits.

How to use this book

The following icons are used throughout the three books in the GCSE Kit series:

When you see this ...	It represents ...
	The opportunity to use a Toolkit Resource from either the English 'Toolkit' unit, or the English Literature 'Toolkit' unit, with specific activities in other units.
	The section of each unit aimed towards the teacher. Teachers are provided with helpful Unit Plans mapping the assessment objectives to the specific resources within the units, supportive introductory text and explanatory text indicating the many ways in which each resource can be used in practice.
	The resource pages within each unit that can be photocopied for use within the classroom.
	Resources that provide opportunities for students to develop their reading skills.
	Resources that provide opportunities for students to develop their writing skills.
	Resources that provide opportunities for students to develop their speaking skills.
	Resources that provide opportunities for students to develop their listening skills.
	Resources that link with the *GCSE Kit: English Literature Pre-1914* and *GCSE Kit: English Literature Post-1914*, or which provide English Literature Examination-style questions.
	Resources that require the use of a shared text.
	Resources that provide suggestions for general assignments that respond to the topic of the unit from a wider range of perspectives. The assignments are particularly suited to coursework, but can also be used as supporting exercises for an examination text.
	Resources that require use of the media of film or video.
	Links to interesting websites that extend learning and promote independent study.
	The specific genre being studied in each unit, in this case: poetry. This is particularly relevant to *GCSE Kit: English Literature Pre-1914* and *GCSE Kit: English Literature Post-1914*.
	The specific genre being studied in each unit, in this case: prose. This is particularly relevant to *GCSE Kit: English Literature Pre-1914* and *GCSE Kit: English Literature Post-1914*.
	The specific genre being studied in each unit, in this case: drama. This is particularly relevant to *GCSE Kit: English Literature Pre-1914* and *GCSE Kit: English Literature Post-1914*.

BOARD SUMMARIES

The table below gives a summary of the requirements of the four main examination boards. Its main purpose is to show how the resources in this book can be used to meet the different specifications. Please note that this table is intended for comparison purposes only. It is based on the latest information available at the time of going to press, but *any planning decisions should be based on the latest version of the boards' full specifications.*

Speaking and listening

To include individual contribution; group discussion and interaction; drama-focused activity.

RANGE	DRAMA-FOCUSED ACTIVITY	GROUP DISCUSSION AND INTERACTION	INDIVIDUAL EXTENDED CONTRIBUTION
ALL BOARDS	Coursework	Coursework	Coursework

Reading

This must cover prose, poetry and drama.

RANGE	AQA A	AQA B	EDEXCEL A	EDEXCEL B	OCR	WJEC
SHAKE-SPEARE	Coursework*	Coursework *	Paper 1 Coursework*	Paper 1 Coursework*	Unit 3 (exam) or 4 (coursework)	Coursework*
LITERARY HERITAGE	Coursework* (prose study pre- or post-1914)	Coursework * (prose study)	Paper 2F/4H (Modern poetry from anthology)	Paper 2F/4H (Modern poetry from anthology)	Unit 3 (exam) or 4 (coursework) poetry pre- or post-1914	'Welsh relevance' (in Wales)
DIFFERENT CULTURES AND TRADITIONS	Paper 2 Section A (poetry from anthology)	Paper 2 Section A (unseen poetry)	Paper 1 Coursework	Paper 2F/4H (pre-released material)	Unit 2	Coursework*
NON-FICTION TEXTS	Paper 1 (unseen)	Paper 1A (unseen non-fiction text)	Paper 2F/4H (anthology)	Paper 3F/5H (unprepared)	Unit 1	Paper 2 Section A
MEDIA TEXTS	Paper 1 (unseen) and coursework	Paper 1A (pre-released news items)	Paper 3F 5H (unprepared)	Paper 1 Coursework	Unit 1	Paper 2 Section A

* 'Crossover' unit

Writing

RANGE	AQA A	AQA B	EDEXCEL A	EDEXCEL B	OCR	WJEC
EXPLORE, IMAGINE, ENTERTAIN	Coursework (original writing)	Coursework (personal writing)	Paper 1 Coursework (personal and imaginative writing)	Paper 1 Coursework (personal and imaginative writing)	Unit 3 (exam) or 4 (coursework)	Paper 1 Section B and coursework
INFORM, EXPLAIN, DESCRIBE	Paper 2 Section B	Coursework (personal writing)	Paper 2F/4H	Paper 2F/4H	Unit 1	Paper 1 Section B
ARGUE, PERSUADE, ADVISE	Paper 1 Section B	Paper 1 Section B	Paper 3F/5H	Paper 3F/5H	Unit 2	Paper 2 Section A and coursework
ANALYSE, REVIEW, COMMENT	Coursework (on media text)	Paper 2 Section B	Paper 3F/5H	Paper 3F/5H	Unit 2	Paper 2 Section A

MAPPING GRID

UNIT TITLE	RANGE (units 2–10 based on reading range)	TEXT (chosen to extend the range of set texts covered by the *GCSE Kits*)	BOARD (be sure to check latest version of specifications)
1. Toolkit	–	–	all
2. *Blood Brothers*	Speaking and listening – drama-focused activity	*Blood Brothers*	all boards for coursework, WJEC literature set text
3. The Talk Project Part 1: For and Against Part 2: Towncester Part 3: Matrices	Speaking and Listening – Group discussion and interaction Individual extended contribution	n/a	all boards for coursework
4. *The Merchant of Venice*	Work based on a play by Shakespeare	*The Merchant of Venice*	all boards/crossover/ AQA B, OCR, WJEC literature set text
5. *Silas Marner*	Literary heritage	*Silas Marner*	WJEC literature set text
6. A Choice of Poets	Literary heritage	*A Choice of Poets*: Blake, Wordsworth, Robert Frost, R. S. Thomas	OCR/WJEC/OCR literature set text
7. *Chinese Cinderella*	Response to a text from another culture or tradition	*Chinese Cinderella*	Edexcel recommended coursework text and set text
8. The Astrology Project	Non-fiction texts	n/a	all boards for coursework
9. *Metropolis*	Media texts	n/a	Edexcel B and all boards for coursework
10. Teenage Rebellion Part 1: *Rebel Without a Cause* Part 2: Songs of the Sixties	Media texts	n/a	Edexcel B and all boards for coursework
11. Advertisements	Media texts	n/a	Edexcel A preparation for unseen media text and all boards for coursework
12. Newspaper articles	Media texts	n/a	AQA A and B coursework and preparation for pre-released texts/Edexcel B/ OCR/WJEC and all boards for coursework

DISCLAIMER: this table is intended for initial planning purposes only. It is based on the latest information available at the time of going to press, but any final plans should be based on the latest version of the boards' full specifications.

UNIT 1: *TOOLKIT*

Introduction

This bank of Toolkit Resources is intended partly as revision of key skills that have been taught in Key Stage 2 and Key Stage 3 and partly as a support for specific activities required in the units. It will be particularly helpful to foundation-tier students, but higher-tier students will also benefit from it. It is recommended that the whole set is photocopied and placed at the front of students' English folders for ease of reference. At an early stage in the GCSE course each one should be made the focus of a short introductory session of 10–15 minutes. This will familiarise students with the resources as well as providing revision of key skills. After this, they should be used on an individual basis as the need arises, or with specific activities in the units as indicated by the Toolkit logo.

Notes on the Resources

1. WORD CLASSES

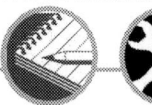

AIM: use a range of sentence structures effectively with accurate punctuation and spelling (AO3iii)

This list differs slightly from the traditional list of parts of speech as articles and interjections have been left out and replaced with connectives as this term is frequently used in the National Literacy Strategy Frameworks, and they are so important in the writing of discursive essays.

This resource is meant as a refresher, as it would be impossible to do justice to eight word classes on one page. All of the word classes will have been covered in previous years by students who have grown up with the National Literacy Strategy. This resource reminds students of the definition of each word class and, in column two, gives them advice about how it can be used to improve their writing.

Supplementary to this resource are the following resource sheets:

2. Adverb Bank
3. Words and Phrases for Argument.

(Answer to question about the ADJECTIVE: the poet chose the adjective *paraplegic*. This is very effective because it describes the way a mosquito's legs dangle as though nerveless.)

2. ADVERB BANK

AIM: use a range of sentence structures effectively with accurate punctuation and spelling (AO3iii)

This resource provides a bank of adverbs to help students describe what people do and what people say. Of course, it can only be a starting point as there are many thousands more adverbs. However, the important thing is for students to get the idea of describing things with more detail and precision.

3. WORDS AND PHRASES FOR ARGUMENT

AIM: use a range of sentence structures effectively with accurate punctuation and spelling (AO3iii)

Written English is different to spoken English as a wider vocabulary and more sophisticated sentence structure takes the place of intonation and gesture. However, the English of formal argument, particularly written argument is even further away from everyday English. This resource is intended to help to bridge the gap. The idea is that students will have it beside them while they write their arguments. It can also be used later during the redrafting process.

4. SPELLING HELPER

AIM: use a range of sentence structures effectively with accurate punctuation and spelling (AO3iii)

Students who have followed the National Literacy Strategy will have benefited from an extended programme of spelling development covering everything from spelling rules to prefixes, roots and suffixes. By the time students start GCSE, it is too late to go over all this again in detail, but all is not lost! This resource can be used as a reminder of the most important spelling skills. The most important being the advice to keep a personal spelling list and keep working at it using Look, Cover, Write, Check (students look carefully at a word, cover it up, try to spell it, then check it). Also important is to encourage students to believe that:

- good spelling really is important.
- they will improve (however slowly) if they keep trying.

5. 80 COMMONLY MISSPELLED WORDS

AIM: use a range of sentence structures effectively with accurate punctuation and spelling (AO3iii)

Students may find it encouraging to be told that most of the words on this resource are regularly misspelled, not just by students, but by adults, and – yes – even by teachers! The list can be used for whole-class or group spelling tests, or used individually as follows.

- Enlarge the list to A3 size to allow space for writing.
- LOOK at a word carefully.
- COVER the word by folding the word list back.
- WRITE the word in the blank column.
- Fold back the page and CHECK the word.

Whichever method is used, it is important that all wrongly spelled words should be transferred to students' personal word lists and learned.

6. PUNCTUATION HELPER

AIM: use a range of sentence structures effectively with accurate punctuation and spelling (AO3iii)

This resource is a reminder of the main types of punctuation. Generally, there has been a trend towards the simplification of punctuation, so two pieces of good advice would be: *keep it simple*, and *if in doubt, leave it out*.

The greatest demand on students' punctuation skills is undoubtedly the writing of dialogue, in which a wide range of punctuation comes thick and fast. However, there are clear and relatively simple rules for the punctuation of dialogue (using commas to mark clauses is conceptually more difficult), so there is no excuse for getting it wrong. If necessary, give students lots of practice.

7. PARAGRAPH STRUCTURE

AIM: organise ideas into sentences, paragraphs and whole texts using a variety of linguistic and structural features (AO3ii)

Paragraphing is another skill in which students can be surprisingly careless. The main thing, as with spelling, seems to be convincing them that it really matters. After that, it is simply a matter of practice.

The first box deals with layout. It is all obvious stuff, but some students, even at GCSE level, still have problems with it. There is nothing conceptually difficult here at all, so anything less than perfect layout should simply not be accepted.

The second box deals with organisation. This is much more difficult than layout. However, a well-constructed plan will automatically translate into good paragraphing, particularly in non-fiction. Throughout the *GCSE Kit*, there are many paragraph plans to help students with this aspect of writing essays. When students have to decide on their own paragraph divisions, they can be helped by a simple rule of thumb – three to four paragraphs per A4 page is about average. In particular, they should avoid the two extremes: if they write a whole A4 page without starting a new paragraph, it is time to check carefully that this is really intended; and if they have a large number of paragraphs, check that they are not making the opposite mistake of making every sentence a paragraph.

The final box in column two deals with the setting out of dialogue. *The rule is: start a new indented line for every change of speaker.* Students who are having difficulty with this will learn most from studying and emulating good models.

8. DISCURSIVE ESSAY TEMPLATE 1

AIM: organise ideas into sentences, paragraphs and whole texts using a variety of linguistic and structural features (AO3ii)

Template 1 is for a discursive essay that attempts to persuade by presenting only one side of an argument. This template can be used to help weaker students plan their essays. It is based on the tried-and-tested five-paragraph plan: an introduction, three arguments and a conclusion. This template includes a sample essay with examples of two different types of introduction and different ways of writing arguments. Of course, there is no reason why the middle section should be restricted to just three arguments, though it is better to have three well-reasoned points than several paragraphs of waffle! Students may find it helpful to use Resource 3, 'Words and Phrases for Argument', Resource 7, 'Paragraph Structure', and Resource 10, 'Types of Argument', alongside this essay.

9. DISCURSIVE ESSAY TEMPLATE 2

AIM: organise ideas into sentences, paragraphs and whole texts using a variety of linguistic and structural features (AO3ii)

Template 2 is a variant of the above that examines both sides of an issue before coming to a conclusion. The template can be used to help weaker students plan their essays. Students should note that the sample essay is necessarily rather short to enable the text to fit the boxes. They should aim for a fuller development of each paragraph. Students may find it helpful to use Resource 3, 'Words and Phrases for Argument', Resource 7, 'Paragraph Structure', and Resource 10, 'Types of Argument', alongside this essay.

10. TYPES OF ARGUMENT

AIM: follow an argument, identifying implications and recognising inconsistencies (AO2iii)

Students can use column two of the resource to find arguments for discursive essays and debate speeches. Column three can be used by the seconding speaker in a debate to find weakness in a speech and plan a quick response to it. It can also be used to evaluate written argument.

11. LITERARY ESSAY TEMPLATE

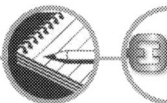

AIM: organise ideas into sentences, paragraphs and whole texts using a variety of linguistic and structural features (AO3ii)

Literary essays vary enormously in format depending on the type of question. However, students can learn a great deal from this basic template – in particular, that a literary essay is a series of points supported by evidence and how to use quotations and references to specific events as evidence. Students may find it helpful to use Resource 3, 'Words and Phrases for Argument', and Resource 7 'Paragraph Structure', alongside this essay.

12. STORY PLANNER

AIM: organise ideas into sentences, paragraphs and whole texts using a variety of linguistic and structural features (AO3ii)

Students should approach this planner with some idea about the story they wish to write. The planner can then be used to refine the idea. Many of the General Assignments provide ideas for stories. Students can also find ideas in Resource 13, 'Story Titles Matrix'.

The beginning of a story is very important because the writer must catch the readers' attention. The first section of the resource sheet suggests different ways of making a beginning interesting, depending on the type of story.

The middle is where the story develops. Students should read about each of the essential story ingredients and think about how their own story idea measures up. Except for a few budding Thomas Hardys, most students will find some weakness in their story idea. For example, the story may lack conflict. They can then go back to their draft and add another character or situation that creates conflict.

Endings are difficult. Students should note the definition in the box: 'the main character's problems are solved and the reader's curiosity is satisfied'. That is all that is needed for most endings. If this is done well, it is enough. However, students might like to try a more dramatic ending, such as a proverb, a twist, anticlimax or a circular ending (bringing the reader back to the beginning).

13. STORY TITLES MATRIX

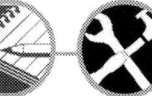

AIM: communicate clearly and imaginatively, using and adapting forms for different readers and purposes (AO3i)

This matrix contains a collection of 36 titles for stories. The matrix can be used simply as a list of titles, or in the form of a game. For this, a number of dice will be needed (or folded papers numbered 1–6).

Students work in groups of 3 to 5. They take it in turn to roll a dice twice (or, in the absence of dice, select folded papers numbered 1–6). The two numbers refer to each axis of the matrix and will randomly select a topic. The student has to improvise a story synopsis for the title. If this is done without undue hestitation and without 'drying up', the student wins a point. At the end of the game, the student with the most points is the winner.

Students can refer back to the matrix whenever they are seeking a story title. Their recollection of the game will give them some ideas for which title to choose, and how to approach it.

The bottom half of the resource contains an additional list of story ideas.

14. BOOK REVIEW

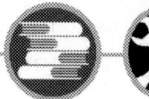

AIM: communicate clearly and imaginatively, using and adapting forms for different readers and purposes (AO3i)

This is intended to be used as a response to wider reading. It would be a good idea to require at least two of these (or similar assignments, e.g. a film review) per year. The format is deliberately literary in approach. Students are asked to focus on plot, characters and themes, and to use quotations from the text as evidence.

15. FILM REVIEW

AIM: communicate clearly and imaginatively, using and adapting forms for different readers and purposes (AO3i)

Film reviews can be written in many formats and it is a good idea for students to read some examples of different kinds (many are available on the Internet – just type in the title of a film followed by 'review'). The following format has been designed to help students think about the production and technical processes in film making, as well as the all-important evaluation.

To complete Section 4, students will need to learn the following terms (see Toolkit Resource 16): long shot, mid-shot, close-up, high angle, mid-angle, low angle, pan, tilt, zoom, cut, fade, wipe. Note that terms vary slightly in different scripts, e.g. 'mid-shot' is sometimes called 'medium shot', 'close-up' 'tight shot', etc. There are many more terms too numerous to list here.

Finally – just for fun, students could post their reviews on a website. These can be set up for free and posted with search engines for free. Just type 'free web space' into any search engine.

16. FILM TECHNIQUES

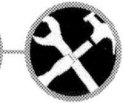

AIM: communicate clearly and imaginatively, using and adapting forms for different readers and purposes (AO3i)

The camera shots and editing techniques listed on this resource are a sort of 'grammar' of film that has built up throughout the twentieth century. As with written grammar, good usage makes the narrative seamless, bad usage draws attention to itself as being clumsy.

Give out the resource, go through it quickly, then ask students to reread it while you set up a video. This should be either a short extract of a film you are studying, or a TV advertisement. Play the extract and ask students to look for and discuss examples of camera shots and editing techniques. The extract could be repeated while students record the time between edits – they will be surprised how short it is.

This resource should be referred to whenever students are writing about a film.

17. FORMS OF WRITING

AIM: communicate clearly and imaginatively, using and adapting forms for different readers and purposes (AO3i)

Within the limited space of this book, only a few important forms can be covered in detail: discursive essay, literary essay, story, book review, film review. This resource includes brief information about a range of forms. It is important that students are familiar with writing in a range of forms, not least because these forms are often specified in directed writing tasks in GCSE examinations. From an examination point of view, students should be taught to do the following:

- read the task carefully
- take particular note of the form

- take note of the purpose and audience
- take note of any models (e.g. a text in an earlier part of the paper).

Throughout the two-year course, students should be given several opportunities to write in each of the forms on the resource sheet. The General Assigments at the end of each unit provide many appropriate tasks, and additional tasks can be generated from the three matrices in Unit 3.

18. FACT AND OPINION

AIM: distinguish between fact and opinion and evaluate how information is presented (AO2ii)

Although the title of this resource is 'Fact and Opinion', it goes one step further to include a third category: reasoned judgement. Definitions are given on the resource sheet. After reading through the resource sheet, students should write their own examples in the box at the bottom of the page and then discuss them.

After the familiarisation process described above, students use this resource to help them identify fact, opinion and reasoned judgement in articles and speeches they are studying.

19. REFERENCE SKILLS

AIM: select material appropriate to their purpose, collate material from different sources, and make cross-references (AO2iv)

The skills covered on this resource sheet are selection, summary, collation and cross-referencing. These skills can be dealt with on separate occasions as the need for the skill arises. However, Unit 8, 'The Astrology Project', has been specifically written to develop these skills.

Selection

This box gives a brief summary of the key reference and research skills that students should have developed in Key Stage 2 and Key Stage 3. It is important to continue to develop them, and this can be done by ensuring that many of the research tasks that appear throughout the book (usually as pre-reading to a literary text) require students to retrieve information from a range of sources. Most students will be comfortable with CD-ROMs and the Internet, but still need to be able to find their way around a library. Make sure that the English section of the library is stocked with appropriate reference works, and ensure that students refer to them.

Summary

A great deal of academic and professional work depends on summary in one form or another, yet summaries are one of the least popular tasks – probably because they are intellectually demanding but not very creative. The box gives a brief explanation of the process of summary and advice about how to cope with different types of summary. Throughout the book there are ample opportunities to use summary skills. For example, many introductory paragraphs in essay templates require a brief summary of the plot and main characters.

Collation

This is an important research and professional skill. At GCSE level it is a skill which is required in several subjects, e.g. history. The box gives a brief explanation and provides a recommended process which will help students to find relevant information, cope with duplication of information, contradictory information, etc.

Cross-referencing

Once again, this is a skill that is more likely to be required in other subject areas than in English, though Unit 8, 'The Astrology Project', has been specifically written to involve students in cross-referencing different texts. The box gives a brief explanation and provides notes about conventions used to refer to other texts.

20. DRAMA TECHNIQUES

AIM: adopt roles and communicate with audiences using a range of techniques (A01iii)

This resource contains a selection from the many drama techniques which have been developed in recent years for exploration and improvisation. They have been set out on cards so that students can use them as a game. To do this, the pack is shuffled and a card dealt out to each student in the group. Each student then has to plan and direct the drama activity on the card in a way that relates to the text being studied. For example, if students were studying *Blood Brothers*, a group of four students might draw the following tasks (all resources referred to below can be found in Unit 2):

- *Hot-seating* – the students might decide to explore Mickey's thoughts and feelings in the part of the play represented by card D (see Resource 21, 'Synopsis').
- *Sociogram* – the student might decide to explore how the different characters relate to one of the characters chosen from the character cards (see Resource 22, 'Main Characters').
- *Improvisation* – the student might decide to explore one of the themes chosen from the theme cards (see Resource 24, 'Themes').
- *Mime* – the student might decide to act out one of the arguments without words.

1. WORD CLASSES

DEFINITION	WHAT TO LOOK OUT FOR
A NOUN is the name of a person, place or thing, e.g. *carpet, clergyman, flying saucer, monkey*, etc. PROPER NOUNS are the names of specific things, e.g. people and places, and take capital letters: *Amanda, Fort Lauderdale, Vauxhall Corsa.*	Don't just write the first noun that comes into your head – there may be a more accurate *synonym*, e.g. instead of ship, *barque, galley, hydrofoil, liner, longship,* etc. might be a more appropriate noun. Use a thesaurus for more ideas.
A PRONOUN can replace a noun. There are several types of pronouns: Personal pronouns: *I, you, he, she, it, we, they, me, him, her, us, them* Possessive pronouns: *mine, yours, his, hers, ours, theirs* There are also demonstrative and relative pronouns.	Use pronouns to achieve paragraph cohesion. For example, don't keep repeating names; use pronouns to refer back to them, e.g. *Zarg was an alien from the planet Krell.* <u>He</u> *had six arms and six legs.* <u>His</u> *skin was green and knobbly.*
An ADJECTIVE describes a noun, e.g. a *yellow* bikini. They can be used in groups, e.g. *teeny, weeny, yellow, polka-dot* bikini. Adjectives are compared by adding *-er* and *-est* to short words, and *more* and *most* before long words (but beware of exceptions!), e.g. *big, bigger, biggest; beautiful, more beautiful, most beautiful.*	Adjectives are your big chance to write great descriptions! The important thing is to choose them carefully. See if you can beat the poet who wrote this line by choosing a better adjective: *… the mosquito with his _____ legs* Take care when writing comparisons of adjectives.
A VERB is a doing word. It is the most important element of a sentence. The form of verbs changes to show the tense: *past, present* or *future* and the time taken and state of completion of an action: *simple* or *continuous.* Modal verbs combine with main verbs to express ability, obligation, permission and volition, e.g. *can, may, must, will, shall.* Verbs can also be changed to emphasise who acted upon whom: *active* or *passive.*	Make sure that every sentence has a main verb. Check agreement of subject and verb. Uncertainties can be clarified by writing out the verb in full in a verb table. Give thought to the choice of verbs, e.g. instead of shows, *exemplifies* or *indicates*, etc. might be more effective (see Resource 3).
An ADVERB describes a verb. Traditionally they are divided into four categories: Time, e.g. *now, never;* Place, e.g. *here, there;* Manner, e.g. *quickly, happily;* Degree, e.g. *almost, very.*	Here is another big chance to improve your descriptions. Think particularly about how people *do* things, and *say* things (see Resource 2) e.g. *… replied Sarah* <u>angrily</u>.
CONJUNCTIONS join statements together. They can join sentences together to avoid a monotonous series of short sentences; or they can join one idea to another in a way that shows the relationship between the two ideas. The most common conjunctions are: *although, and, as, because, but, for, until, when.*	If your writing has too many short sentences, join those with related ideas with an appropriate conjunction, e.g. *I wanted to be on time today, but I was abducted by an alien.*
CONNECTIVES are words and short phrases which link ideas together, and are therefore important in discursive writing. Some common examples are: *however, in addition, in other words, meanwhile, moreover, nevertheless.*	When you are writing a discursive essay, it is a good idea to have a list of connectives beside you, as the right choice of connective can help you to place exactly the right emphasis on a point and any qualifications or additions you wish to make to it (see Resource 3).
A PREPOSITION shows the relationship of a noun to another word. The most common prepositions are: *about, above, across, after, among, at, before, behind, below, between, by, down, during, for, from, in.*	Bread-and-butter stuff and usually no problem, though there are a few problems words, e.g. is it *different to, different from* or *different than?*

2. ADVERB BANK

Adverbs to describe how people do things

artistically	honourably
attentively	kindly
audibly	lazily
big-headedly	loyally
bravely	methodically
cautiously	nervously
charmingly	orderly
clearly	patiently
cleverly	rashly
clumsily	reluctantly
correctly	romantically
deeply	secretively
dreamily	sensibly
friendlily	skilfully
generously	slightly
gloomily	smoothly
greedily	soundly
happily	strongly
helpfully	wastefully
honestly	well

Adverbs to describe how people say things

angrily	icily
apologetically	loudly
bluntly	miserably
boastfully	moodily
brightly	nervously
calmly	politely
cheekily	proudly
cheerfully	quietly
childishly	sadly
coolly	scornfully
crossly	sharply
deceitfully	shyly
eagerly	snappily
enthusiastically	softly
excitedly	spitefully
frankly	sulkily
frostily	sweetly
grumpily	tactfully
hesitantly	wisely
hopefully	wittily

3. WORDS AND PHRASES FOR ARGUMENT

When writing a discursive essay, or preparing a speech, refer to this list for words and phrases that will help to put your arguments together in the most effective way.

Verbs

allows	generates	mirrors	represents
creates	indicates	problems	reveals
discloses	influences	produces	shows
exemplifies	initiates	provokes	suggests
expresses	inspires	reflects	symbolises

Connectives

afterwards	for instance	next
again	further	next to
also	furthermore	notwithstanding
alternatively	here	on the contrary
although	however	on the other hand
another point is	in addition	on the whole
as a result	in any case	otherwise
as I have said	in any event	secondly
at the same time	in brief	similarly
besides	in fact	sooner or later
but	in other words	still
consequently	in short	therefore
equally important	later	thirdly
eventually	meanwhile	to sum up
finally	moreover	what is more
first	nearby	whereas
for example	nevertheless	

Phrases

an outcome of . . .	After examining both sides of the argument . . .
as a consequence of . . .	However, on closer inspection . . .
as a result of . . .	In discussing whether or not . . .
as an effect of . . .	It is often argued that . . .
brought about . . .	My conclusion is that . . .
caused by . . .	My point of view is . . .
contributed to . . .	On one side of the issue . . .
produced by . . .	On the other side of the issue . . .
shows evidence of . . .	There are both advantages and disadvantages in . . .
stemmed from . . .	Therefore, after examining all the arguments . . .

4. SPELLING HELPER

◆ Write 'i' before 'e' except after 'c' when the sound is 'ee', e.g. *believe, thief, ceiling, perceive*. Exceptions: *seize, weird, weir, counterfeit, neither, foreign, either*.

◆ Words ending in a silent 'e' lose this 'e' when adding a suffix, e.g. *love – loving, move – moving, change – changing*.

◆ Words ending in 'y' (sounding as 'i' in *pit*) have plural ending 'ies', e.g. *forty – forties, laboratory – laboratories*.

◆ Words ending in 'f' change to 'ves' in the plural. For example, *shelf* becomes *shelves*. Common exceptions: *dwarfs, roofs, chiefs*.

◆ Note that many words double the consonant before an ending is added, e.g. *sit – sitting, rob – robbing*.

◆ When trying to spell a long word try to break it down into smaller units that you know, e.g. with *acknowledging* – begin with 'know' or 'knowledge', add the prefix 'ack', apply the second rule (above) then add the ending 'ing'.

◆ Many words in English are not spelled exactly as they sound. Therefore it often helps to say the word as it is spelled, e.g. when learning *criticised*, say 'critic – ised'. This will help you to remember that the 's' sound in the middle is written with a 'c'.

◆ Learn this list of common words with silent letters:

answer	gnat	rhubarb
argue	government	rhinoceros
biscuit	guess	rhyme
bomb	half	sign
calm	island	solemn
castle	knew	Wednesday
daughter	knife	whether
debt	knight	whistle
February	pneumonia	who
fought	queue	whole

◆ Learn this list of irregular plurals:

SINGULAR	PLURAL	SINGULAR	PLURAL
aquarium	aquaria	man	men
child	children	mouse	mice
deer	deer	oasis	oases
diagnosis	diagnoses	ox	oxen
goose	geese	phenomenon	phenomena
gymnasium	gymnasia	stimulus	stimuli

◆ Learn the list of 80 commonly misspelled words in Resource 5.

◆ MOST IMPORTANT OF ALL – KEEP A LIST OF ALL THE WORDS YOU GET WRONG AND KEEP GOING OVER IT USING LOOK, COVER, WRITE, CHECK.

5. 80 COMMONLY MISSPELLED WORDS

1	absence		41	irrelevant
2	although		42	judge
3	answer		43	knowledge
4	appearance		44	leisure
5	argue		45	lovable
6	argument		46	maintain
7	beautiful		47	maintenance
8	because		48	manageable
9	beginning		49	mischief
10	believe		50	misspelled
11	business		51	naive
12	ceiling		52	necessary
13	chimney		53	neighbour
14	conscientious		54	noticeable
15	convenient		55	occasionally
16	courageous		56	occur
17	criticism		57	panicked
18	deceive		58	parallel
19	decision		59	patient
20	definitely		60	possess
21	describe		61	priest
22	disappear		62	professor
23	discipline		63	pursue
24	enough		64	queue
25	especially		65	receive
26	essential		66	remember
27	except		67	restaurant
28	exercise		68	rhyme
29	existence		69	rhythm
30	February		70	seize
31	fought		71	separate
32	government		72	similar
33	guard		73	sincerely
34	height		74	solemn
35	humorous		75	success
36	humour		76	surprise
37	immediate		77	thorough
38	independent		78	twelfth
39	insistent		79	unnecessary
40	instalment		80	vicious

6. PUNCTUATION HELPER

Keep this resource handy and consult it whenever you are unsure about punctuation.

SYMBOL	NAME	USE
'	apostrophe	1. Shows where letters have been omitted in shortened forms: *do not/don't.* 2. Shows possession: *Sara's key.* Note: if a word ends in 's' because it is spelled that way, or because it is plural, the apostrophe is placed *after* the 's': *Students' Union.*
:	colon	Points forward to the next sentence, a list or an example: *We have the following books by Crichton:* Jurassic Park, Eaters of the Dead *and* Sphere.
,	comma	1. Marks certain phrases and clauses in a sentence: *Sally, who is a socialist, spoke next.* 2. Separates items in a list: *A wheel, a tyre, a valve and an axle.* 3. Used, with speech marks, to mark direct speech (see below).
—	dash (note: longer than a hyphen with spaces before and after)	Shows a dramatic change of thought or contradiction: *The ghost was – me!*
!	exclamation mark	Used instead of a full stop or comma to show the reader that a word or group of words was said with force or excitement.
.	full stop/period	1. Used to show the end of sentences. 2. Used to show abbreviations, e.g. etc.
-	hyphen (note: shorter than a dash, no spaces)	1. Used in compound words: *twenty-three, mother-in-law.* 2. Used to split syllables in words that will not fit the end of a line.
?	question mark	Used to show that the preceding words are in the form of a question.
;	semicolon	1. Used instead of a full stop when the next sentence is strongly related. 2. Marks groups of items in a complex list. *I need a pencil, ruler and paper; a large board; and a place to work quietly.* Should be used sparingly.
" "	speech marks/ quotation marks/ inverted commas (note: often single in printed text: ' ')	Direct speech begins with speech marks and a capital letter, ends with . , ? or ! and speech marks. *'Where is my mobile?' said Sarah* or *Sarah said, 'Where is my mobile?'*

7. PARAGRAPH STRUCTURE

Layout

INDENTED	BLOCK	SEMI-BLOCK
◆ always used with hand-writing. ◆ used for stories ◆ the first line of each paragraph is indented by 1 cm; no blank lines between paragraphs	◆ often used for printed non-fiction and office correspondence ◆ no indentation ◆ whole blank line between paragraphs	◆ sometimes used for printed non-fiction and more often for office correspondence ◆ like indented paragraphs, but with a whole blank line between paragraphs

Organisation

NON-FICTION	FICTION
Beginning New paragraphs are started to introduce a new sub-topic of the main topic. The first sentence is usually the TOPIC SENTENCE: This states what the paragraph is about.	**Beginning** New paragraphs may be started for: ◆ a step forward in time ◆ a flashback ◆ a change of scene ◆ a change of viewpoint ◆ the introduction of a new character.
Development A paragraph is developed by additional information about the idea expressed in the topic sentence. For example, by: ◆ adding details ◆ stating facts ◆ giving examples ◆ relating an incident ◆ giving reasons.	**Development** A paragraph is developed by: ◆ descriptive detail ◆ dialogue ◆ a series of events.
Concluding sentence This is the sentence that rounds off the paragraph.	**Dialogue** This is set out with a new indented line for each speaker, like paragraphs. Dialogue is one reason why fiction rarely uses block paragraphs – it would take too much space to have a blank line after every speaker! Study an example of the way dialogue is set out.

8. DISCURSIVE ESSAY TEMPLATE 1

PLAN: USE FOR ANY ISSUE	EXAMPLE: END THE TV LICENCE FEE
Introduction Write a paragraph in which you explain the issue. Give key names, dates, facts and explain any difficult terms.	*The TV licence fee costs £114 per year for a colour television, and I believe that the public is getting such poor value for money it should be abolished at once.*
Alternative introduction Go for a 'shock horror' introduction to grab the reader's attention – but make sure you still get the basic information across.	*How would you feel if you were told that you had to pay for 70 people to go on a luxury holiday in South Africa? Well, that's exactly what you are doing. The BBC is sending 70 people to the Earth Summit at a cost of £120,000 – paid for by your licence fee. That is one reason why I think the licence fee should be abolished.*
Argument 1 The three arguments could be in 'ascending' or 'descending' order, i.e. with the strongest first, or the strongest last.	*The BBC used to spend the licence fee money on good-quality programming that gave us such quality programmes as* The Forsyte Saga *and* Civilization. *But now we get endless repeats and 'dumbed-down' news, while the licence fee is wasted on new channels that nobody watches – BBC Choice and BBC 4 get only 91,000 viewers a day.*
Argument 2 Try to make at least one of your arguments appeal to the reader's emotions – for example, relate a human interest story, describe suffering caused to those involved or give information that will make them angry.	*That brings me back to the Earth Summit. It says in today's newspaper that 70 staff will be staying in £120-a-day apartments in Sandton near Johannesburg, with maids and 24-hour security. Admittedly, when the BBC got wind of public opinion, they cut back the number to 50, but does it really take 50 staff to provide good-quality news coverage?*
Argument 3 One of your arguments could be to attack one of the opposition's arguments, as in this example.	*It could be argued that a licence fee is important to ensure that the BBC can concentrate on producing quality programming and introducing new developments such as 625 lines, colour and CEEFAX. However, new developments, such as satellite and cable, have been paid for by private companies which charge viewers a fee for their service, so the licence fee means we are paying twice!*
Conclusion Try not to introduce any new information or arguments. Sum up on the key points and try to end with a memorable sentence. This conclusion refers to two earlier points – the decrease in quality programming and the new technology. The last sentence is memorable and makes the key point in an interesting way.	*Now that hundreds of channels are available, the only thing that could make the BBC worthwhile is quality programming, and since they don't seem to be able to make them any more, I'd rather keep the licence fee and use it to pay for some extra channels of my choice – FilmFour, for example.*

9. DISCURSIVE ESSAY TEMPLATE 2

PLAN: USE FOR ANY ISSUE	EXAMPLE: CLONING
Introduction Write a paragraph in which you explain the issue. Give key names, dates, facts, etc. Explain any difficult terms, e.g. cloning.	*Cloning is the process of creating groups of genetically identical cells. The cells themselves can be modified by adding DNA from any source. The process allows scientists to modify the genetic structure of any living thing, or to create perfect copies of any living thing.*
One side of the issue Write at least *two* paragraphs giving evidence, examples or arguments to support one side of the issue.	*This knowledge will greatly improve medicine. For example, babies could have their genes modified to protect against common diseases. It will also be possible to regrow damaged limbs and organs. Scientists could also modify genes to ensure that the next generation is not only healthier, but more intelligent and better looking.* *Another advantage of cloning is that a new generation of plants can be created which will be resistant to disease and will provide greater nutrition. This could help to feed the starving people in third world countries.*
The other side of the issue Write at least *two* paragraphs giving evidence, examples or arguments to support the other side of the issue.	*The most serious argument against tampering with genes is that harmful bacteria might be produced by accident – indeed, some people believe that this is where AIDS came from (though this cannot be proved). Another problem is that cloning will reduce the gene pool because all the clones have exactly the same genes as the parent.* *Also, can we be sure that these new 'Frankenstein foods' will not affect our health?* *There is also a moral issue: Is it right to tamper with the genetic material of living creatures, especially humans?*
Conclusion State which of the above arguments you find most convincing, and state which side of the issue you support.	*This is a difficult issue, and I do think the dangers are very real. However, I believe that we have to pursue these developments because of the good they can do. If scientists do this with very great care, and with due respect for the moral issues, humanity will surely benefit overall.*

10. TYPES OF ARGUMENT

TYPE OF ARGUMENT	PRESENTING AN ARGUMENT	EVALUATING AND RESPONDING TO AN ARGUMENT
Information	Researching your topic so that you are able to give detailed information about it will help you to win the argument. Also, if you are well prepared you will be better placed to respond to a challenge from the opposition.	This works both ways – detailed knowledge can also be used to evaluate and attack an argument. Make sure that you know at least as much about the topic, and preferably more.
Facts or statistics	Give facts or statistics to support your case.	Are the facts really facts, or are they just opinions? Are the facts or statistics accurate? Have statistics been correctly interpreted? Are they relevant to the argument?
Giving an example	An example can often inject 'human interest'.	Examples are a weak form of argument because they do not prove general rules. Is it a good example? Can you think of an example that proves the opposite?
Giving opinions	The best way to present an opinion is to make it sound like a fact or a reasoned argument.	Opinions are one of the easiest things to attack. Respond by exposing the point as a mere expression of opinion and by countering the opinion with a hard fact.
Referring to expert opinion	This can take the form of named 'experts', or to more general expert opinion such as 'medical research', 'doctors', 'scientists'.	How credible is the expert opinion? Often it is possible to find experts who take the opposite view.
Appealing to emotions	Paint a vivid picture of suffering that is caused by the opposition's point of view, e.g. suffering animals, nuclear war, etc.	Any individual case can be used to excite emotions, but this does not necessarily prove anything. Respond with the same tactic: appeal to the emotions even more strongly *or* expose the emotive appeal as exaggerated and misleading.
Refuting the opposition's arguments in advance	This will take 'take the wind out of the sails' of the opposition. No matter how effective an argument, it is less effective if it has already been discredited in advance.	How effectively has the argument been discredited? Is there a weakness or a loophole that will enable you to fight back?

11. LITERARY ESSAY TEMPLATE

PLAN: USE FOR ANY ISSUE	EXAMPLE: Courage in *Chinese Cinderella*
Introduction Give basic background information about the book and the main characters. Introduce the subject of the essay.	The *Chinese Cinderella* Adeline Yen Mah. When her father remarries she and her brothers and sisters have to take second place to the two new children. As the youngest, she is the 'Cinderella' of the whole family. However, she is supported by Aunt Baba and grandfather Ye Ye at home, and by her teachers and friends at school. Finally, because of her courage, she fulfils her dearest wish – to be sent to university in England.
Point 1 These two paragraphs show how to make a point and support it with a quotation. Long quotations (one line or more) are set out with a blank line before and after them, and are indented from the margin (quotation marks are optional, but help to make clear that this is a quotation). Note that an additional analysis follows the quotation.	Her courage is evident from a very early age, when she starts school in Hong Kong. Ye Ye has been paying the children's tram fare, but when Niang finds out she says they must apologise or she will not give them the tram fare. All the children apologise except Adeline. The reason she does not apologise is: 'Something to do with loyalty, fair play, and a sense of obligation.' This shows her courage, but also her honour. She is not standing up to Niang out of stubbornness, but because of important princples.
Point 2 This paragraph shows how to make a point and support it – not with a quotation, but with a detailed reference to a specific incident.	Another example of her courage is how she responds to the nasty trick played by third brother. He offers her a drink of orange juice, but it turns out to be urine. Even though she is very hurt and upset, she still thinks that the saddest thing about the incident is that it shows that third brother was losing his integrity.
Point 3 This paragraph shows how short quotations (less than one line) are integrated with the text. Quotation marks are essential here so that it is clear where the quotation begins and ends.	Adeline draws strength from her life outside the home, particularly school and friends: 'My friends respect me.' She wins several prizes and even becomes class president. This helps to give her self-esteem, and ultimately to win the prize that persuades her father to let her go to university in England.
Conclusion Try not to introduce any new points. Sum up on the key points and try to end with a memorable sentence.	Adeline's courage helped her to overcome a series of cruel incidents. She was supported by her friends and by her success at school, and was able to fulfil her dream.

12. STORY PLANNER

BEGINNING – there are many ways to begin a story, but here are some of the most popular:			
Description of a place	**Description of a person**	**Dialogue**	**Action**
This is a good way to begin when the setting is important, e.g. in a horror story or travel story.	This is a good way to begin when the story focuses on one main character.	This launches the reader straight into the story. The reader finds out about the characters and emerging plot from what is said.	To grab the reader's interest, begin with an exciting action scene. Introduce the details of characters and setting in the next scene.

MIDDLE – the middle is the main part of the story. It may consist of some or all of the following:	
Suspense	Suspense is a tense feeling of worrying what will happen next. It can be created in many ways, but it usually hinges on something which has to be done to stop something terrible happening.
Conflict	Conflict is the struggle at the heart of every story ever written. It may be a conflict between people, or a trial of strength between a person and nature. The cause of the conflict should be established as early as possible in the story, because it is interest in the conflict that will make the reader want to read on. This conflict should develop throughout the story and reach its highest point in the climax (see below).
Plot	The plot is the plan of how the conflict unfolds. Many types of plot are possible, e.g. a plot with flashbacks; a circular plot in which the hero ends up more or less where he or she began; a parallel plot, in which two branches of the plot are developed before coming together at the end. Many longer stories also have subplots. These are mini-plots, stories in themselves, which interweave with the main plot.
Complications	Complications add interest and suspense. They can include unexpected setbacks, new characters who cause problems, a subplot interweaving with the main plot, a new source of conflict, etc.
Crisis	The crisis is the 'make or break' point in the story. The hero or heroine could fail or succeed, and the reader is not sure whether it is going to be a happy or a tragic ending.
Climax	The climax is the highest point of action in the story. This is the point where the Prince gets the Princess and the One Ring is thrown into the Cracks of Doom.

ENDING – this is the resolution to the climax, where the main character's problems are solved and the reader's curiosity is satisfied.

13. STORY TITLES MATRIX

Choose a title for a story, or choose at random by rolling a dice twice. This will give a number for each axis of the matrix.

	1	2	3	4	5	6
1	A Night in a Haunted House	A Night to Remember	Witch Hunt	Difficult Journey	Broken Promises	Before Eden
2	Down to a Sunless Sea	Gamblers Never Win	Sleepless Night	Leave him Alone – He's Only a Kid	The Silent Eyes of Time	No Going Back
3	Set a Thief to Catch a Thief	The Ghost, the Girl and the Gold	The Silent Eyes of Time	The Lies People Tell	The Whole Thing Had Started as a Joke	The Day My Mother Made Me Wear That Awful Dress
4	The Secret of Crookhill Hall	The Kiss	The Human Element	Who Dares Wins	Locked Out	Dancing
5	Depressed by a Bad Book of Poetry	Dark Night Scare	Devil in the Fog	All Alone	Missed Opportunity	Love on the Dole
6	It was a Bitter-sweet Experience	Cheri	Accident	What a Way to Go!	A Stitch in Time	You Can't Win Them All

More story ideas

1. Write a school story from the point of view of the teacher.
2. Write a story about a child who is bullied at school but who eventually learns to stick up for himself/herself.
3. Write a story about someone who overcomes a handicap.
4. Write a story based on the idea: 'I wish I had the chance to do it all over again.'
5. Write a story based upon the wish: 'If only...'
6. Write a story beginning, 'It was a short narrow street of tall, thin houses and it ended in a railway embankment. I wasn't sure which house I was looking for.'
7. Write a story beginning, 'There was hardly anybody about ...'
8. Write a story in which any *two* or more of the following play an important part: an old newspaper, a broken gate, a taxi ride, a shopkeeper, a lost child, a dog, a cheeseburger, a telephone.
9. Write a story including the words 'We opened it and to our horror ...'
10. Write a story including the words 'You should have seen the mess!'
11. Write a story involving some lost money.
12. Write a story which ends, 'There was no hope left.'
13. Write a story about somebody writing a story.

14. BOOK REVIEW

Introduction

Give some information about the author and a brief outline of the story.

Paragraph 1

Describe the main character as he or she is introduced at the beginning of the story. Use two or three quotations from the text as evidence.

Paragraph 2

Explain the main problem or problems that the character has to face and how the character attempts to solve them. Describe any low points or crises in the character's life. Use one or two quotations where appropriate.

Paragraph 3

Describe how the character has changed and developed by the end of the novel and what he or she has learned as a result of his or her experiences. Use one or two quotations as evidence.

Paragraph 4

Explore any themes in the novel. A theme is an idea such as love, war, growing up, etc. What does the novel say about the theme? What events or actions of characters help to put it across. Use one or two appropriate quotations.

Paragraph 5

Describe the language and style of the writer. A good way to do this is to analyse a passage of description or narrative in detail.

Conclusion

End by giving your personal response. Say what you liked and disliked about the novel, what various scenes made you think and feel, and how it has helped your understanding of the main theme.

15. FILM REVIEW

Introduction
List key information, title of film, date, studio, director, cast, etc.

Section 1
Write a brief synopsis of the film.

Section 2
Briefly discuss the themes explored in the film.

Section 3
Write brief notes on each of the following:

direction

script

casting

acting

music

costume

locations

special effects

Section 4
Analyse one scene in detail using the technical terms explained in Resource 16.

Section 5
Write your overall evaluation of the film.

16. FILM TECHNIQUES

This repertoire of camera shots and editing techniques was developed in the early days of cinema by directors such as Fritz Lang and D. W. Griffith. They are also used today for television.

CAMERA SHOTS	DESCRIPTION	USE
long shot/establishing shot	shows the whole of a scene	establishes where the action is taking place
mid-shot/medium shot	shows one person or a group	used for most scenes in which characters interact
close-up/tight shot	head and shoulders or full face	used to show emotions or reactions of characters
two-shot favouring A	shows two characters but emphasises character A	emphasises the character who is speaking or reacting, as appropriate
high angle	looking down on a scene	suggests power and menace or the position of the onlooker
mid-angle	the normal human viewpoint	used for most scenes
low angle	looking up on a scene	suggests helplessness or the position of the onlooker

16. FILM TECHNIQUES

continued

CAMERA SHOTS	DESCRIPTION	USE
pan	following action from side to side	useful for following movement – often done with the camera on a crane or trolley
tilt	an up/down movement of the camera	useful for following movement or 'scanning' tall buildings and landscapes
zoom in/out	moving into or out of a scene	an effective way of making a transition between long, mid- and close-up shots

EDITING TECHNIQUES	DESCRIPTION	USE
cut	an abrupt change from one scene to another	the usual way of changing scenes – note that most scenes only last from about 1 to 5 seconds
intercut	change back and forward between two scenes	useful to show things like telephone conversations
fade	the image darkens to blackness	emphasises the end of a scene
wipe	a new scene is moved in from one side to replace the previous scene	one of many special effects which can be used to change scenes

Analyse a short section of film in detail. Describe the camera shots, and editing techniques using the terms above, and try to explain the effect they have.

17. FORMS OF WRITING

FORM	KEY FEATURES
Advertisement	Must catch the attention. Usually relies more on images than words, though the few words are carefully chosen. There is usually a slogan, key information and small print.
Article	Look for information about the purpose and audience of the article and write in an appropriate style. If it is a newspaper article, try to use journalistic features such as a headline, subheadings and bylines. If it is an article for a more serious magazine or journal, write continuous text in paragraphs without subheadings. Articles are usually written in the present tense, with extensive use of connectives and subordinate clauses.
Essay (see Resources 8, 9 and 11 for detailed information)	The essay can take many forms, the commonest of which are the discursive essay and the literary essay. The discursive essay argues a point of view. Remember the five-paragraph essay plan as a starting point. The literary essay should consist of a series of points supported by evidence from the text. Essays are usually formal and impersonal in style. They are usually written in the present tense, with extensive use of connectives and subordinate clauses.
Journal/diary	Journals and diaries are similar, though the term 'journal' is usually given to an extended and reflective style of writing, and 'diary' to the shorter, more anecdotal style. Journals and diaries are by their nature personal and informal in style. They make extensive use of the first person, past tense and chronological order.
Letter	It is important to know how to address both a formal and an informal letter, though writing the address is not usually required in examinations. Use appropriate forms of salutation and closure depending on whether the letter is formal or informal. Letters range from very formal and impersonal, to very informal and personal in style – so make sure you take note of the audience and purpose.
Non-fiction text	Non-fiction texts vary from texts with chapters of continuous prose and few illustrations, to texts based mainly around the 'double-page spread' with text in boxes, subheadings, illustrations, charts, etc. This depends very much on purpose and audience. Non-fiction texts are impersonal in style, and use present tense and non-chronological order.
Novel/story (see Resources 12 and 13)	A novel or story has a beginning, a middle and an end and consists of characters, who interact in a plot, which often expresses a theme or themes. They are written in the past tense and use the first or third person.
Poem	The unit of organisation in a poem is the line. Line length is usually decided by rhythm (the number of stressed syllables). Lines are often grouped into stanzas, which often have a pattern of rhyme. Poems use a wide range of figures of speech and effects of sound.
Review (see Resources 14 and 15)	The main focus of a review is what a book, film, play, etc. was like and whether it is worth reading, seeing, buying, etc. Reviews vary in degree of formality. They are often quite personal, as the reviewer is giving his or her personal opinion. They are usually written in the present tense with extensive use of connectives and subordinate clauses.
Script	A script consists of dialogue plus directions. Layout conventions vary depending on whether the script is for stage, radio, TV or film. Note that the dialogue is written without speech marks.

18. FACT AND OPINION

FACT

Something known to be true; something you can check or prove

Example: *The death penalty in Britain was abolished in 1964.*

OPINION

A belief or point of view about a subject

ASK YOURSELF

Is it possible to check this statement? If not, be suspicious.

LOOK OUT FOR

◆ words and phrases which signal an opinion, e.g. *appear, could, I believe, I feel, I suggest, I think, in my opinion, might, often, on occasion, ought, perhaps, probably, seem, should, sometimes, usually, would.*

◆ emotive words and phrases, e.g. *shocking, horrifying, reckless, depressing.*

◆ words and phrases implying value-judgements, e.g. *beautiful, ugly, safe, dangerous, evil, attractive, well-dressed, good, vicious, sophisticated.*

Example: *The death penalty should be brought back.*

REASONED JUDGEMENT

A logical conclusion based on reasoned arguments (see Toolkit Resource 10, 'Types of Argument', for examples of effective arguments)

EXAMPLE: *The death penalty should be brought back because violent crime is rising. It would act as a deterrent, and victims' families would see it as a just punishment.*

YOUR EXAMPLES

Write your examples of fact, opinion and reasoned judgement:

19. REFERENCE SKILLS

SELECTION

Selection is finding the information you want in a library, on a CD-ROM or the Internet. The first step is finding an appropriate text, CD-ROM or website, the second step is to find relevant information within the text, CD-ROM or website.

◆ Find the text you want using library research skills such as a knowledge of the Dewey Decimal cataloguing system.
◆ Find out how to get the best out of Internet search engines.
◆ Make full use of contents, index and glossaries.
◆ Use skimming and scanning techniques – don't read the whole text in detail.
◆ Use a search facility to search an electronic text for key terms.

SUMMARY

A summary is a shortened version of a text. Usually the main points are rewritten in a shorter form. This is different from an *abridgement* in which the author's words are preserved and the shortening is achieved by making cuts.

◆ Highlight or underline the main points.
◆ Count the highlighted words.
◆ If there are too many, decide which are the least important and delete them. If there are too few, highlight some of the less important points.
◆ Rewrite the highlighted points into a paragraph, changing words, phrases and sentences in order to make it read well.

COLLATION

Collation is bringing together information from different sources.

◆ Highlight useful information in each source.
◆ Where there is duplication of information, decide which source to use.
◆ Where sources disagree, use the information which you think is most accurate *or* write an account of the different information (this will depend on your audience and purpose).
◆ Decide how to organise the material you have selected from different sources.
◆ Rewrite the highlighted material in a *consistent style*. The choice of style will depend on audience and purpose.

CROSS-REFERENCING

Cross-referencing is giving references from one part of a book to another, or from one text to another.

If you are writing a serious article, it is a good idea to give references to the source of your information. This enables the reader to check your information, and thus adds strength to any points you make. There are several ways to make references or cross-references.

◆ Include the reference in the sentence e.g. *This is how Stephen Hawking describes black holes in* A Brief History of Time.
◆ Use brackets – e.g. *Black holes are created when the gravity of a body is so great that light waves cannot escape (see* A Brief History of Time *by Stephen Hawking).*
◆ Numbered footnotes – a small number in the text refers to a number at the bottom of the page.

Note: academic articles require much more detail in cross-references.

20. DRAMA TECHNIQUES

TURNING POINT

Points in the play where important choices are made, or chance events occur that have a significant effect on everything that follows. These points are worth examining in detail through some of the other techniques on this page.

THEATRE FORUM

Students perform an improvisation, which is stopped, and the audience intervenes to change the direction/emphasis of the drama. This may then involve members of the audience taking an active role in the continuation of the improvisation.

FREEZE FRAME

At a word from the director, the action is frozen at a key moment. This provides an opportunity to adjust posture and gesture to ensure that the significance of the moment is fully expressed and for a range of other techniques, such as hot-seating.

HOT-SEATING

One of the characters is questioned in role. This could be during a 'freeze-frame' moment, or the character could be taken out of the play and questioned separately. It is a way of exploring a character's inner life, such as emotion and motivation.

IMPROVISATION

This involves making up dialogue and some details of action as the play unfolds while following a general plan.

MIME

Conveying character and/or plot through body movement only. It is a valuable exercise, as without dialogue everyone is much more focused on movement.

SOCIOGRAM

The actors position themselves as near to or as far away from a specified character as they feel emotionally. This can be followed up by hot-seating or thought-tracking so that characters have to explain their positioning.

THOUGHT-TRACKING

Characters are asked express their thoughts whilst remaining in character. They can be prompted to do this by name or by discreet tapping on the shoulder.

UNIT 2: *BLOOD BROTHERS*

RESOURCES: *Blood Brothers*, Willy Russell, Methuen Student Edition, ed. Mulligan, ISBN 0–413–69510–7 (contains excellent introduction and teaching notes)

CD: *Blood Brothers*, London Revival Cast, RCA Victor, 1988 (or any other recording)

BOARD: Any for English or English literature coursework; WJEC for English literature examination (Note: check current specifications).

RANGE: Speaking and listening: Drama-focused activity

AO	TEACHING SEQUENCE	RESOURCES	OUTCOMES
AO2i	Read the text and listen to the songs on CD and/or see a performance.	Text, CD	Knowledge of plot and characters
AO2i	Put a jumbled-up synopsis in order	21, 'Synopsis'	Reinforcement of knowledge of plot
AO1 i–iii	Explore character through group discussion and presentation	22, 'Main characters'	Detailed knowledge of six major characters Assessment opportunity for group discussion and interaction
AO1 i–iii	Compare the two main characters, through note-taking, discussion and role play	23, 'Mickey and Edward'	Detailed knowledge of the two main characters and the issues arising from their different upbringing
AO1 i–iii	Explore themes through group discussion and presentation	24, 'Themes'	Detailed knowledge of six main themes Assessment opportunity for group discussion and interaction
AO1 i–iii	Explore plot, characters and themes through a range of drama techniques	Toolkit 20, 'Drama Techniques'	Assessment opportunity for drama-focused activity
AO2 i, v **AO3 i–iii**	Students do one or more of the general assignments (optional)	25, 'General Assignments'	One or more general assignments
LIT AO1–4	If students are preparing the text for examination, answer one or more examination-style questions	26, 'English Literature Examination-Style Questions' Toolkit 11, 'Literary Essay Template'	One or more literary essays

Introduction

Blood Brothers is a musical play which tells the story of twin brothers who are separated at birth. Mickey stays with his poverty-stricken mother, while Eddie is brought up by the wealthy Mrs Lyons. Their very different life chances are explored in the play. A series of coincidences brings them together and involves them in a quarrel over a girl, which eventually leads to both their deaths.

The activities in this unit focus on exploring the play through drama to meet the requirements of English language coursework (all boards). However, some suggestions for written work, and examples of examination-style questions, are included for students who are studying the play as a set text for WJEC English Literature.

As this is a 'musical play' (not a musical as such because of the predominance of dialogue), the CD is an essential resource. Details of current performances may be found at
http://www.musicalstages.co.uk/listings/bloodbrothers_londonlisting.htm

Note: as this unit will be one of the main drama-focused activities during the course, particular care must be taken to plan for the involvement of all students in a range of assessable activities. In addition to the resources in this unit, Toolkit Resource 20, 'Drama Techniques', provides for a very wide range of permutations on the activities in this unit, which can be used to provide assessment opportunities for every student.

Notes on the Resources

21. SYNOPSIS

AIM: plot familiarisation

Working in pairs, students put the paragraphs of the plot synopsis in the correct order. This can be done by writing numbers under the letters in the left-hand column, or by cutting out the paragraphs and shuffling them around until they are in the correct order. The correct order is as follows: A6 B9 C11 D8 E7 F4 G3 H10 I2 J5 K1.

This resource can be used later with Toolkit Resource 20, 'Drama Techniques', as the basis for role play and improvisation.

22. MAIN CHARACTERS

AIM: detailed knowledge of main characters

There are a number of ways in which these cards can be used. Students should write their notes neatly on the cards, as they will be needed later for reference.

Pair work

Students, working in pairs, make notes on each of the characters, referring to the text for information as necessary.

Jigsaw groups

The class is divided into groups of six, and each group is given a set of cards. Students choose a card at random and then the groups reform so that students who have drawn the same character card are working together. They brainstorm ideas about the character, referring to the text for information as necessary, and make notes on the cards. Finally, the original groups reform, and each student reports back on his or her character.

Improvisation

Working in pairs, students randomly select a card, then improvise a dialogue between the two characters. This can be more closely related to the plot by selecting at random one of the synopsis cards. Students then improvise the dialogue that might have taken place at this particular point in the play. See Resource 20, 'Drama Techniques', for additional ideas for improvisation.

Writing

If the play is being studied as a set text, the notes on the cards can be used as the basis for an essay on one or more of the characters.

23. MICKEY AND EDWARD

AIM: understanding the similarities and differences between Mickey and Edward and exploration of the theme of class

Working in pairs, students complete the two columns of the resource sheet. One way to do this is for each student of the pair to focus on a different character, and then read and discuss their findings, collaborating on the activities at the bottom of the resource sheet.

24. THEMES

AIM: understanding the main themes in the play

Each card contains an outline of ideas that students can expand with more detail from the play. Students should work in groups of four, which can be subdivided or reorganised for different purposes.

Pair work

Students, working in pairs, make notes on each of the characters, referring to the text for information as necessary.

Jigsaw groups

The class is divided into groups of four, and each group is given a set of cards. Students choose a card at random and then the groups reform so that students who have drawn the same character card are working together. They brainstorm ideas about the character, referring to the text for information as necessary, and make notes on the cards. Finally, the original groups reform, and each student reports back on his or her character.

Improvisation

See Resource 20, 'Drama Techniques'.

Writing

If the play is being studied as a set text, the notes on the cards can be used as the basis for an essay on one or more of the themes.

25. GENERAL ASSIGNMENTS

AIM: explore the play from a wider range of perspectives

The resource sheet provides a list of suggestions for responding to the play from a wider range of perspectives. The activities are particularly suited to coursework, but can also be used as supporting exercises for an examination text. Toolkit Resources – for example, Toolkit Resource 17, 'Forms of Writing' – can be used to support several of the assignments on this resource.

26. ENGLISH LITERATURE EXAMINATION-STYLE QUESTIONS

AIM: prepare and practise for examination

These questions can be used for practice by students who are preparing the text for WJEC English Literature. Foundation-tier students may find it helpful to use Toolkit Resource 11, 'Literary Essay Template', as a support for their writing.

21. SYNOPSIS

Put this synopsis in order by writing the number of the paragraph underneath the letter in the first column.

No.	SYNOPSIS
A	Eddie is sent to private school and Mickey to the local school. He gets into trouble at school and also with the police. Eddie and Mickey meet again when Mrs Johnstone is rehoused in the country not far from the Lyons'. Eddie persuades Mickey to ask Linda out. 'Linda, for Christ's sake will you go out with me?' 'Yeh.' Once again the three become inseparable.
B	Linda seeks comfort in Eddie who has recently become Counsellor Lyons. 'Suddenly they kiss.'
C	Mickey bursts into the meeting to tell Eddie exactly what he thinks of him. Mrs Johnstone follows with two armed policemen. Seeing Mickey with the gun and panicking, she blurts out the truth about the brothers. He replies bitterly: 'I could have been him!' His uncontrolled rage causes the gun to go off, killing Edward. Mickey turns to the police as they open fire, losing control of the gun and simultaneously an armed policeman takes action. The narrator spells out the moral: 'Could it be what we, the English, have come to know as class.'
D	Mickey, who is unemployed and desperate for money, helps his brother Sammy with an armed robbery and is caught and sent to jail for seven years. He is released early but is suffering from acute depression and is reliant on medication. 'I get depressed and I need to take these 'cos they make me better.'
E	When they turn eighteen, Edward goes away to university and Mickey gets Linda pregnant. They are married while Eddie is away. Mickey is made redundant from his factory job. 'I've been walking around all day, every day, lookin' for a job.'
F	The babies are born. Mrs Johnstone keeps Mickey and Edward is brought up by Mr and Mrs Lyons. Eddie is brought up in a middle-class area with everything money can buy, and Mickey is brought up on a council estate.
G	Mrs Lyons asks Mrs Johnstone to give one of the new babies to her so that she can trick her husband into believing she became pregnant before he went away on business: 'Give one to me.' Mrs Johnstone agrees and they swear on the Bible that neither will reveal the truth. 'There's a pact been sealed.'
H	Mrs Johnstone sees Eddie and Linda together, and tells Mickey about it. He wrongly assumes they are having an affair. Armed with his brother's gun, he rushes to a meeting that Eddie is chairing at the town hall.
I	Mrs Johnstone works as a cleaner for the wealthy Mrs Lyons who is unable to have children and is desperate for a baby. 'We've been trying for such a long time now.'
J	When they are both seven they meet and become friends and 'blood brothers'. 'Now, you say after me: "I will always defend my brother".' They go around with Linda, a girl from the same estate as Mickey. Mickey and Linda are always getting Edward into trouble. 'I'm not sure I'd let him mix with the likes of them in the future.' Mr and Mrs Lyons forbid Edward to see Mickey and they move away.
K	Mrs Johnstone has seven children. She discovers she is pregnant yet again with twins. Her husband has just left her 'for a girl they say who looks a bit like Marilyn Monroe'.

22. MAIN CHARACTERS

```
┌ ─ ─ ─ ─ ─ ─ ─ ─ ─ ─ ─ ─ ┐
        MRS JOHNSTONE
```

```
        MRS LYONS
```

```
        MICKEY
```

```
        EDDIE
```

```
        SAMMY
```

```
        LINDA
```

23. MICKEY AND EDWARD

Mickey and Edward are genetically identical, but as a result of their upbringing they become very different people. Working in pairs, list the main differences in the main stages of their lives.

	MICKEY	EDWARD
AT BIRTH		
AS YOUNG CHILDREN		
AT SCHOOL		
AT UNIVERSITY/ AT WORK		

Role play

Extend the conversation that Mickey and Edward have in Act II at Christmas (page 71). Role-play them comparing their life experiences so far, using the table above as a basis.

Discussion

What point is Willy Russell making about the opportunities available to working-class and middle-class youth? Do you agree with his views?

24. THEMES

CLASS

Though genetically identical, Mickey is working class, Eddie is middle class. Explore how this affects their life chances, particularly:

◆ education
◆ housing
◆ the way they speak
◆ their jobs.

Discuss how far you think the same is true today.

NURTURE VS. NATURE

Explore which aspects of the two main characters are the result of nurture and which aspects are the result of nature.

Nurture:
Eddie's polished accent, manners and behaviour compared to Mickey's rough accent, manners and behaviour. Eddie has better life opportunities, e.g. university. He is confident, e.g. speaking to girls. Mickey is tongue-tied; he daren't ask Linda out, even though he knows she likes him.

Nature:
They have similar personalities, they instinctively like each other and become blood brothers, they love the same girl.

Overall, does nurture or nature have the greatest effect on their life chances?

FATE

Explore the role of Fate in the play. For example:

◆ Mrs Lyons' choice at the beginning of the play.
◆ Eddie and Mickey meet and become 'blood brothers'.
◆ Mrs Johnstone is rehoused to the place where Mrs Lyons moved.
◆ Eddie and Mickey fall in love with the same girl.
◆ Mrs Lyons tells Mickey about seeing Eddie with Linda.
◆ Events at the court house lead to the accidental shooting of Eddie by Mickey.

Do you think the characters in this play have any free will, or was the ending predestined from the moment the twins were born?

SUPERSTITION

There are many references to superstitious beliefs during the play, though Eddie and Mrs Lyons scoff at such beliefs:

◆ Bogeyman
◆ Shoes on the table
◆ One magpie (note the old rhyme: 'One for sorrow, two for joy/Three for a girl and four for a boy').
◆ Spilled salt
◆ Cracked mirror

(See Narrator's speeches for more examples.)

At the end of the play, the narrator asks the question: 'Was the tragedy caused by superstition or class?' What do you think?

25. GENERAL ASSIGNMENTS

Note: Students using the Methuen Student Edition (ISBN 0–413–69510–7) will find an excellent commentary and a range of activities at the back of the book.

Speaking and listening

Devise through a combination of improvisation and writing a similar play which explores the same themes, but through a different story and characters.

Reading

Find out about social conditions in Liverpool today.

Blood Brothers has often been compared to Greek tragedy. Find out about Greek tragedy and make the comparison for yourself. If possible, read or watch a Greek tragedy by Sophocles or Aeschylus.

Writing

Plan how you would stage the play.

Use the information in the play as the basis for an article or TV documentary on social class and its effect on people's life chances.

Write the newspaper front page that might have appeared after the shoot-out in the council meeting.

Retell the story, or a scene from the story, in a different form, e.g. short story, series of diary entries, ballad, etc.

The wider curriculum

Analyse some of the songs by looking carefully at tempo, mood, instrumentation, and what the song contributes to the play at that particular moment.

Spiritual, moral, ethical, social and cultural issues

Discuss: can it ever be right to sell or give away a child? Note that the practice is sadly still common – for example, the recent case of a Korean child bought by a childless American couple.

The issue explored in the play has been revived in recent years in the debate about 'surrogate mothers' who give birth to a baby conceived by the sperm of another woman's partner. What legal and ethical considerations should control the process?

ICT

Visit http://www.bradley.edu/academics/abroad/eji/the131/blood.htm for a review of the play. Write a response to the review. Write your own review of the play.

The European dimension

Discuss: could *Blood Brothers* have been set in any other European country, or could the play only be set in the UK because of its class structure?

26. ENGLISH LITERATURE EXAMINATION-STYLE QUESTIONS

Foundation tier

Describe the character of Mickey and show how he is a victim of his upbringing. In your answer, you should:

◆ explain the basic idea behind the plot
◆ describe Mickey's personality
◆ show how the life chances of Mickey and Eddie are different because one is brought up in a working-class home, and the other in a middle-class home
◆ show how circumstances lead Mickey into crime and gun use.

Compare the characters of Mrs Lyons and Mrs Johnstone. In your answer, you should:

◆ explain the difference in social circumstances and how it shapes their characters
◆ describe what motivates them (Mrs Lyons is driven by the need for a child, Mrs Johnstone by the need to survive and her love for her children).

Write about *two* of the following themes in the play: the class system, violence, love, fate, superstition.

Read from page 22, 'Edward, also aged 7 appears . . .' to page 27, 'before the bogeyman gets you'. Show how the language and attitude of each boy reveals the effects of his upbringing.

Higher tier

'Likable but overly sentimental low-concept musical' (Nick Curtis, *Evening Standard*). Do you agree with this judgement of *Blood Brothers*?

What is the role of the Narrator in the play? In your answer, you should:

◆ study the speeches of the Narrator and analyse what he has to say about the events of the play
◆ consider his relationship with the audience
◆ consider whether he is a sinister figure, or just a storyteller.

At the end of the play, the narrator says, 'Do we blame superstition for what came to pass?' Examine the role of superstition in the play.

Throughout the play, there are frequent allusions to Marilyn Monroe. Examine each of these allusions and discuss how it contributes to our understanding of characters and themes.

Read the ending to the original play (before it was changed into a musical) on pages 96–99. Which do you think is most effective and why?

UNIT 3: THE TALK PROJECT

RESOURCES: Photocopiable resources in Unit and Toolkit – no additional resources required

BOARD: Any for English coursework

RANGE: Speaking and listening: Group discussion and interaction and Individual extended contribution

AO	TEACHING SEQUENCE*	RESOURCES	OUTCOMES
PART 1: FOR AND AGAINST			
A01 ii	Develop arguments for and against a topic in more detail (higher-tier students can omit this stage)	27a, b, c, 'For and Against Cards' Toolkit Resource 10, 'Types of Argument'	Group discussion Increasing ability to develop an argument in more detail
A01 i–iii	Research a topic in depth and prepare it for a debate speech or presentation.	28, 'Preparing a Speech or Presentation' Toolkit Resource 10, 'Types of Argument'	Debate speech or presentation
PART 2: TOWNCESTER			
A01 i–iii	Students work in groups of 4 to 6 to orally improvise stories based on the Towncester resources, followed by a review of the oral stories and the preparation of a carefully planned group narration.	29, 'Towncester Characters' 30, 'Towncester Plan'	Oral story improvisation Group narration of the Towncester soap
PART 3: MATRICES			
A01ii	Students play the discussion games using Resource 33, 'Discuss, Argue, Persuade Matrix'	33, 'Discuss, Argue, Persuade Matrix'	Familiarisation with a range of discussion topics Increased confidence in discussion
A01 i–iii	Students play a game with the matrix which will introduce them to a range of topics, then choose one or more topics to develop into a talk or presentation	31, 'Explain, Describe, Narrate Matrix'	Talk or presentation on one of the topics
A01 i–iii	Students play a game with the matrix which will introduce them to a range of topics, then choose one or more topics to develop into a talk or presentation	32, 'Explore, Analyse, Imagine Matrix'	Talk or presentation on one of the topics
Various	Students choose one or more activities from Resource 34, 'General Assignments'	34, 'General Assignments'	One or more General Assignments

Note: spread out these activities throughout the course and combine with oral work arising from language and literature work.

Introduction

The majority of oral activities in any English course should be process-based. In other words, they should be planned as part of the process of studying language, media and literature. However, some activities, particularly the individual extended contribution, will need to be separately planned. This unit offers a range of activities for group discussion and interaction and the individual contribution, but unlike other units it is not intended that they should be covered as a block. It would be far more effective to space out opportunities for planned discussion, debate and individual contributions over the whole course.

Notes on the Resources

27a. b. and c. FOR AND AGAINST CARDS

AIM: stimulate ideas for discussion and debate and support the development of arguments

The For and Against Cards can be used in a variety of ways as a stimulus for discussion and debate:

- A group of four students is given the topic – two students brainstorm arguments for the topic, and two against the topic. They jot down their main arguments, and then they can be given the cards to compare their own ideas with those on the cards. The students are then ready to try out their arguments in a discussion between the two pairs of students.
- Students with limited experience of developing arguments could be given the cards straight away as a starting point. After studying the For and Against Cards in pairs, they can then join up for a group discussion.
- Students working in groups of 2 to 4 could browse through the topics, discussing them as they go, until they find a topic that interests them. This can then be a focus for further development.

The next step is for students working alone or in pairs to choose a topic for further development into a debate speech or presentation. Resource 28, 'Preparing a Speech for Presentation', will help them to do this. Toolkit Resource 10, 'Types of Argument', will also be helpful.

28. PREPARING A SPEECH OR PRESENTATION

AIM: provide support for preparing, planning and delivering a speech or presentation

This resource gives a range of advice to help students prepare, plan and present their topics. It is not necessary to give every student a copy, as it can be displayed on an OHT. The relevant section of the OHT can be displayed before each stage of the process, as for some students the whole thing may be too much to take in at once. Before starting their preparation, students need to know whether they are preparing for a debate speech or presentation. During the two-year course, it should be possible to give all students an opportunity to take the lead in both.

- *A traditional debate* – the topic titles will need to be adapted into motions (e.g. this house believes that testing on animals is wrong and should be banned). Two speakers for the motion and two against, the role of the supporting speakers being to respond to the opposing team's main speech. This is followed by questions from the floor and a final vote.
- *A presentation* – one or two students prepare a presentation to the class on one of the topics. This could be longer and more detailed than a debate speech and could be supported by computer or OHT slides. The presentation could be followed by a discussion chaired by the speakers. A variation on this is for the student or students to use both cards to present a balanced view of the issue before throwing it open for discussion.

Toolkit Resource 10, 'Types of Argument', is referred to on the resource sheet and is worth consulting, as it will help students to build up a wide range of arguments, and to prepare a defence against the opposition.

Note: students should be reminded not to merely read the points on the slides and instead see them as aides-mémoire for themselves and the audience. Suggest that they plan a few sentences to expand each point. Advise that they keep any video or audio clips SHORT.

29. TOWNCESTER CHARACTERS and 30. TOWNCESTER PLAN

AIM: to provide a context for narrative talk

These two resource sheets provide a starting point for oral storytelling in the soap opera genre.

Students work in groups of 4 to 6.

Cut out the character cards. For each one they should make up additional background information: family (if any), where he or she lives, his or her personality. Jot the agreed information on the back of the card in pencil as a reminder.

Study the plan of Towncester (this is easier to work with if it can be enlarged to A3 size). The places on the plan will suggest a range of stories, e.g.

- Rupert meets Amanda at the Dog and Bone and asks her for a date – but his wife finds out
- Mike organises a protest against congestion charging
- Marion is mugged for her mobile phone and is angry that the local police station has been closed down
- A day in the life of Bob
- Sarah's bright ideas to increase her congregation.

There are two ways to develop the resources:

Game

Students take it in turns to select a character card at random. They then have to orally improvise a story about that character.

When all students have had a turn, the whole group takes the best ideas and interweaves them into a long soap opera story.

Plan

Students take each character and carefully plan a series of stories that will link them all up.

Drama

Students choose a character to role-play and orally improvise various situations suggested by the plan.

Presentation

Whatever the development process, each group then has to devise a way to present their soap opera to the rest of the class.

31. EXPLAIN, DESCRIBE, NARRATE MATRIX

AIM: explore a range of topics to explain, describe and narrate

This matrix contains a collection of 36 additional topics for students to explain, describe and narrate. The matrix can be used simply as a list of topics, or in the form of a game. For this, a number of dice will be needed (or folded papers numbered 1–6).

Students work in groups of 3 to 5. They take it in turn to roll a dice twice (or, in the absence of dice, select folded papers numbered 1–6). The two numbers refer to each axis of the matrix and will randomly select a topic. The student has to talk on that topic for a specified number of minutes (this will vary from half a minute to two minutes, depending on the ability of the group). Students who 'dry up' get a black mark. The student with the fewest black marks at the end of the game is the winner.

Students can refer back to the matrix whenever they are seeking a topic to explain, describe or narrate in speech or writing. Their recollection of the game will give them some ideas for which topic to choose, and how to approach it.

32. EXPLORE, ANALYSE, IMAGINE MATRIX

AIM: explore a range of topics to explore, analyse and imagine

With thanks to John Lennon for some of the 'Imagine' topics. This matrix is used in exactly the same way as the 'Explain, Describe, Narrate Matrix'.

33. DISCUSS, ARGUE, PERSUADE MATRIX

AIM: explore a range of topics to discuss and argue

This matrix contains a collection of 36 additional topics for students to discuss and argue. It is used slightly differently from the two previous matrices.

For students with little experience of discussion, or low confidence, it is better to play the exploratory rather than the competitive version of the discussion game. This works as follows:

- Students work in groups of 2 to 5.
- They take it in turn to roll the dice twice (or in the absence of dice, select folded papers numbered 1–6). The two numbers refer to each axis of the matrix and will randomly select a discussion topic. The student has to express his or her opinion on that topic.
- This is followed by a brief discussion.
- Other students in the group do the same.

The game can be made more competitive in the following way:

- Students play in groups of three, one student acting as a referee.
- The player whose turn it is decides which side of the topic is easiest to argue for and puts his or her case for that point of view.
- The other player argues from the opposite point of view.
- The referee decides who has put forward the most convincing arguments.
- The winner is the one who has won the discussion on most topics.

Students can refer back to the matrix whenever they are seeking a topic for discussion, debate or discursive writing. Their recollection of the discussion game will give them some ideas which topic to choose, and what arguments to use.

34. GENERAL ASSIGNMENTS

AIM: explore the resources from a wider range of perspectives

The resource sheet provides a list of suggestions for responding to the resources from a wider range of perspectives. Students can be allowed a degree of choice of assignment, but it is important to ensure that over the two-year course they have covered a wide range of different types of assignment. The list of forms on Resource 17, 'Forms of Writing', can be used as a way to audit this.

27a. FOR AND AGAINST CARDS

ABORTION – FOR
- ◆ Abortion was legalised in 1967 following pressure from women's groups and problems with back-street abortionists.
- ◆ An unwanted baby causes suffering to mother and child.
- ◆ 'Gymslip' mums can have their lives ruined by a baby.
- ◆ Women should have freedom of choice over all matters affecting their own bodies.

ABORTION – AGAINST
- ◆ The Roman Catholic Church bans it.
- ◆ It can never be right to take a human life except where there is a medical problem for mother or child.
- ◆ The 1990 act allows termination up to 24 weeks into the pregnancy – but a baby is fully formed by then.
- ◆ Why not have unwanted babies adopted? There is a long waiting list for adoption.

ALIENS HAVE VISITED EARTH – FOR
- ◆ There is a great deal of evidence to prove that aliens have visited Earth:
  - a) UFO debris was found at Roswell, New Mexico in 1947.
  - b) Area 51 is a secret American base where crashed UFOs are stored.
- ◆ Many people say that they have been abducted by aliens.
- ◆ There is extensive photographic and film evidence.
- ◆ With billions of planets in the universe, there must be some with intelligent life.

ALIENS HAVE VISITED EARTH – AGAINST
- ◆ There is no hard evidence.
- ◆ The American military state categorically that the Roswell incident and Area 51 have nothing to do with UFOs.
- ◆ Most of the photographs are faked, or are natural phenomena.
- ◆ There may be other intelligent life in the universe, but there is no evidence that it has visited Earth.

ANIMAL TESTING – FOR
- ◆ Surely it is better to test new products on animals first than to risk human lives.
- ◆ Animal testing helps us to find a cure for diseases such as cancer.
- ◆ Animals such as laboratory rats are specially bred for testing, so it is not as if they would have a better life if it stopped. In fact, they would have no life at all.
- ◆ There is no alternative – computer simulations can only go so far.

ANIMAL TESTING – AGAINST
- ◆ Animals suffer pain and death during testing.
- ◆ Testing products on animals is ethically questionable.
- ◆ The majority of testing is not for life-saving drugs, but for cosmetics and vanity products.
- ◆ Watch out! The animal rights activists will be on your case!

27b. FOR AND AGAINST CARDS

COSMETIC SURGERY – FOR

◆ Cosmetic surgery is just another way to keep young and healthy, like a good diet and regular exercise.

◆ It can boost confidence – if you look good, you'll feel good.

◆ It can improve your relationships with the opposite sex.

◆ It can further a career – in today's world, looks are important.

◆ More and more people are having it done.

COSMETIC SURGERY – AGAINST

◆ Okay for real problems such as burns, etc., or reconstructive surgery *BUT* it is morally wrong to spend money on vanity when millions are starving.

◆ It can go wrong, leaving people scarred for life.

◆ It is sometimes a displacement activity – in other words, people with problems think that cosmetic surgery will solve them – they should tackle the root problem instead.

◆ It can be addictive. Some people just cannot stop – look at Michael Jackson!

DESIGNER BABIES – FOR

◆ They will improve the physical appearance and health of the human race.

◆ They will boost examination results.

◆ Some of them will be geniuses – such as Einstein and Beethoven – who improve the quality of life for all.

◆ People have a right to choose, so why should they not choose the characteristics of their babies?

DESIGNER BABIES AGAINST

◆ Cloning techniques run the risk of reducing the gene pool.

◆ Creating designer babies is not natural and could work against evolution.

◆ It could go wrong in unexpected ways, producing a generation of Frankenstein monsters.

◆ The new 'super race' might despise their parents.

◆ The geniuses might be evil geniuses, such as Hitler.

DIVORCE IS TOO EASY – FOR

◆ Britain has the highest divorce rate in Europe (in 2002, 2 in 5 marriages ended in divorce).

◆ It creates single-parent families, which are economically disadvantaged.

◆ Children suffer economically and emotionally.

◆ Four out of five second marriages also end in divorce.

◆ If divorces were harder to get, people would try harder to make marriage work.

DIVORCE IS TOO EASY – AGAINST

◆ People should be able to escape from a bad marriage; for example, in cases of domestic violence.

◆ Life expectancy is longer and people change as they get older. It is not reasonable to expect two people to stay together for so long.

◆ In modern life, people expect to change everything regularly – e.g. cars – so why not partners?

◆ What is the point of carrying on with a relationship that is making both partners unhappy?

27c. FOR & AGAINST CARDS

GLOBAL WARMING IS A PROBLEM – FOR

◆ Scientists agree that since 1900 the world's climate has risen by 0.4°C.
◆ Recent freak weather conditions show that the problem is real, e.g. freak storms in the autumn of 2001, freak floods in the summer of 2002 – and that's only in Europe!
◆ Greenpeace have taken photographs to show that the polar glaciers are melting.
◆ We must cut emissions of greenhouse gases at once if we are to save the planet.

GLOBAL WARMING IS A PROBLEM – AGAINST

◆ Global warming is a good example of a 'modern myth' or 'urban legend'.
◆ It is true that the average temperature has risen but this is just one of a series of regular climate changes.
◆ There have always been freak weather events, hurricanes, floods, etc. and Greenpeace chose to photograph a receding glacier. Norwegian scientists pointed out that there was an advancing glacier in the next bay!

INTERNET BAN FOR UNDER 12s – FOR

◆ Paedophiles use Internet chatrooms to make contact with children.
◆ Pornography is widely available on the Internet.
◆ Many sites contain biased or misleading information.
◆ Filters are ineffective and children soon learn to bypass them.
◆ The Internet can be addictive.

INTERNET BAN FOR UNDER 12s – AGAINST

◆ The Internet is very educational – it is like an encyclopedia with millions of pages.
◆ The content of TV, books and magazines can also be harmful.
◆ It can be counter-productive to shelter children too much.
◆ It is better to supervise Internet use than to ban it all together.

LEGALISATION OF DRUGS – FOR

◆ The current situation in which cannabis has been reclassified as a class C drug is an improvement, but does not go far enough.
◆ Legalisation would take drug sales away from dealers.
◆ It would take away the 'forbidden fruit' effect that makes drug-taking glamorous.
◆ It would make it easier to treat addicts properly.
◆ The United States' experience with Prohibition in the 1920s is a good example of how criminals take over when a substance is banned.

LEGALISATION OF DRUGS – AGAINST

◆ The experiment with the reclassification of cannabis in Brixton shows the dangers of this idea. Drug-dealing in all drugs now takes place openly, and drug abuse is increasing.
◆ All drugs, even cannabis, are dangerous.
◆ Every year, hundreds of young people die because of drug abuse.
◆ Sweden has the lowest number of drug addicts in Europe – but it has tough laws on drugs.

28. PREPARING A SPEECH OR PRESENTATION

Define any difficult or vague terms in the topic title

(*Note*: titles are taken from Resource 33.)

- **Scientific or technical terms** For example, 'GM crops' means genetically modified crops. Check that you understand the term: genetically modified means that the genetic structure of the crop has been changed to increase yields and make it more resistant to disease. Remember to explain this to your audience in your introduction.

- **Slang** For example, 'The police have "lost it".' What does the slang phrase 'lost it' mean? (That they have lost control of crime.)

- **Interpretation** For example, in the topic title 'Computers are taking over the world', 'taking over the world' is open to interpretation. It could mean that computers are taking over from labour-intensive manual systems in every sphere of work and therefore making things more efficient, or it could mean that computers are taking the human element out of things and making the world a more impersonal, soulless place. Choose the interpretation that favours your line of argument.

Research

Good research can make the presentation of a point of view much more powerful. Here are some of the things you should look for in your research:

- **Facts and statistics** These persuade by appealing to the audience's reason.

- **Anecdotes** These add human interest and persuade by appealing to the audience's emotions.

- **Illustrations, video clips, graphs, charts, bulleted lists, etc**. These add interest and can help to express key points more powerfully. Note that they are suitable for all kinds of presentation (e.g. a debate speech) and also that they are easy to misuse.

Planning

Review your research material and plan your speech or presentation.

- **Introduction** State your line of argument, define any difficult or vague terms, and give some background information about the topic. Another approach is to begin with an 'attention-grabber' – for example, a harrowing anecdote about the effects of a cosmetics test on a puppy. If your take this approach, remember to follow up your 'attention-grabber' with the basic information outlined above.

- **Series of arguments** See resource 10, 'Types of Argument', for ideas about the kind of arguments that are most effective. The For and Against Cards (Resources 27a, b and c) contain specific suggestions for each topic. However, these need fleshing out. Remember to make good use of facts and statistics and anecdotes. You could also use humour, but be careful! Nothing sounds worse than forced humour. Only use it if it arises naturally from the point you are making. Finally, it is a good idea to respond to (or anticipate, if you are speaking first) the opposition's main points.

- **Conclusion** Sum up your main points and try to leave the audience with a memorable thought. For example, you could refer back to your description of the suffering puppy, and say that this need never happen again if animal testing is made illegal. Whatever you do, don't end with a downbeat comment like 'That's it' or 'Was that OK, Sir/Miss?'

29. TOWNCESTER CHARACTERS

RUPERT

Accountant
'I'm worried that they'll convert Harwell Hall into a centre for asylum seekers. I think the steel works site would be more suitable.'

BILL

Police constable
'I'm fed up with criticisms of the police. Crime is soaring and we're undermanned and swamped in paperwork.'

SALLY

Call-centre worker
'There's a lot of pressure and the pay's not great, and we're all worried the centre will be relocated to India.'

BOB

Beggar and drug addict
'My pitch is just outside Central Station. I can make £100 on a good day. Of course, I blow it on drugs as soon as I get it.'

RAJID

Owner of 'Latenite' corner shop
'It's a tough job! If I get attacked again, I'm going to sell up and retire.'

AMANDA

Barmaid at the Dog and Bone
'It's a great town for pubs and clubs. Mind you, it gets a bit rough at chucking-out time!'

SARAH

Vicar
'I feel that I've been accepted, but congregations are declining. There are more worshippers at the mosque now.'

MIKE

Department store Manager
'I'm worried about how these congestion charges will affect business – and, to make it worse, they're planning an out-of-town shopping mall!'

MARION

Teacher
'Archways is a wonderful school. I'm so glad I transferred from Sunny Hill Comp. The kids used to swear at me and fight in class – it was impossible to teach!'

30. TOWNCESTER PLAN

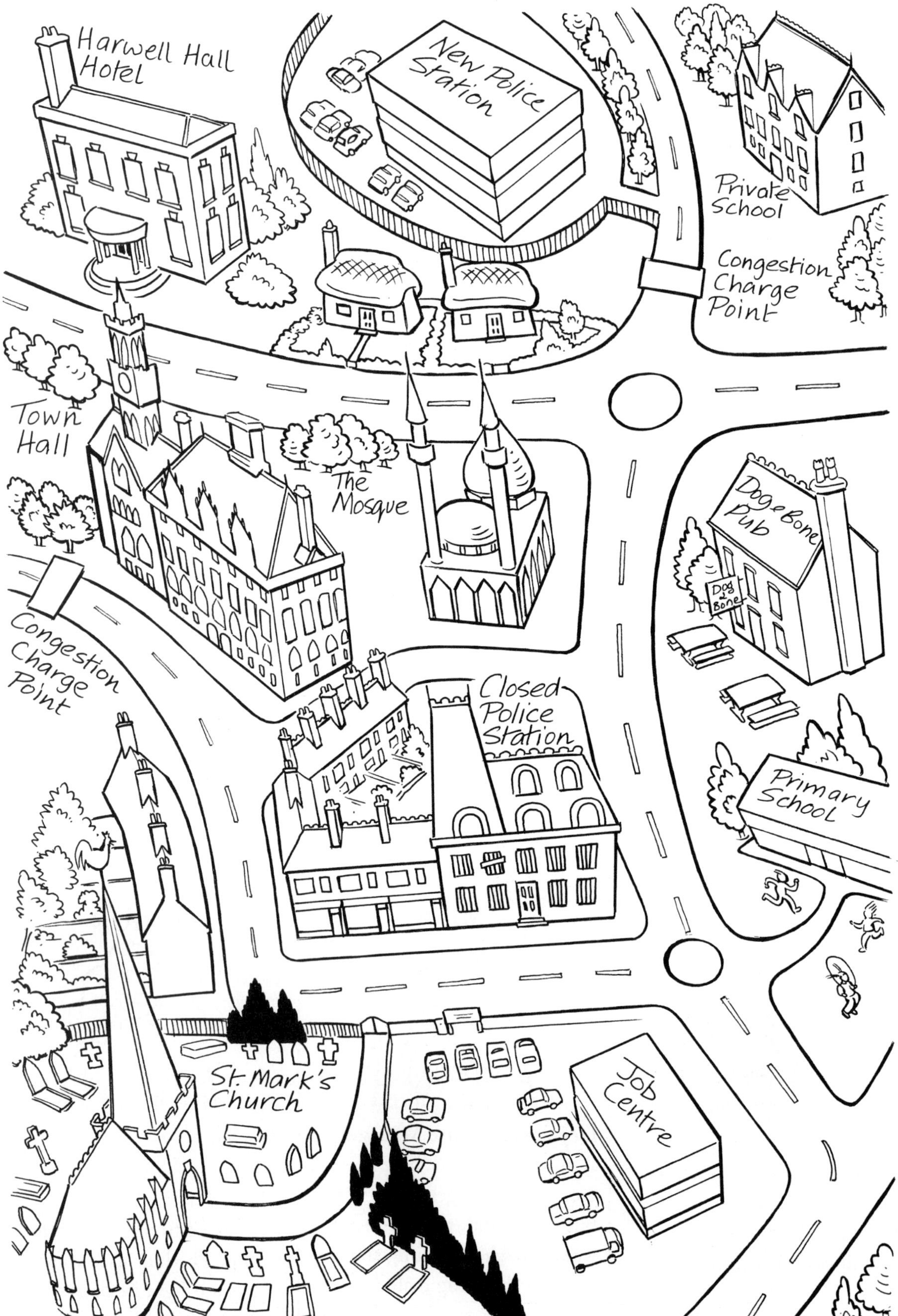

Harwell Hall Hotel

New Police Station

Private School

Congestion Charge Point

Town Hall

The Mosque

Dog Bone Pub

Congestion Charge Point

Primary School

Closed Police Station

St. Mark's Church

Job Centre

31. EXPLAIN, DESCRIBE, NARRATE MATRIX

Choose a topic to explain, describe or narrate, or choose at random by rolling a dice twice. This will give a number for each axis of the matrix.

	1	2	3	4	5	6
1	Explain a scientific theory	Describe a book or film	Narrate a fairy tale	Explain how you made something	Describe a place	Narrate an urban legend
2	Explain how something is operated	Describe a famous person	Narrate a family argument	Explain how you overcame a problem	Describe your best friend	Narrate the plot of your favourite book
3	Explain how to chat up a boy/girl	Describe a dream	Narrate a fantasy about a night out with your favourite celebrity	Explain the main theme in a poem, a book or a film	Describe your ambition	Narrate the plot of your favourite film
4	Explain how to cook your favourite meal	Describe a hobby	Narrate a fantasy about your future	Explain why you like a particular piece of music	Describe your family	Narrate what happened on your first date
5	Explain how to look after something, e.g. a pet	Describe a holiday	Narrate a ghost story	Explain why you were late/wrong/made a mistake	Describe your fears	Narrate what happened on your first day at school
6	Explain how you carried out a task	Describe a personal achievement	Narrate a joke	Explain your philosophy of life	Describe your pet	Narrate your most embarrassing moment

32. EXPLORE, ANALYSE, IMAGINE MATRIX

Choose a topic to explore, analyse or imagine, or choose at random by rolling a dice twice. This will give a number for each axis of the matrix.

	1	2	3	4	5	6
1	Explore a concept through concept-mapping	Analyse (psychoanalyse) a real person	Imagine a better world	Explore a holiday plan	Analyse a character in a novel you have read	Imagine all the people living for today
2	Explore a novel through discussion and role-play	Analyse a person's motives for doing something	Imagine all the people living life in peace	Explore a problem through brainstorming	Analyse a poem	Imagine all the people sharing all the world
3	Explore alternative solutions to a problem	Analyse a problem	Imagine being an animal	Explore an idea or philosophy	Analyse a relationship	Imagine living on another planet
4	Explore an imaginary world	Analyse a TV advertisement	Imagine no possessions	Explore the weak points in a plan or idea	Analyse an argument in an essay or article	Imagine there were no countries
5	Explore different interpretations of a book or film	Analyse the film techniques used in a film	Imagine there is no heaven	Explore the implications of a decision	Analyse the pros and cons of a decision	Imagine what it would be like to be disabled
6	Explore the meaning of a figure of speech	Analyse where you went wrong last time you made a mistake	Imagine what it would be like to be somebody else	Explore your shared assumptions	Analyse your own personality	Imagine what life will be like in the year 3000

33. DISCUSS, ARGUE, PERSUADE MATRIX

Choose a topic for discussion, debate or presentation, or choose at random by rolling a dice twice. This will give a number for each axis of the matrix.

	1	2	3	4	5	6
1	AS levels should be abolished	Books are more satisfying than films	Britain should become the 51st American State	Brussels bureaucrats are ruining Britain	Cars should be taxed out of existence	CCTV cameras are an invasion of privacy
2	Computers are taking over the world	Corporal punishment	Every job should have the same salary	Everyone should be on a diet	Factory farming	Footballers are overpaid
3	Globalisation	GM crops	Happiness is more important than money	Immigration	Islam is the religion of the future	Life exists on other planets
4	Marriage is an outmoded institution	Nuclear power should be abolished	Polygamy should be legal	Pop music has been declining since the 1990s	Pornography exploits women and should be illegal	Private education should be abolished
5	Racism is no longer a problem in Britain	Religion	Which five people have contributed most to Britain?	Sex changes should be available on the NHS	Sustainable development	The BBC no longer deserves its licence fee
6	The existence of God	The monarchy	The police have 'lost it'	Third World debt should be written off	TV can seriously damage your brain	Women are taking over the world

34. GENERAL ASSIGNMENTS

Speaking and listening

Further develop the Towncester soap by introducing some of the issues from the 'Discuss, Argue, Persuade Matrix'.

Improvise what might happen if some of the characters from a literary text you are reading visited Towncester and interacted with some of the characters there.

Reading

Select some of the issues from the from the 'Discuss, Argue, Persuade Matrix' and look them up in an encyclopedia or type them into an Internet search engine.

Read the latest newspaper and compile a list of current issues for discussion and debate.

Writing

Write about some of the topics from the 'Discuss, Argue, Persuade Matrix' and the 'Explain, Describe, Narrate Matrix'.

Produce the front page of the *Towncester Times*.

The wider curriculum

Many of the topics relate to other areas of the curriculum. If time allows, explore them in other subject lessons and get help from teachers of those subjects, e.g. get a physics teacher to help with research on global warming. Get his or her views and the reasons behind them.

Spiritual, moral, ethical, social and cultural issues

Some of the topics relate to the above areas and could be investigated further in subjects such as RE, PHSE and Citizenship.

What social issues are explored in the Towncester soap? Do you think a soap opera can make a valid contribution to debate on serious issues (consider, for example, *EastEnders*, particularly in its earlier days)?

ICT

Enter the 'Discuss, Argue, Persuade Matrix' and the 'Explain, Describe, Narrate Matrix' into a database and continue to add to the list of topics.

Design and post an Internet site expressing your views on one of the 'Discuss, Argue, Persuade' topics.

European dimension

Explore (with the help of a modern languages teacher, if possible) what would be better, worse or just different if Towncester were a European town.

Write about what happens when students from Sunny Hill Comprehensive go on a trip to Paris.

UNIT 4: *THE MERCHANT OF VENICE*

RESOURCES: *The Merchant of Venice* any edition

VIDEO: (optional): *The Merchant of Venice*, Jonathan Miller, John Sichel, 1973 (or any other version)

BOARD: Any for English or English literature coursework; AQA, OCR and WJEC for English literature examination (*Note*: check current specifications)

RANGE: Work based on a play by Shakespeare

AO	TEACHING SEQUENCE	RESOURCES	OUTCOMES
A02iv	Pre-reading: research Judaism	Library, Internet	Understanding of why Shylock is an outsider in Venetian society, and why Antonio berates him for lending money at interest
A02i A01 i–iii	Students read Act 1, Scene 2 and then play 'The Caskets Game' in groups of 4 to 6; after playing the game, students read from Act 1, Scene 2, to Act 3, Scene 2	35, 'The Caskets Game'	Knowledge of the text and understanding of some of the issues to do with appearance and reality
A02i A01 i–iii	Students read to the end of Act 3, then play 'The Trial Game'; then read Act 4, Scene 1 to find out what actually happened at the trial Students read play to the end	36, 'The Trial Game'	Knowledge of the text and understanding of some of the issues to do with revenge, justice, racism, etc.
A02i	Working in pairs, students use the resource sheet to study the character of Bassanio	37, 'Bassanio'	Knowledge of character Essay on this character and/or one of the other characters studied in detail
A02i	Working in pairs, students use the resource sheet to study the character of Antonio	38, 'Antonio'	Knowledge of character Essay on this character and/or one of the other characters studied in detail
A02i	Working in pairs, students use the resource sheet to study the character of Jessica	39, 'Jessica'	Knowledge of character Essay on this character and/or one of the other characters studied in detail
A02i	Working in pairs, students use the resource sheet to study the character of Shylock Students make notes on the minor characters in the play (optional)	40, 'Shylock'	Knowledge of character Essay on this character and/or one of the other characters studied in detail Knowledge of minor characters
A02i A01 i–iii	In groups of 3 or 4, students research one theme, then share their findings with the rest of the class	41, 'Themes'	A short essay on one of the themes to share with the rest of the class
Various	One or more general assignments from Resource 43	43, 'General Assignments'	As appropriate
LIT A01–4	If the text is being studied for the English literature examination, use these questions for practice and revision	26, 'English Literature Examination-Style Questions' Toolkit 11, 'Literary Essay Template'	One or more literary essays using notes made in previous lessons

Introduction

The Merchant of Venice consists of three interwoven plots. The Casket Plot is about an heiress named Portia who, according to her father's will, must be won by selecting one of three caskets which contains her portrait. Bassanio asks his wealthy merchant friend Antonio for a loan so he can woo Portia. This introduces the Bond Plot. Antonio cannot lend money to his friend as he has invested everything in some 'argosies' (merchant ships). He therefore agrees to stand as surety for a loan of 3000 ducats from Shylock, a Jewish moneylender, on the condition that if the loan cannot be repaid in time Antonio will forfeit a pound of flesh. Bassanio uses the money to woo Portia and succeeds in selecting the casket which contains her portrait, and he and Portia marry. After the wedding, they hear that Antonio's ships have been lost and Shylock is demanding his pound of flesh. Bassanio rushes to help him, and so does Portia – disguised as a young lawyer (Balthazar). She decrees that he must take flesh only, and that if any blood is spilled he must die. Shylock is ordered to give half of his estate to Antonio, who agrees not to take the money if Shylock converts to Christianity. The play ends with the Ring Plot, in which Portia, disguised as Balthazar, demands the wedding ring she gave to Bassanio as a gift. He is compelled to give it, and she punishes him playfully at the end of the play.

The Merchant of Venice is a good choice of Shakespeare play for GCSE as it is relatively easy to read, has a strong plot and characters, and raises some interesting issues.

Notes on the Resources

35. THE CASKETS GAME

AIM: to find out about the caskets plot by playing it as a game

There are two ways to present this activity. For each group, cut out the three caskets from a resource sheet and fold them over backwards. The caskets should be laid face up on the table and students instructed not to look at the other side of the fold until they have made their choice. A quicker way is to make two OHTs of the resource sheet, one with the 'inside' box (on the right) blanked out, and the other one complete.

Students read Act I, scene ii before playing the game, as this explains its purpose in the play. (Portia's father left a will saying that any suitor would have to choose one of the caskets. If he chose correctly, he would find a picture of Portia within and would win her for his wife.)

Students work in groups of 4 to 6. On each table, place the three 'caskets' face up and ask them to discuss which they would choose and why. When all students have chosen, the casket cards can be turned over and the scrolls read. Discuss the object and message in each scroll.

Students then read from Act I, scene ii to Act III, scene ii to find out the choices Portia's suitors made, and how Bassanio gets his loan and is able to woo Portia and choose the right casket.

Finally students discuss whether they think that, in the words of Nerissa, the casket test was a 'good inspiration'. In other words, do they think it acted as an effective way of filtering out unsuitable suitors?

36. THE TRIAL GAME

AIM: to explore the issues raised by Antonio's trial

The game should be played when students have read to the end of Act II, but *before* they have read Act IV. Of course, some students will know the play, or may have read ahead, but the important principle is that the case should be decided on the evidence.

Divide the class into two halves. One half should research evidence for column one of the resource sheet, and the other half for column two.

Groups of students should now argue the case. One way to do this is in groups of five, with two students arguing in defence of Shylock and two in prosecution of Shylock. The fifth student could act as judge and pronounce sentence.

- Ensure that students are clear what the case is about: Shylock wants to take Antonio to court to get his 'bond' (a pound of flesh). He refuses repayment of even three times the amount because he wants revenge on Antonio for the way he has treated him.
- Students should decide the case on the basis of their own judgement, not what happens in the play (should any of them know this).
- Since no students can know the laws of sixteenth-century Venice and few are likely to know enough modern law, the case should be decided on the basis of *what is fair*.

When students have role-played the trial, the results should be discussed by the whole class. This should be followed by reading Act IV, scene ii. The class then discuss the judgement on Shylock, in particular how it compares to their own judgements and the question, Is it fair?

37. BASSANIO

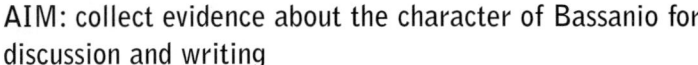

AIM: collect evidence about the character of Bassanio for discussion and writing

The quotation on the resource sheet is from Act I, scene i and is a key piece of evidence about Bassanio. Working in pairs, students read the quotation and then discuss the questions below, making notes on their answers. The first task involves bringing together all the basic background information about Bassanio; those that follow explore his character in more depth as well as his motive for wanting more money and to marry Portia. Overall, he does not emerge as a very attractive character: he has got into debt through living beyond his means, and wants to borrow more money to win Portia so that he can benefit from her fortune.

As a follow-up students could discuss the Bassanios of the modern world. In other words, people who live beyond their means in order to impress others.

Writing

Students use the information to write an essay on this character and/or one of the others studied in detail.

38. ANTONIO

AIM: collect evidence about the character of Antonio for discussion and writing
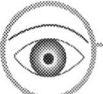

This extract from Act I, scene iii shows the negative side of Antonio's character. Working in pairs, students read the extract and then discuss the questions below, making notes on their answers. The first task involves bringing together all the basic background information about Antonio. This should include information about his profession and personality, in particular, his great friendliness and generosity. It could be argued that he is so friendly and generous that people like Bassanio take advantage of him. Contrasted to this is his vitriolic treatment of Shylock, which the third and fourth questions explore.

As a follow-up, students could 'hot-seat' Antonio and ask him why, when he is generally so friendly, he treats Shylock in this way.

Writing

Students use the information to write an essay on this character and/or one of the others studied in detail.

39. JESSICA

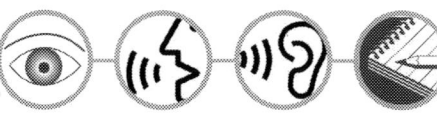

AIM: collect evidence about the character of Jessica for discussion and writing

The quotation on the resource sheet is from the beginning of Act II, scene iii and is a key piece of evidence about Jessica's attitude to her life with her father. Working in pairs, students read the quotation and then discuss the questions below, making notes on their answers.

As a follow-up, students could discuss the Jessicas of the modern world, in other words, teenage girls who are treated strictly by their parents, especially those from cultures where arranged marriages are common.

Writing

Students use the information to write an essay on this character and/or one of the others studied in detail.

40. SHYLOCK

AIM: collect evidence about the character of Shylock for discussion and writing

The extract on the resource sheet is from Act III, scene i and is a key piece of evidence about Shylock's mistreatment at the hands of Christians. Working in pairs, students read the quotation and then discuss the questions below, making notes on their answers.

Today's students may know very little about the traditional Jew stereotype, or it may have become confused with stereotypes arising from more recent world events such as the conflict in the Middle East. The stereotype arose because Jews were often immigrants confined by law to ghettos. Most types of work were denied to them, so they resorted to moneylending. They were thought to be greedy, grasping, miserly and extortionate. The Nazis even went so far as to portray them as subhuman.

When students compare this stereotype with Shylock, they will find that he fits the stereotype. However, Shakespeare has added a very important human dimension. This famous speech emphasises that he is just as human as a Christian.

Writing

Students use the information to write an essay on this character and/or one of the others studied in detail.

If the play is being prepared for examination, it is worth asking students to make brief notes on the minor characters in the play. This work could be shared around the class by asking a pair of students to research each character and then report back while others take notes. The minor characters in the play are:

PRINCE OF MOROCCO, suitor to Portia
PRINCE OF ARRAGON, suitor to Portia
SOLANIO, friend to Antonio and Bassanio
SALERIO, friend to Antonio and Bassanio
GRATIANO, friend to Antonio and Bassanio
TUBAL, a Jew, Shylock's friend
LAUNCELOT GOBBO, a clown, servant to Shylock
OLD GOBBO, father to Launcelot
LEONARDO, servant to Bassanio
BALTHASAR, servant to Portia

STEPHANO, servant to Portia
PORTIA, a rich heiress
NERISSA, her waiting maid.

41. THEMES

AIM: explore the main themes of the play

Students work in groups of 3 or 4 to research a theme. Each group can be allocated a different theme and asked to report back to the rest of the class. This way, all students study one theme in detail and get to know something about all the others.

This could be followed up by asking each group to write about their theme on one A4 page. The pages can then be duplicated for the rest of the class.

42. IMAGERY

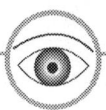

AIM: examine how imagery is used throughout the play to add to our impression of Shylock

Working in pairs, students examine the imagery and figures of speech which are used to describe Shylock. Before starting the activity, students may need to revise the following terms that can be used for this purpose:

connotation – the associations of a word
extended metaphor – a metaphor developed to include other aspects of the basic comparison
figure of speech – a way of saying something
imagery – figures of speech which are 'word pictures'
metaphor – a direct comparison between one thing and another
play on words – exploiting the double meaning of different words which sound the same or similar
sarcasm – humour or irony which is intended to hurt
simile – a comparison using 'like' or 'as'.

Even more important than identifying the imagery and figures of speech is to comment on their cumulative effect, which is extremely negative.

An interesting follow-up would be to compare the imagery used to describe another character, e.g. Antonio or Portia.

43. GENERAL ASSIGNMENTS

AIM: explore the play from a wider range of perspectives

The resource sheet provides a list of suggestions for responding to the play from a wider range of perspectives. The activities are particularly suited to coursework, but can also be used as supporting exercises for an examination text. Toolkit resources, for example Toolkit Resource 17, 'Forms of Writing', can be used to support several of the assignments on this resource.

44. ENGLISH LITERATURE EXAMINATION-STYLE QUESTIONS

AIM: prepare and practice for examination

These questions can be used for practice by students who are preparing the text for Edexcel English Literature. Foundation-tier students may find it helpful to use Toolkit Resource 11, 'Literary Essay Template', as a support for their writing.

35. THE CASKETS GAME

Who chooseth me shall gain what many men desire.

FOLD BACKWARDS ALONG THIS LINE

All that glisters is not gold,
Often have you heard that told;
Many a man his life hath sold
But my outside to behold.
Gilded tombs do worms infold.
Had you been as wise as bold,
Young in limbs, in judgment old,
Your answer had not been inscroll'd.
Fare you well, your suit is cold.

Who chooseth me shall get as much as he deserves

FOLD BACKWARDS ALONG THIS LINE

The fire seven times tried this;
Seven times tried that judgment is
That did never choose amiss.
Some there be that shadows kiss,
Such have but a shadow's bliss.
There be fools alive iwis
Silver'd o'er, and so was this.
Take what wife you will to bed,
I will ever be your head.
So be gone; you are sped.

Who chooseth me must give and hazard all he hath

FOLD BACKWARDS ALONG THIS LINE

You that choose not by the view,
Chance as fair and choose as true!
Since this fortune falls to you,
Be content and seek no new.
If you be well pleas'd with this,
And hold your fortune for your bliss,
Turn to where your lady is
And claim her with a loving kiss.

36. THE TRIAL GAME

Collect evidence from the play to support one of the following cases:

EVIDENCE IN DEFENCE OF SHYLOCK	EVIDENCE IN PROSECUTION OF SHYLOCK

37. BASSANIO

BASSANIO. 'Tis not unknown to you, Antonio,
How much I have disabled mine estate
By something showing a more swelling port
Than my faint means would grant continuance;
Nor do I now make moan to be abridg'd
From such a noble rate; but my chief care
Is to come fairly off from the great debts
Wherein my time, something too prodigal,
Hath left me gag'd. To you, Antonio,
I owe the most, in money and in love;
And from your love I have a warranty
To unburden all my plots and purposes
How to get clear of all the debts I owe.

- Jot down basic information about Bassanio.

- Why is he in debt and why does he want to borrow more money?

- Why does he want to marry Portia?

- Do you think these motives justify making his friend sign such a serious 'bond'?

38. ANTONIO

SHYLOCK. Signior Antonio, many a time and oft

    In the Rialto you have rated me

    About my moneys and my usances;

    Still have I borne it with a patient shrug,

    For suff'rance is the badge of all our tribe;

    You call me misbeliever, cut-throat dog,

    And spit upon my Jewish gaberdine,

    And all for use of that which is mine own . . .

ANTONIO. I am as like to call thee so again,

    To spit on thee again, to spurn thee too.

    If thou wilt lend this money, lend it not

    As to thy friends, for when did friendship take

    A breed for barren metal of his friend? . . .

- Jot down everything you know about Antonio: personality, profession, behaviour towards his friends, etc.

- Why is Antonio sad at the beginning of the play?

- Discuss the above conversation. How do you explain Antonio's attitude towards Shylock? What does he dislike about him? Does his attitude lower your opinion of his personality, or is it excusable in the context of the times?

39. JESSICA

JESSICA. I am sorry thou wilt leave my father so.
　　Our house is hell; and thou, a merry devil,
　　Didst rob it of some taste of tediousness.
　　But fare thee well; there is a ducat for thee;
　　And, Launcelot, soon at supper shalt thou see
　　Lorenzo, who is thy new master's guest.
　　Give him this letter; do it secretly.
　　And so farewell. I would not have my father
　　See me in talk with thee.

- What does this speech show about Jessica's feelings about life in her father's house?

- Describe the plot she has made with Lorenzo.

- Who do you think is most to blame for Jessica's elopement and why (Shylock, Lorenzo or Jessica herself)?

40. SHYLOCK

SALERIO. Why, I am sure, if he forfeit, thou wilt not take his flesh. What's that good for?

SHYLOCK. To bait fish withal. If it will feed nothing else, it will feed my revenge. He hath disgrac'd me and hind'red me half a million; laugh'd at my losses, mock'd at my gains, scorned my nation, thwarted my bargains, cooled my friends, heated mine enemies. And what's his reason? I am a Jew ... If you prick us, do we not bleed? If you tickle us, do we not laugh? If you poison us, do we not die? And if you wrong us, shall we not revenge? If we are like you in the rest, we will resemble you in that. If a Jew wrong a Christian, what is his humility? Revenge. If a Christian wrong a Jew, what should his sufferance be by Christian example? Why, revenge. The villainy you teach me I will execute; and it shall go hard but I will better the instruction.

- Jot down everything you know about the stereotype of the typical Jew as portrayed in history and literature pre-twentieth century. How have events of the twentieth and twenty-first century changed those stereotypes?

- Jot down everything you know about Shylock – his personality, how he makes a living, etc. Discuss his plea to be treated as a human being. How far is his behaviour a result of the way he has been treated by Christians?

- Discuss how far the character of Shylock conforms to or differs from the pre-twentieth-century stereotype of Jews. Does Shakespeare present him as a stereotype or as a rounded human being?

41. THEMES

Choose one of the following themes and make notes on it using the table below.

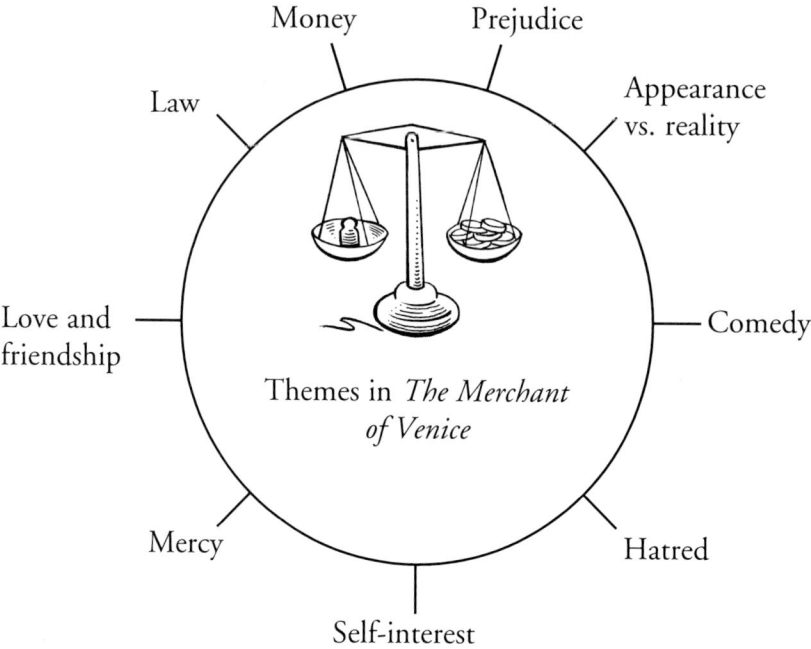

CHARACTERS
EVENTS
KEY SCENES
QUOTATIONS

42. IMAGERY

In the 'Notes' column, explain what figure of speech is used in each quotation and what effect it has.

QUOTATION	NOTES
1. The devil can cite Scripture for his purpose. An evil soul producing holy witness Is like a villain with a smiling cheek, A goodly apple rotten at the heart. O, what a goodly outside falsehood hath!	
2. What should I say to you? Should I not say 'Hath a dog money? Is it possible A cur can lend three thousand ducats?'	
3. Hie thee, gentle Jew. The Hebrew will turn Christian: he grows kind.	
4. Certainly the Jew is the very devil incarnation;	
5. There is more difference between thy flesh and hers than between jet and ivory; more between your bloods than there is between red wine and Rhenish	
6. Thou call'dst me dog before thou hadst a cause, But, since I am a dog, beware my fangs; The Duke shall grant me justice.	
7. Truly then I fear you are damn'd both by father and mother; thus when I shun Scylla, your father, I fall into Charybdis, your mother; well, you are gone both ways.	
8. We all expect a gentle answer, Jew.	
9. Thy currish spirit Govern'd a wolf who, hang'd for human slaughter, Even from the gallows did his fell soul fleet, And, whilst thou layest in thy unhallowed dam, Infus'd itself in thee; for thy desires Are wolfish, bloody, starv'd and ravenous	

Now: examine the overall effect of the imagery used to describe Shylock throughout the play.

43. GENERAL ASSIGNMENTS

Speaking and listening

Role-play what might have happened if the Prince of Morocco or the Prince of Arragon had chosen the right casket, or Bassanio had chosen the wrong one.

Role-play what would happen if Shylock had a lawyer to speak for him and he raised these points:

◆ *flesh* means physical body of man as distinct from the spiritual, and therefore includes, blood, bones, skin, etc.

◆ Shylock is not on trial and therefore the court can only rule whether or not the bond is forfeit, and not take any action against Shylock.

◆ Shylock wishes to bring a second action against Antonio – of racism.

Explore the play using a range of drama techniques (see Toolkit Resource 20, 'Drama Techniques').

Reading

Read Marlowe's *Jew of Malta* and compare Barabas with Shylock.

Writing

What changes would you make to turn the play into a tragedy? Write an outline of your new plot, and one or two new scenes in detail.

Imagine that your school is planning a performance of the play and a Jewish parent writes a letter urging you to choose another play on the grounds that *The Merchant of Venice* is racist. What would you say in your letter of reply?

Watch a performance or a video (for example, the Jonathan Miller version, 1973) and write a review (see Toolkit Resource 15, 'Film Review').

The wider curriculum

Lending money at interest (*usury*) was forbidden to Christians but allowed under Jewish law. Find out when this changed and why. Do some research into interest rates charged by different credit card companies and work out how much you would have to pay back if you borrowed £3000 for three months. Discuss how far you think the public is being exploited.

Spiritual, moral, ethical, social and cultural issues

Find out about Judaism and compare it with the related religions of Christianity and Islam.

Explore anti-Semitism in medieval and modern Europe.

Investigate other groups that have been stereotyped and denied their full human rights in recent history.

ICT

Download the electronic text of the play from http://etext.lib.virginia.edu/shakespeare/works/ and experiment with searching for key words and phrases, e.g. *Christian, cur, dog, ducats, friend, Jew, mercy, money*, or the names of characters.

European dimension

Find out about the history of the Venetian Republic.

44. ENGLISH LITERATURE EXAMINATION-STYLE QUESTIONS

Foundation tier

Four things are important to Shylock. Put them in order of importance, giving a detailed explanation for the position you have given to each one:

◆ money (his ducats)

◆ his daughter, Jessica

◆ revenge on Antonio

◆ to be accepted as a human being.

Write about *one* of the following pairs of themes in *The Merchant of Venice*: law and mercy, love and money, humanity and racism, appearance and reality.

Though *The Merchant of Venice* explores some serious issues and comes close to tragedy, it is still very much a comedy. Explore this statement by referring to:

◆ the comic characters (Launcelot Gobbo and his father, Old Gobbo)

◆ disguise (Portia and Nerissa)

◆ teasing (the ring plot).

Higher tier

Describing the comic elements in the play, one critic wrote that: 'It is the earliest example of a pantomime.' Discuss this statement by considering:

◆ the three caskets and three different choices by three suitors

◆ the evil villain (Shylock)

◆ the 'prince' in 'drag' (Portia as Balthazar) who saves the hero with a twist of words

◆ the sexual teasing in the ring plot

◆ the important differences between this play and a pantomime.

In Shylock, Shakespeare has created a character that is more than a stereotype. Discuss this statement by referring to:

◆ the aspects of his character, such as miserliness, that conform to the stereotype

◆ the way the Christian characters have provoked Shylock

◆ his passionate plea for his humanity to be recognised.

'How shalt thou hope for mercy, rend'ring none?' Discuss the theme of mercy in the play. You may wish to write about:

◆ Antonio's treatment of Shylock – did he show any mercy?

◆ Shylock's lust for revenge – how far could it be justified or at least understood?

◆ the Duke's plea to Shylock

◆ Portia's speech about mercy

◆ the Duke's final sentence on Shylock – is it really merciful?

Reread the Prince of Morocco's speech in Act II, scene vii, the Prince of Arragon's speech in Act II, scene ix and Bassanio's speech in Act III, scene ii. Describe the decision-making process that each suitor goes through, what it reveals about him and how it relates to the themes of the play.

UNIT 5: *SILAS MARNER*

RESOURCES: *Silas Marner* by George Eliot. Any edition, but note that OCR specify, for 2005, *Silas Marner* by George Eliot, Wordsworth 1853262218

FILM: *Silas Marner*, directed by Giles Foster, BBC, 1985

BOARD: WJEC terminal examination 2004, OCR terminal examination 2005

RANGE: Prose pre-1914

AO	TEACHING SEQUENCE	RESOURCES	OUTCOMES
A02iv	Pre-reading: historical and geographical background, brief biography of Eliot	Library, internet, see The Victorian Web at //65.107.211.206/victor.html	Understanding of the context of the novel
A02i	Read the novel in three sections, each followed by discussion: Chapters 1–7 Chapters 8–15 Chapters 16–Conclusion	*Silas Marner*	Notes on discussion topics
A02 i, iv	In pairs, students draw up a Plot Chart and paste events cut from Resource 45a in correct sequence (use Resource 45b to check)	45a, 'Plot Sequence', 45b, 'Plot Sequence'	Main events in plot mapped onto Plot Chart
A02 i, iv A03 i–iii	Students study the characters in the book by completing Resource 46 and 47 and cutting and pasting them onto the Plot Chart Essay on one of the main characters using Resrouce 48 as a basis General assignment (optional)	46, 'Characters' 47, 'Character Quotations' 48, 'The Two Main Characters' 54, 'General Assignments'	Characters mapped onto plot chart Essay on one of the main characters General assignment (optional)
A02 i, iv A03 i–iii	Students complete Resource sheets 49, 'Objects' and 50, 'Opposites' and map them onto the Plot Chart; all students complete the resource sheets for all four themes but choose one as the basis of an essay General assignment (optional)	49, 'Objects' 50, 'Opposites' 51a, 'Religion and Love' 51b, 'Social Class and Prejudice' 54, 'General assignments'	'Objects', 'Opposites' and themes mapped onto Plot Chart Essay on a theme General assignment (optional)
A02v A03 i–iii	Students complete Resources 52 and 53, and choose one as the basis for an essay	52, 'Language' 53, 'Novel or Moral Fable?'	Essay on 'Language' or 'Novel or Moral Fable?'
Various	One or more General assignments from Resource 54	54, 'General Assignments'	As appropriate
LIT AO 1–4	If the text is being studied for the English literature examination, use these questions for practice and revision	56, 'English Literature Examination-Style Questions'	One or more literary essays using notes made in previous lessons

Introduction

Silas Marner was written in 1861. It tells the story of a weaver, Silas Marner, who came to the village of Raveloe after being rejected by his church for a crime which he did not commit. He fills the emptiness of his life with love of gold, which he gloats over every evening. One day his gold is stolen and he nearly goes out of his mind, but he is saved by his love for a child who crawls in through his open doorway. The child, whom Silas names Eppie, is the daughter of a woman who has died from an opium overdose near his house. (She is the unacknowledged wife of Godfrey Cass, the squire's son, and her death frees him to marry the woman of his choice, Nancy Lammeter.) In the second half of the novel, Godfrey wants to adopt the child, but it is too late, as she has grown to love Silas and has become too much a part of the humble village milieu, for example – by her engagement to a local working lad. The book ends with her wedding.

Silas Marner is a blend of novel and moral fable. For this reason it has sometimes been dismissed as too trivial for serious study by critics (among them, F. R. Leavis). However, its critical reputation has risen in recent years. As a GCSE text, it may lack the appeal of some other titles, but the simple plot and characterisation mean that the book is relatively easy to teach.

Many of the activities in this unit are based on a Plot Chart. This is most effective for students working in pairs. The chart is prepared with the following resources (for each pair of students):

- a sheet of A2-sized paper
- ruler
- pencil
- paste, e.g. Pritt stick.

Drawing up the chart

The Plot Chart can be displayed on OHP or drawn on the board for students to copy. The chart should take up the whole width of the A2 page. The best way to measure it out is by folding it in half, then in half again, and then to go over the folds in pencil. An alternative is for the teacher to supervise contributions to one master chart displayed in a prominent place in the classroom.

A CHARACTERS, OBJECTS, THEMES	B MAIN PLOT	C SUBPLOT	D CHARACTERS OBJECTS, THEMES, etc. (SUBPLOT)

Notes on the Resources

45a. and 45b. PLOT SEQUENCE

AIM: knowledge of plot sequence and understanding of plot structure

This resource can be used in several ways. It can be used as a simple sequencing exercise in which students place the events in the correct sequence by numbering the boxes in the left-hand column. Ask students to do this in pencil so that they can make changes.

The best way to use this resource is for students to cut out the events and to paste them in sequence in the appropriate column ('main plot' or 'subplot') of the grid. Another approach is to ask students to complete the plot grid without the help of this resource, and to cross-check it using Resource 45b. This could be displayed on OHP for correction and completion of any of the above sequencing exercises.

When the plot sequence has been pasted onto the Plot Chart, use it to discuss the structure of the novel. Students will see that it has a highly symmetrical stucture. The main plot and subplot develop side by side and occasionally come together. Also, the plot is divided into two separate parts with a fifteen-year gap between them.

46. CHARACTERS

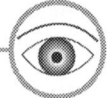

AIM: basic knowledge of the characters in the novel

This resource can be used by itself, or in conjunction with the Plot Chart. Working in pairs, students find information about all the characters listed on the resource sheet and make notes in the appropriate boxes. If they are using this with the Plot Chart, they should then cut out each character strip and paste it in the appropriate column (A or D) at the first appearance of the character.

The following example of how to complete the boxes can be given to any students who need help:

DUNSTAN CASS is the Squire's younger son who is an evil character – a 'spiteful, jeering fellow'. He is blackmailing Godfrey by threatening to reveal his secret marriage to Molly Farren. He persuades Godfrey to let him sell his horse, Wildfire, but rides it to death at a hunt before he can collect the money. He then steals Silas' gold and disappears. His body turns up years later when the stone pits are drained.

The exercise can be extended by drawing up a similar resource sheet on the following minor characters (students could provide their own illustrations):

Aaron Winthrop Mr Snell
Dolly Winthrop Squire Cass
Mr Macey The Pedlar
Mr Lammeter

47. CHARACTER QUOTATIONS

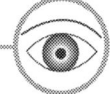

AIM: make good use of quotations to support views about a character in a literary text

This resource can be used by itself, or in conjunction with the Plot Chart. Working in pairs, students read the quotations and try to identify who said it and when. The quotations can then be cut out and pasted on the chart in the appropriate place. The quotations should also be used to support key points in essays on character (see below).

Answers to exercise

1. Eliot explaining how Silas' love for Eppie helps to save him from loneliness and obsession (Chapter 14)
2. Said by Silas to Godfrey when Godfrey offers to adopt Eppie (Chapter 19)
3. Eliot explaining how Silas discovers Eppie (Chapter 12)
4. Nancy to Godfrey after talking to Silas and Eppie about her adoption (Chapter 20)
5. Eliot explaining how Silas began to be integrated into the community (Chapter 16)
6. Silas to Dolly after his trip to Lantern Yard (Chapter 21)
7. Silas to Godfrey trying to explain his feeling that there is a mysterious link between the money and the child (Chapter 14)

8.   Eliot explaining how Silas' religion turned to bitterness (Chapter 1)
9.   Eliot explaining the effect on Godfrey of his 'dark secret' (Chapter 3)
10. Silas talking to Dolly after his trip to the northern city (Chapter 16)
11. Eliot explaining Molly's plan to expose Godfrey (Chapter 12)
12. Eppie to Godfrey explaining why she wants to stay with Silas (Chapter 19)

48. THE TWO MAIN CHARACTERS

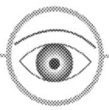

AIM: analyse relevant details of character relating them to interpretation

Silas and Godfrey are the only fully rounded and developed characters in the novel – all the others being simple two-dimensional stereotypes. This resource provides a template for studying the two characters in detail and writing an essay about either or both of them. The template can also be used by higher-tier students to write an essay comparing the two characters.

Students should fill out the information on the template with other information from the text (e.g. explain Silas' trip to Lantern Yard and discuss its significance in terms of his character development). Scanning the Plot Chart may suggest other details for discussion. They should also support main points with quotations. Resource 47, 'Character Quotations', will help with this.

49. OBJECTS

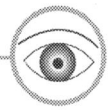

AIM: understand the symbolic significance of certain objects in the novel

Many of the objects in the text are *symbols*. Check that students understand the meaning of this term. *A symbol is something that stands for something else*; for example, a red cross is a symbol for medical aid. An example from the text is Squire Cass's tankards. These are much more than something to drink beer out of, as they stand for or symbolise the antiquity of his family (see below). When the resource sheet has been completed, each object can be cut out and pasted in the appropriate place in columns A or D of the Plot Chart.

The following example of how to complete the boxes can be given to any students who need help:

The tankards are 'older than King George'. They are a symbol of the ancestry of Squire Cass's family, but they are neglected (they smell of 'flat ale') until Nancy marries Godfrey, when they are kept polished. This symbolises the reviving fortunes of the Cass family.

50. OPPOSITES

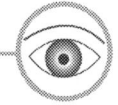

AIM: to analyse the thematic structure of the novel

Literary theorists would call these 'binary oppositions'. Plotting these oppositions gives an indication of the overall thematic structure of the book. Students make notes about each of the opposites on the resource sheet. The next step is to draw lines on the Plot Chart showing the opposites. Finally, they should study the lines on the Plot Chart and comment on any interesting patterns or relationships.

51a. RELIGION AND LOVE and 51b. SOCIAL CLASS AND PREJUDICE

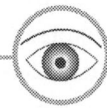

AIM: show insight into issues raised (themes)

Students work in pairs or small groups to complete the two resource sheets. Each student should then choose one of the themes to develop into an essay.

The resource sheet is designed to focus attention on four scenes in which the theme is explored or developed. They make notes on each scene on the resource sheet. The notes should give brief information about the scene and, above all, should bring out the significance of the scene in terms of the theme. An example is given below. They should also include an appropriate quotation from the text.

Religion

Silas belonged to a non-conformist religious sect in Lantern Yard. He is wrongfully accused of stealing church money and sadly realises that he has been duped by his friend, William Dane. The church community cast lots to find out the truth and he is found guilty. Sarah ends their engagement and Silas leaves Lantern Yard with his religious feelings 'turned to bitterness' (Chapter 1).

After the theft of his gold, Dolly visits Silas to bring some lard-cakes on which she has printed the letters 'IHS'. Silas reads these and they start talking about church. Dolly tries to persuade him to go, especially at Christmas. She says there's 'no telling the good it'll do you.' Before Dolly leaves, she begs Silas not to work on the loom on Sundays, as he always does. Aaron sings a Christmas carol, but their efforts to persuade him are 'like a report of unknown objects, which his imagination could not fashion. The fountains of human love and divine faith had not yet been unlocked' (Chapter 10).

In Chapter 14, Dolly advises Silas that Eppie should be christened. He is doubtful at first, but accepts her advice: 'He had no distinct idea about the baptism and the church-going, except that Dolly had said it was for the good of the child.' This shows that, in his desire to do the right thing for Eppie, he has begun to accept the customs and religion of Raveloe.

Silas visits Lantern Yard in the hope that he can clear his name at last, but the church and the minister are no longer there. Dolly comforts him with her usual words of wisdom: 'it seems as you'll never know the rights of it; but that doesn't hinder there being a rights.' This shows he is learning that love and faith are more important than proof (Chapter 21).

The strips for each scene can be cut out and pasted on the Plot Chart. This will enable students to get an overview of the way the theme is developed throughout the novel and perhaps to identify other places where the theme is explored.

The next step is to research the theme further by finding out if there is anything relevant to the theme in:

- the author's life
- the social and historical context
- other scenes in the novel
- other characters in the novel.

Writing

This information can then be presented in an essay. A simple structure (for foundation-tier candidates) would be a six-paragraph essay as follows:

Paragraph 1: introduction stating which theme is to be explored, and commenting briefly on any background information
Paragraph 2: expansion of the notes on scene 1
Paragraph 3: expansion of the notes on scene 2
Paragraph 4: expansion of the notes on scene 3
Paragraph 5: expansion of the notes on scene 4
Paragraph 6: conclusion bringing together the main points made in the previous paragraphs.

Higher-tier candidates should use a more flexible structure, to make the most of a deeper investigation into the themes in the novel.

52. LANGUAGE

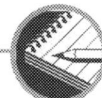

AIM: examine closely relevant details of language

Students analyse the language of Eliot's narrative by rereading the first five sentences of Chapter 1 and completing the table on the resource sheet. The first two columns ('Number of words in sentence' and 'Number of Words with Three or More Syllables') are simply a matter of counting (check that students know what a *syllable* is). The third column, 'List of Difficult, Unusual or Archaic Words', is partly a matter of interpretation. Foundation-tier students will find more difficult and unusual words than higher-tier students. However, in a sense this variation is valid, because it affects the student's perception of the difficulty of the text.

When students are ready to describe the language of Eliot's narrative style, ask them to use information from the table and to pick out two or three words from the box below it. Warn them that not all of the words are appropriate.

In their answer, they will probably express surprise at the long sentences, and comment on one or two archaic terms. They may well choose words like 'difficult', 'serious' and 'old-fashioned'. Some of the abler students may find it 'straightforward', as Eliot's language in this novel is easier than in many other novels of the period.

The second part of the resource analyses Eliot's use of local dialect. Before starting, check that students understand the distinction between the terms *accent* and *dialect* and discuss the difficulties of representing dialect in a novel (if the author tries to represent it too accurately, it is hard to read – see Tennyson's 'Northern Farmer' as an example).

Writing

Finally, students could bring together the information arising from the resource sheet to write an essay on Eliot's language in *Silas Marner*.

53. NOVEL OR MORAL FABLE?

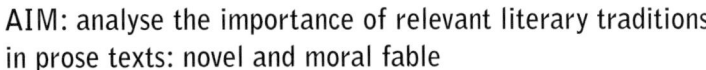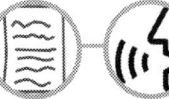

AIM: analyse the importance of relevant literary traditions in prose texts: novel and moral fable

Pre-teaching could include a brief investigation into the history of the moral fable from Aesop and folk-tales to nineteenth-century moral tales; and the history of the novel and the social conditions which allowed the form to flourish. Check understanding of the term *stereotype*. The term comes from a method of printing. When applied to people it means that every person of a particular category is expected to have the same characteristics, whereas in real life (and good literature) every person is a different mixture of good and bad qualities.

Explain to students that *every box in both columns* of the table should be completed (because *Silas Marner* has elements of both forms). Students who are in doubt could be shown the example below.

NOVEL	MORAL FABLE
Characters are fully developed, complex, true-to-life human beings. *Two of the characters, Silas and Godfrey, are fully developed. Both have two sides to their character and both change as a result of their experiences throughout the novel.*	Characters are stereotypes, one-sided, and not very true to life. *Apart from Silas and Godfrey, the characters are stereotypes. Dunsey is the stereotypical aristocratic villain, and Eppie the stereotypical dutiful daughter. Her naughtiness and lack of punishment as a child is an opportunity to develop the character that Eliot chose not to explore.*

Using the information students have noted on the resource sheet, discuss the question, 'Is *Silas Marner* a novel or a moral fable?' (The answer is that it has elements of both, and that the elements of moral fable have caused many critics to undervalue it as a novel.)

Writing

Finally, students could use the information to write an essay on the question. They could use the table as an essay plan using appropriate connectives ('on the other hand', 'however', etc.) to move from one side to the other and to show that *Silas Marner* has elements of both novel and moral tale.

54. GENERAL ASSIGNMENTS

AIM: to explore the text in the widest possible sense through a range of creative, exploratory and open-ended responses

This resource sheet contains a wide range of assignments which help students to get to know the text better, even though many of them are not directly suited to examination (note that creative responses to texts are less frequently set for examination than in the past). However, it is worth considering setting some of these assignments as alternatives to literary essays (where appropriate) or to provide light relief from examination preparation. They are particularly valuable when a text has been chosen for coursework.

55. ENGLISH LITERATURE EXAMINATION-STYLE QUESTIONS

AIM: to prepare for writing examination-style essays

The resource sheet contains a range of examination-style questions which can be used for practice and revision. Students studying a text for examination should write full answers to some of the questions, and essay plans for all of them at some stage during the course. Support for writing literary essays may be found on English Toolkit Resource 11, 'Literary Essay Template'.

45a. PLOT SEQUENCE

Number the events in the order they occur or cut out the events and paste them on a plot chart.

	A tinderbox is found near the stone pits that could have belonged to a pedlar who recently visited the village.
	At the Christmas party, Godfrey asks Nancy Lammeter to forgive him for his past mistakes.
	Dunsey 'stakes' Wildfire in the hunt and the horse dies.
	Dunsey disappears – and everyone thinks it is because of the Wildfire incident.
	Dunsey does not pay back Fowler's rent money to Godfrey. He threatens to reveal Godfrey's dark secret if he does not pay the money himself.
	Dunsey takes Wildfire to a hunt, where he finds a buyer (for £120).
	Dunsey, desperate for money now that he has killed Wildfire, steals Silas's gold.
	Eppie and Aaron are married and they live together with Silas in his house, which has been enlarged with money given by Godfrey.
	Eppie refuses to go to live with Godfrey and Nancy because she loves Silas, has been brought up as a working girl and wants to marry a working man – Aaron.
	Godfrey and Nancy visit Silas's cottage, where they ask Eppie if she wants to become their daughter.
	Godfrey is now married to Nancy Lammeter, but they are childless.
	Godfrey reluctantly agrees that Dunsey can sell his horse, Wildfire.
	Godfrey tells his dark secret to Nancy and suggests that they adopt Eppie. Nancy agrees.
	Godfrey tells Squire Cass about the missing rent money.
	Godfrey wants to marry Nancy Lammeter, but can't because of his dark secret – he is already married to Molly Farren.
	Molly Farren, carrying her baby to Squire Cass's party to expose Godfrey, dies of an opium overdose.
	Molly's baby girl comes in through Silas's door.
	Silas came to Raveloe because he was falsely accused of stealing the church money.
	Silas decides to try to clear his name by visiting Lantern Yard, but it has been swallowed up by a factory.
	Silas finds that his gold is missing and goes to report the theft.
	Silas keeps the child, whom he calls Eppie. Godfrey agrees to this and gives money to help.
	Silas lives alone for the next fifteen years and becomes a miser.
	Silas Marner has worked as a weaver in the village of Raveloe for fifteen years.
	Silas thinks his gold has returned, but it turns out to be a blonde-haired baby. He looks outside and finds her dead mother.
	Silas used to be a member of a church in Lantern Yard – a place in a northern town.
	Silas, helped by Dolly, looks after Eppie and she brings him more happiness than gold.
	Sixteen years later, now grown up, Eppie tells Silas she would like to marry Aaron Winthrop.
	The stone pits are drained. Dunsey's body, Godfrey's whip and Silas's gold are found.

45b. PLOT SEQUENCE

Use this chart to cross-check or complete any of the sequencing exercises.

1.	Silas Marner has worked as a weaver in the village of Raveloe for fifteen years.
2.	Silas used to be a member of a church in Lantern Yard – a place in a northern town.
3.	Silas came to Raveloe because he was falsely accused of stealing the church money
4.	Silas lives alone for the next fifteen years and becomes a miser.
5.	*Dunsey does not pay back Fowler's rent money to Godfrey. He threatens to reveal Godfrey's dark secret if he does not pay the money himself.
6.	*Godfrey wants to marry Nancy Lammeter, but can't because of his dark secret. He is already married in secret to Molly Farren.
7.	*Godfrey reluctantly agrees that Dunsey can sell his horse, Wildfire.
8.	*Dunsey takes Wildfire to a hunt, where he finds a buyer (for £120).
9.	*Dunsey 'stakes' Wildfire in the hunt and the horse dies.
10.	*Dunsey, desperate for money now that he has killed Wildfire, steals Silas's gold.
11.	Silas finds that his gold is missing and goes to report the theft.
12.	A tinderbox is found near the stone pits that could have belonged to a pedlar who recently visited the village.
13.	*Dunsey disappears – and everyone thinks it is because of the Wildfire incident.
14.	*Godfrey tells Squire Cass about the missing rent money.
15.	*At the Christmas party, Godfrey asks Nancy Lammeter to forgive him for his past mistakes.
16.	**Molly Farren, carrying her baby to Squire Cass's party to expose Godfrey, dies of an opium overdose.
17.	Molly's baby girl comes in through Silas's door.
18.	Silas thinks his gold has returned, but it turns out to be a blonde-haired baby. He looks outside and finds her dead mother.
19.	Silas keeps the child, whom he calls Eppie. Godfrey agrees to this and gives money to help.
20.	Silas, helped by Dolly, looks after Eppie and she brings him more happiness than gold.
21.	Sixteen years later, now grown up, Eppie tells Silas she would like to marry Aaron Winthrop.
22.	*Godfrey is now married to Nancy Lammeter, but they are childless.
23.	The stone pits are drained. Dunsey's body, Godfrey's whip and Silas's gold are found.
24.	*Godfrey tells his dark secret to Nancy and suggests that they adopt Eppie. Nancy agrees.
25.	*Godfrey and Nancy visit Silas's cottage, where they ask Eppie if she wants to become their daughter.
26.	**Eppie refuses to go to live with Godfrey and Nancy because she loves Silas, has been brought up as a working girl and wants to marry a working man – Aaron.
27.	Silas decides to try to clear his name by visiting Lantern Yard, but it has been swallowed up by a factory.
28.	Eppie and Aaron are married and they live together with Silas in his house, which has been enlarged with money given by Godfrey.

Note: Single asterisks denote subplot; double asterisks denote main plot and subplot coming together.

46. CHARACTERS

In each box, write notes about the characters.

Dunstan (Dunsey) Cass	
Eppie (Hephzibah)	
Godfrey Cass	
Molly Farren	
Nancy Lammeter	
Silas Marner	
Squire Cass	

47. CHARACTER QUOTATIONS

QUOTATION	WHO SAYS IT AND WHEN?
1. 'As her life unfolded, his soul, long stupefied in a cold narrow prison, was unfolding too, and trembling gradually into full consciousness.'	
2. 'God gave her to me because you turned your back on her, and He looks upon her as mine; you've no right to her! When a man turns a blessing from his door, it falls to them as take it in.'	
3. 'He leaned forward at last, and stretched forth his hand; but instead of the hard coin with the familiar resisting outline, his fingers encountered soft warm curls.'	
4. 'It wouldn't be right to want to force her to come to us against her will. We can't alter her bringing up and what's come of it.'	
5. 'Nobody was jealous of the weaver, for he was regarded as an exceptional person, whose claim on neighbourly help were not to be matched in Raveloe.'	
6. 'Since the time the child was sent to me and I've come to love her as myself, I've had light enough to trusten by; and now she says she'll never leave me, I think I shall trusten till I die.'	
7. 'My money's gone, I don't know where – and this is come from I don't know where. I know nothing – I'm partly mazed.'	
8. 'The Power in which he had vainly trusted among the streets and in the prayer-meetings, was very far away from this land in which he had taken refuge, where men lived in careless abundance, knowing and needing nothing of that trust, which, for him, had been turned to bitterness.'	
9. 'The yoke a man creates for himself by wrong-doing will breed hate in the kindliest nature; and the good-humoured, affectionate-hearted Godfrey Cass, was fast becoming a bitter man, visited by cruel wishes . . .'	
10. 'There's good in this world – I've a feeling o' that now; and it makes a man feel as there's a good more nor he can see, in spite o' the trouble and the wickedness. That drawing o' the lots is dark; but the child was sent to me.'	
11. 'This journey on New Year's Eve was a premeditated act of vengeance which she had kept in her heart ever since Godfrey, in a fit of passion, had told her he would sooner die than acknowledge her as his wife.'	
12. 'We've been used to be happy together every day, and I can't think o' no happiness without him. And he says he'd nobody in the world till I was sent to him, and he'd have nothing when I was gone.'	

48. THE TWO MAIN CHARACTERS

	SILAS	GODFREY
B E F O R E E P P I E	◆ Describe Silas at the beginning of the novel. Explain why he left Lantern Yard and how this affected him. ◆ Explain how he was seen by the villagers of Raveloe, and how his appearance, job and skill with healing herbs reinforced their prejudices. ◆ Show how these influences led him to adopt the life of a lonely miser. ◆ The crisis for Silas is when his gold is stolen.	◆ Describe Godfrey at the beginning of the novel. Explain his dark secret and how Dunsey uses this to blackmail him. ◆ Show how he is pulled in two ways. His love for Nancy makes him want to be a better person, but his fear of Dunsey causes him to be bad-tempered, drink too much and manage his affairs badly. ◆ The crisis for Godfrey is when he finally agrees to sell Wildfire.
A F T E R E P P I E	◆ Because of the strange way in which she came, and her blonde hair, Silas sees Eppie as his gold coming back to him. ◆ Explain how this completely changes his life by referring to how he learns to love a person instead of money and becomes integrated into society.	◆ Because Molly died of an opium overdose, Godfrey is free to marry Nancy. Also, Dunsey disappears. ◆ Explain how these events completely change his life.
I N P A R T T W O	◆ The discovery of Dunsey's body brings back the past. For Silas, this means his gold, but now he only sees it as providing a future for Eppie. ◆ But the discovery of Dunsey's body also prompts Godfrey to confess his secret to Nancy and they decide to adopt Eppie. ◆ Discuss how Silas handles this situation. Note how he puts Eppie's needs first in a self-sacrificing way. ◆ Conclude by explaining how he has grown as a person throughout the novel.	◆ The discovery of Dunsey's body brings back the past. For Godfrey, this means that his dark secret will come out if he doesn't confess it. Describe how he tells Nancy, and explain their decision to adopt Eppie. ◆ Discuss the initial arrogance and thoughtlessness of the offer to Eppie, and explore the significance of Godfrey's final acceptance of the situation. ◆ Conclude by explaining how he has grown as a person throughout the novel.

49. OBJECTS

In each box, write a few notes about the significance of each object in the story.

Squire Cass's old silver tankards	*The tankards are 'older than King George'. They are a symbol of the ancestry of Squire Cass's family, but they are neglected (they smell of 'flat ale') until Nancy marries Godfrey, when they are kept polished. This symbolises the reviving fortunes of the Cass family.*
Dolly's lard-cakes	
Silas's gold	
Silas's loom	
The phial of opium	
The tinderbox	
Wildfire	

50. OPPOSITES

Write notes on the ways in which the following are opposites. Think of other opposites and write about them.

NANCY LAMMETER	**MOLLY FARRELL**
GODFREY	**DUNSEY**
SILAS THE LOVING STEPFATHER	**SILAS THE MISER**
EPPIE	**SILAS'S GOLD**
RAVELOE	**LANTERN YARD**
WORKING CLASS	**UPPER CLASS**
ACCEPTANCE	**PREJUDICE**
RAVELOE CHURCH	**LANTERN YARD**

51a. RELIGION AND LOVE

Write notes on four scenes that develop each of the two themes below.

Religion

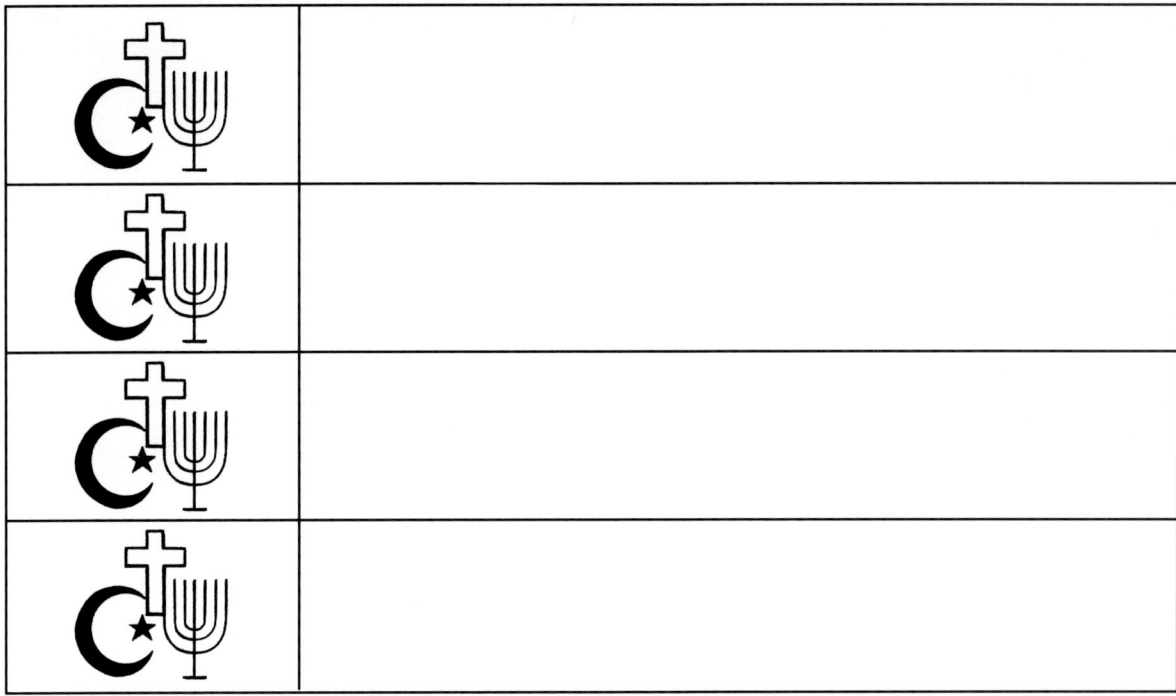

Love

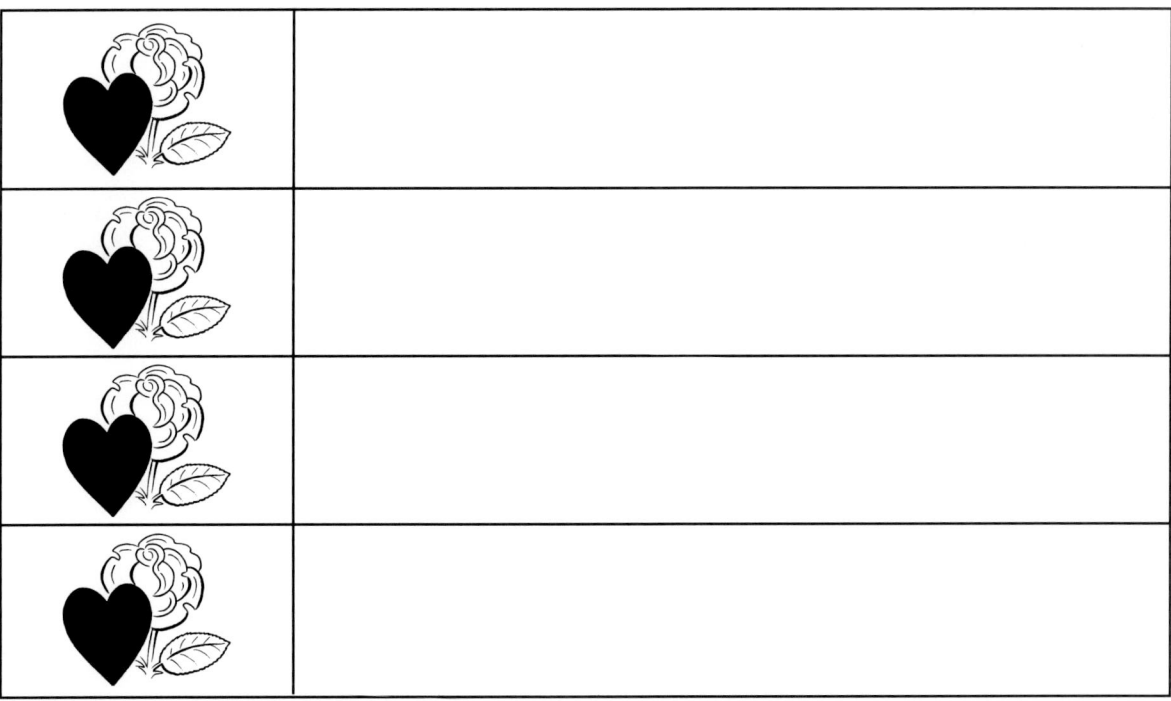

51b. SOCIAL CLASS AND PREJUDICE

Write notes on four scenes that develop each of the two themes below.

Social class

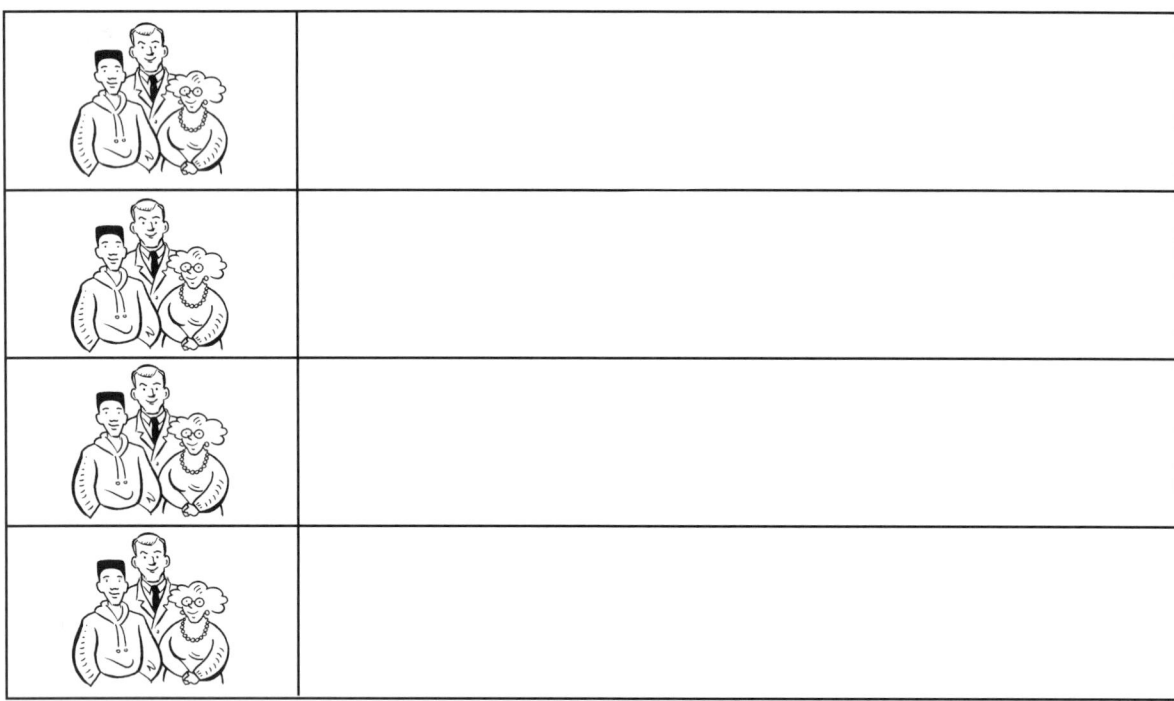

Prejudice

52. LANGUAGE

Eliot's narration

◆ Reread the first five sentences in Chapter 1, then analyse them using the following table. If you have time, analyse another five sentences of narration in the same way.

SEN-TENCE NUMBER	NUMBER OF WORDS IN SENTENCE	NUMBER OF WORDS WITH THREE OR MORE SYLLABLES	LIST OF DIFFICULT, UNUSUAL OR ARCHAIC WORDS
1	64	6	*thread-lace, bosom, pallid, remnants, disinherited*
2			
3			
4			
5			

◆ Describe Eliot's narrative style using information from the table above and adjectives chosen from the box below.

archaic	long-winded	serious
difficult	old-fashioned	solemn
dignified	pompous	straightforward
formal	pretentious	unusual

Eliot's representation of dialect

◆ Reread Chapter 6. This chapter consists entirely of conversation between the local people at the local inn, the Rainbow, and is a good opportunity to study how Eliot represents their dialect. To study the dialect, reread the chapter and fill in the chart until you have about ten words in each category.

ACCENT (DIFFERENT PRONUNCIATION)		DIALECT (DIFFERENT WORD OR GRAMMATICAL STRUCTURE)	
WORD *'ud*	**MEANING** *would*	**WORD** *folks*	**MEANING** *people*

◆ Make notes on the topics the local people talk about and the way they interact.

◆ What is the effect of Eliot's extensive use of local dialect throughout the novel?

53. NOVEL OR MORAL FABLE?

In each box, make a comment about whether the point applies or does not apply to *Silas Marner*. Refer to specific examples wherever possible.

NOVEL	MORAL FABLE
Characters are fully developed, complex, true-to-life human beings.	Characters are stereotypes, one-sided and not very true to life.
Plot develops in a believable way. There are no magic solutions to problems or 'fairytale' endings.	The plot is not believable. Problems are solved by external forces, not by a character's own efforts. The plot is manipulated by the author to express a message.
The main focus is the development of character and plot for their own sakes, not to present a message.	The main focus is the moral message of the fable.
Narrative style is realistic. The author wishes to convey an accurate sense of place and character. Dialogue is true to life.	Narrative style is formal, often following set formulas, e.g. 'three wishes'. Dialogue is limited and unrealistic.

54. GENERAL ASSIGNMENTS

Speaking and listening

In pairs or small groups, act out what might have happened if:

◆ Molly turned up at the Red house with her child

◆ Dunsey was not drowned, but turned up to blackmail Godfrey just before his marriage

◆ Eppie decided to live with Godfrey and Nancy.

After each performance, the audience question the characters and students answer 'in role'.

Explore the story using some of the ideas on Toolkit Resource 20, 'Drama Techniques'.

Reading

Read some examples of moral fables and analyse their key features. Examples may be found at www.allaboutfrogs.org/stories/fables.html and www.2020site.org/aesop/

Writing

Write an extra chapter for the book which shows how Godfrey fell in love with Molly and how she became addicted to opium.

Extend the scene in which Silas and Eppie visit the 'northern manufacturing town'. You could:

◆ add vivid descriptions of black, smoky factories, rows of back-to-back slums, etc.

◆ introduce a dramatic incident, e.g. Eppie gets lost

◆ change the outcome – Silas finds the minister who condemned him – what happens?

Write the newspaper front page article for the following headlines:

◆ 'THEFT OF GOLD'

◆ 'BODY FOUND IN CHALK PITS'

◆ 'WEDDING OF MR A. WINTHROP & MISS E. MARNER'

The wider curriculum

Explore this historical and geographical context in more detail – in particular, the contrast between a country village and a northern manufacturing town at this period.

Spiritual, moral, ethical, social and cultural issues

'There's one of 'em you must choose – ayther smacking or the coal-hole – else she'll get so masterful, there'll be no holding her.' What would have happened if this warning of Dolly's had come true? *Either* write the plan, *or* one scene in detail, of a different part two, in which Eppie grows up to be a 'problem' teenager. Discuss the role of rewards and punishment in bringing up children.

ICT

Visit 'The Victorian Web' at //65.107.211.206/victor.html

55. ENGLISH LITERATURE EXAMINATION-STYLE QUESTIONS

Foundation tier

How does Eppie change Silas's life? Write about:

- why Silas is bitter at the beginning of the novel
- why he develops a miserly love for gold
- what happens when he finds Eppie
- what he has learned by the end of the novel.

What are your feelings about Godfrey? Do you think he really deserves Nancy? You may wish to consider:

- his foolishness in marrying secretly
- his weakness in giving in to blackmail
- the fact that he is saved by an accident (Molly's death) not by anything he does himself.

Reread Chapter 12, from 'While Godfrey Cass was taking draughts of forgetfulness . . .' to '. . . by which the event could have been brought about.' Describe the character of Molly and explain how you think she may have got to this state. In your answer, you should:

- bring together all the information about Molly from the passage
- add other information about her life from the rest of the book
- express your opinion about how she came to be a drug addict.

Higher tier

Silas Marner is full of parallels – for example, in plot structure, characterisation, places, objects, etc. Examine some of these parallels and show how Eliot uses them to express the main message of her story.

'The character of Eppie is particularly shallow and one-dimensional.' Discuss this criticism of the novel. You could approach this question by:

- describing the character of Eppie, showing that she is 'too good to be true'
- examining in detail the implications of Silas's unwillingness to punish her
- showing how this flaw in Eppie's upbringing is not developed by the author.

Note: Doing the linked exploratory task about the reward and punishment of children (see page 87) is a good way of preparing the ground for this essay.

'*Silas Marner* is little more than a moral tale and is not worthy of serious study.' Do you agree with this opinion?

Reread Chapter 6, in which the locals talk to the landlord of the Rainbow. Make a list of the characters and briefly describe each one. Explain what we learn from this chapter about the village and its characters and customs.

UNIT 6: A CHOICE OF POETS

RESOURCES: The choice of poets in the title could be *A Choice of Poets* by R. P. Hewitt, ISBN 0–245–59316–0, which is set for both pre-1914 and post-1914 for AQA English Literature or any other selection of poetry, e.g. the examination boards' anthologies.

BOARD: Any for English or English literature coursework; AQA for English literature examination (*Note*: check current specifications)

RANGE: Poetry Pre-1914

AO	TEACHING SEQUENCE	RESOURCES	OUTCOMES
A02i	Investigate literary tradition and historical and cultural contexts relevant to the specific poet, or collection of poems studied*	Library, Internet	Notes on literary tradition and historical and cultural contexts
A02i A03 i, ii	Analyse the subject and theme of 'Ozymandias' and one other poem* Experiment with writing about a subject in a way that expresses a theme	56, 'Mini-Anthology' 57, 'Subject and Theme'	A draft paragraph on the subject and theme of two poems Draft of own free verse poem
A02i A03 i, ii	Analyse the verse form of 'An Essay on Criticism' and one other poem* Experiment with writing different verse forms	56, 'Mini-Anthology' 58, 'Verse Form'	A draft paragraph on the verse form of two poems Drafts of rhyming poems
A02i A03 i, ii	Analyse the figures of speech in 'Death Be Not Proud' and one other poem* Experiment with figures of speech	56, 'Mini-Anthology' 60, 'Figures of Speech'	A draft paragraph on the figures of speech in two poems Revisions of drafts including figures of speech
A02i A03 i, ii	Analyse the diction in 'Cargoes' and one other poem* Use a thesaurus to experiment with own diction	56, 'Mini-Anthology' 59, 'Diction'	A draft paragraph on the diction of two poems Revisions of drafts with enhanced diction
A02i	(Higher-tier only) analyse the tone and mood of 'Futility' and one other poem*	56, 'Mini-Anthology' 61, 'Tone and Mood'	A draft paragraph on tone and mood in two poems
A02i A03 i, ii	Analyse every aspect, of 'The Charge of the Light Brigade' and one other poem* Complete own poems	62, 'Poetry Analyser'	Draft paragraphs on every aspect of a poem Literary essay on a poem Final draft of one or more of own poems
LIT A0 1–4	Choose one or more general assignments if the poetry is being studied for English or literature coursework	63, 'General Assignments'	One or more General Assignments
LIT A0 1–4	If the poetry is being studied for the English literature examination, practise answering examination-style questions	64, 'English Literature Examination-Style Questions'	One or more literary essays

* See the Introduction to this unit on page 90.

Introduction

The resources in this unit are content-free and can thus be used with any collection of poems, for example, examining board anthologies or English literature set texts. A mini-anthology is included for exemplification purposes, but it is intended that students will focus on a selection of poetry which meets the requirements of an English or English literature specification, for example, *A Choice of Poets* set by AQA.

This unit teaches students to examine five (six for higher-tier students) aspects of a poem. Each aspect is taught through a poem which lends itself to analysis of that aspect (see 56, 'Mini-Anthology'). This is shown in the table below. The table also gives suggestions about how to teach Blake and Wordsworth (AQA English Literature, Pre-1914) or Frost and R. S. Thomas (AQA English Literature, Post-1914) alongside the examples.

In tandem with learning to read and write about poems, this unit also gives students the opportunity to write their own poetry. Doing this will enable them to learn more about each aspect of poetry through experimentation, and will at the same time provide good models for their own writing.

The two different aims are indicated in the 'aims statement' by AT2 (the Reading aim) and AT3 (the Writing aim).

	MINI-ANTHOLOGY	**BLAKE**∗	**WORDS-WORTH**∗	**ROBERT FROST**∗	**R. S. THOMAS**∗
SUBJECT AND THEME	'Ozymandias'	'The Tiger'	'The Prelude (I)'	'Stopping by Woods on a Snowy Evening'	'Farm Child'
VERSE FORM	'Essay on Criticism'	'The Divine Image'	'The Prelude (II)'	'After Apple-Picking'	'Lore'
FIGURES OF SPEECH	'Death Be Not Proud'	'A Poison Tree'	'The World is Too Much With Us'	'The Silken Tent'	'A Blackbird Singing'
DICTION	'Cargoes'	'The Garden of Love'	'Nutting'	'Mowing'	'Children's Song'
(TONE AND MOOD)†	'Futility'	'Holy Thursday'	'The Solitary Reaper'	'An Old Man's Winter Night'	'Cynddylan on a Tractor'
INTERPRE-TATION	'The Charge of the Light Brigade'	'London'	'Westminster Bridge'	'Mending Wall'	'The Evacuee'

∗ See current specification for complete list of poems.
† Higher tier only.
Note: an alternative approach to the analysis of poetry can be found on Literature Toolkit Resource 1, 'Literary Terms', which may be found in *GCSE Kit: English Literature Pre-1914*.

Notes on the Resources

56. MINI-ANTHOLOGY

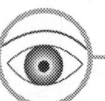

AIM: examine key aspects of poetry in an anthology of specially selected poems

With a sudden enthusiasm for anthologies by examining boards, why another one? The poems in this anthology have been specially selected to illustrate important aspects of poetry. Work on this mini-anthology thus provides an introduction to any other selection of poems ranging from the examination board anthologies to set texts. Details of how to study the different aspects of poetry can be found in the teachers' notes for the following resources.

57. SUBJECT AND THEME

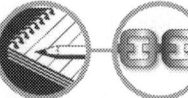

AIM: AT2: learn to distinguish between subject and theme; AT3: experiment with writing about a subject in a way that develops a theme

Reading

Begin by teaching or revising the following definitions.

SUBJECT – this is what the poem is about on the surface level.

THEME – this is the idea or ideas that are expressed in the poem.

Students read the poem 'Ozymandias', on Resource 56, 'Mini-Anthology', then, working in pairs or small groups, try to identify the subject and theme. Discussion can be followed by a plenary in which ideas are shared and possibly written on an OHT of the resource sheet. The end result should be something like this:

SUBJECT

A traveller describes a huge broken statue which he has seen in the desert. On the statue is written 'My name is Ozymandias, king of kings;/Look on my works, ye Mighty, and despair!' but around the statue there is nothing but empty sand.

THEME

The theme of the poem is the transitoriness of earthly power. However great Ozymandias was when he was alive, time has swept away everything he created.

The next step is for students to repeat the process with a poet they are studying (see Introduction).

Writing

Students experiment with writing short free verse poems in which the subject is used to express an idea (theme).

58. VERSE FORM

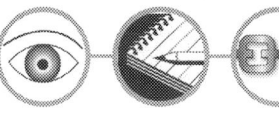

AIM: AT2: understand the basic principles of English prosody; AT3: experiment with different verse forms

Reading

Verse form in English poetry is accentual-syllabic (i.e. it depends on both the stressed syllables in a line of poetry and the total number of syllables). Therefore students will need to revise or be taught the following:

SYLLABLE – this is a sound uttered with a single effort of the voice (articulation). For example, 'drink' has one syllable, 'bouncer' two syllables, and 'discotheque' has three syllables. Activity: students identify the number of syllables in a range of words until they are confident.

STRESS – apart from being one of the problems of modern life, 'stress' means an extra emphasis given to a syllable. The metre of a line of poetry is created by arranging the stressed syllables of words into a regular pattern. Stressed syllables are shown with a mark like a French acute accent. Activity: students identify and mark the stressed syllables in a range of words, then in single lines of poetry. Encourage them to read the line out loud with more emphasis than usual and listen for the stresses. Example:

/   /   /   /   /
Shall I compare thee to a summer's day?

Students are now ready to use the resource sheet. Working in pairs, they should read the explanation of some of the most common verse forms, then find examples of each verse form in the poet they are studying (where appropriate). A few lines of the poem should be written in the 'Example' box. Any verse forms not used by this poet can be left blank and completed later when studying an appropriate poet. Other verse forms can be added on a similar blank grid when they are encountered.

The next step – which is more difficult, but is the key to the whole exercise – is to try to explain the effect of the verse form. In other words, *why* has the poet chosen to express his or her ideas in this particular form?

- Some basic ideas are given in the explanations in the first column.
- Part of the explanation could be the poet's cultural and historical context.
- Finally, look carefully at what the poet is actually saying and then consider the appropriateness of the verse form.

Writing

A template to help students write about verse forms is given at the bottom of the resource sheet, with an example from Pope's 'Essay on Criticism' (see Resource 56, 'Mini-Anthology'). Students should use the template to help them write about the verse form of a poem they are studying (see Introduction).

Extension

It is important that students build up their experience of dealing with these basic concepts, as their ability to understand *why* a poet has chosen a particular verse form will depend partly on comparisons with the way other poets have used verse. However, when students have fully mastered the above, they could move on to a study of the poetic foot, particularly the iamb and the trochee.

Writing

The best way to understand the different verse forms and the effect they can have is for students to experiment with them in their own writing.

59. FIGURES OF SPEECH

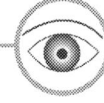 

AIM: AT2: recognise and explain the most important figures of speech; AT3: experiment with own figures of speech

Reading

The resource sheet covers the main figures of speech that students should know for GCSE. There are, of course, many more, but it is better for students to achieve fluency in writing about these seven terms than to learn more terms and risk becoming confused.

Working in pairs, they should read the explanation of the seven most common terms for figures of speech, then find examples in the poet they are studying and write one or two in the 'Example' box. Any figures of speech not used by this poet can be left blank.

The next step, which is more difficult, but is the key to the whole exercise, is to try to explain figures of speech. A template is given to help students to do this. They should try it for themselves on the poet they are studying, for example, by writing about figures of speech in 'Lore' by R. S. Thomas.

Writing

The best way to understand figures of speech and the effect that can have is for students to experiment with them in their own writing. One way to do this is to return to the short free verse poems and see if they can be enhanced by adding one or more figures of speech.

60. DICTION

AIM: AT2: understand how writers use chosen words to express an exact shade of meaning; AT3: students try to refine their own use of words

Reading

There are about 500,000 words in the English language, many of them synonyms (words of similar meaning). With so many words to choose from, writers can express themselves very precisely by using the ones which have exactly the right shade of meaning. Students can explore this for themselves by looking up some common words in a thesaurus. For example, *Roget's Thesaurus* lists over 100 synonyms of 'ship'. The meaning of these words can be further defined or enhanced by the use of adjectives and adverbs.

Poets choose their words more carefully than writers in any other form. The prose writer is usually concerned only with a word's meaning, but the poet is interested in its sound as well, which may be used for rhyme, rhythm or other effects, such as alliteration. For this reason, it is particularly important to consider a poet's diction.

Students work in pairs to complete the resource sheet. This can be used either for a specific poem, or a group of poems by one poet. Of course, not all the categories will apply to every poem or poet.

The next step is to try to explain the poet's use of diction. A template is given to help students to do this, with an example from 'Cargoes' by Masefield (see Resource 56, 'Mini-Anthology'). Students should try it for themselves on the poet they are studying (see Introduction).

Writing

Students use a combination of brainstorming and a thesaurus to find better ways of expressing the ideas in their draft free verse poems.

61. TONE AND MOOD

AIM: AT2: recognise and explain the tone and mood of a poem

Reading

Tone and mood are difficult concepts, which are probably best reserved for higher-tier students. The topic can be introduced by defining both terms and then showing how they apply to a specific poem ('Futility' by Wilfred Owen).

TONE – the poet's attitude towards the subject.

MOOD – the emotions created in the reader.

Note: the tone and mood of a poem are often similar, though there are examples where they can be very different. For example, if the tone of Tennyson's 'The Charge of the Light Brigade' is ironic (which is one possible interpretation), then the mood would be one of sorrow and anger at the unnecessary waste of human life. On the other hand, the tone could be one of celebration of bravery – in which case, the mood would be one of admiration and honour.

Students read 'Futility' and then discuss tone and mood. Discussion can be followed by a plenary in which ideas are shared and possibly written on an OHT of the resource sheet. The end result might be something like this:

TONE

The tone of the first stanza is hopeful. This is shown in phrases such as 'always it woke him', 'kind old sun'. In the second stanza the tone changes to despair – 'Was it for this the clay grew tall?' – and then bitterness: 'O what made fatuous sunbeams toil/To break earth's sleep at all?'

MOOD

The main emotion created in the reader is one of pity. This poem shows how hard it is for the soldier's friends to accept that he is dead – 'Move him into the sun'. At first they cherish false hopes – 'Always it woke him'. At the end of the poem the mood deepens into a tragic sense of the waste of human life – 'Are limbs, so dear achieved . . . too hard to stir?'

Students can then try to identify the tone and mood in a poem by a poet they are studying (see Introduction).

62. POETRY ANALYSER

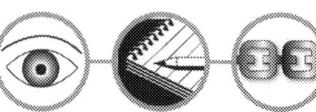

AIM: AT2: analyse a complete poem, connections and comparisons between poems, the work of a poet; AT3: write about a poem

Reading

Now that students have practised analysing different aspects of poems separately, they are ready to analyse all the aspects together and then attempt an overall interpretation. The example below is based on 'The Charge of the Light Brigade' on Resource 56, 'Mini-Anthology'.

Students, working in pairs or small groups, should first read the poem, and then make notes on the first four aspects (five, if tone and mood are included).

The final step is to discuss what the poem *means* (interpretation), drawing on the information in the notes already made. Sometimes, alternative interpretations are possible and equally valid ('The Charge of the Light Brigade' was chosen as an example).

Key points should be supported by evidence (usually a quotation from the poem). The point should then be further developed.

The draft paragraphs on 'The Charge of the Light Brigade' can be developed into a literary essay with the support of other students and the teacher. Students can then use this as a model for an independently written essay on a poem by a poet they are studying (see Introduction).

Four ways to write about poetry

WRITING ABOUT A POEM

Resource 62, 'Poetry Analyser', can be used as an essay plan for an essay on a poem. Note that the subject and theme should be described briefly, as this will serve as the introduction to the essay. The following aspects should be explained in a paragraph each, quoting examples where appropriate. The final section, 'Interpretation', should receive the fullest treatment.

CONNECTIONS AND COMPARISONS BETWEEN TWO POEMS

Lay two completed Resource 62s side by side and compare each aspect of the poems in the order in which they appear.

AN ESSAY ON A POET

- *Introduction* – brief information about biography, literary tradition and historical and social context.
- *Themes* – an exploration of the main themes covered by the poet with specific reference to several poems.

- *Style* – write about the poet's verse forms, figures of speech and diction, with specific reference to several poems.
- *Conclusion* – give a brief personal response to the poet's work.

COMPARING POETS

This can be a 'double' version of the above essay plan. The introduction gives brief information about biography, literary tradition and historical and social context of both poets, pointing out similarities or differences which affect their work. The themes and style of the poets are compared and contrasted. The conclusion gives a brief personal response to the work of both poets.

Writing

To develop one or more of their draft poems, students bring together everything they have learned from the models they have studied.

63. GENERAL ASSIGNMENTS

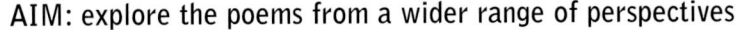

AIM: explore the poems from a wider range of perspectives

The resource sheet provides a list of suggestions for responding to the poems from a wider range of perspectives. The activities are particularly suited to coursework, but can also be used as supporting exercises for an examination text.

64. ENGLISH LITERATURE EXAMINATION-STYLE QUESTIONS

AIM: prepare and practise for examination

These questions can be used for practice by students who are preparing the text for English literature examination. Note that some of the questions are specific to the selections of Blake and Wordsworth (Pre-1914) and Robert Frost and R. S. Thomas (Post-1914) in *A Choice of Poets* (see current AQA specification for details), and some can be used with any selection of poems.

56. MINI-ANTHOLOGY

OZYMANDIAS

I met a traveller from an antique land,
Who said: Two vast and trunkless legs of stone
Stand in the desert. Near them, on the sand,
Half sunk, a shattered visage lies, whose frown,
And wrinkled lip, and sneer of cold command,
Tell that its sculptor well those passions read
Which yet survive (stamped on these lifeless things),
The hand that mocked them and the hand that fed;
And on the pedestal these words appear:
'My name is Ozymandias, king of kings:
Look on my works, ye Mighty, and despair!'
Nothing beside remains. Round the decay
Of that colossal wreck, boundless and bare,
The lone and level sands stretch far away.

Percy Bysshe Shelley (1792–1822)

From AN ESSAY ON CRITICISM (extract)

True ease in writing comes from art, not chance,
As those move easiest who have learn'd to dance.
'Tis not enough no harshness gives offence,
The sound must seem an echo to the sense.
Soft is the strain when Zephyr gently blows,
And the smooth stream in smoother numbers flows;
But when loud surges lash the sounding shore,
The hoarse, rough verse should like a torrent roar.
When Ajax strives some rock's vast weight to throw,
The line too labours, and the words move slow;
Not so, when swift Camilla scours the plain,
Flies o'er th' unbending corn, and skims along the main.

Alexander Pope (1688–1744)

56. MINI-ANTHOLOGY

continued

DEATH BE NOT PROUD

Death, be not proud, though some have called thee
Mighty and dreadful, for thou art not so;
For those whom thou think'st thou dost overthrow,
Die not, poor Death; nor yet canst thou kill me.
From rest and sleep, which but thy pictures be,
Much pleasure; then from thee much more must flow;
And sooner our best men with thee do go –
Rest of their bones, and souls' delivery!
Thou'rt slave to fate, chance, kings, and desperate men,
And dost with poison, war, and sickness dwell;
And poppy or charms can make us sleep as well
And better than they stroke. Why swell'st thou then?
One short sleep past, we wake eternally,
And Death shall be no more: Death, thou shalt die!

John Donne (1572–1631)

CARGOES

Quinquereme of Nineveh from distant Ophir
Rowing home to haven in sunny Palestine,
With a cargo of ivory,
And apes and peacocks,
Sandalwood, cedarwood, and sweet white wine.

Stately Spanish galleon coming from the Isthmus,
Dipping through the Tropics by the palm-green shores,
With a Cargo of diamonds,
Emeralds, amethysts,
Topazes, and cinnamon, and gold moidores.

Dirty British coaster with a salt-caked smoke stack
Butting through the Channel in the mad March days,
With a cargo of Tyne coal,
Road-rail, pig lead,
Firewood, iron-ware, and cheap tin trays.

John Masefield (1878–1967)

56. MINI-ANTHOLOGY

continued

FUTILITY

Move him into the sun—
Gently its touch awoke him once,
At home, whispering of fields half-sown.
Always it woke him, even in France,
Until this morning and this snow.
If anything might rouse him now
The kind old sun will know.

Think how it wakes the seeds—
Woke once the clays of a cold star.
Are limbs, so dear achieved, are sides
Full-nerved, still warm, too hard to stir?
Was it for this the clay grew tall?
—O what made fatuous sunbeams toil
To break earth's sleep at all?

Wilfred Owen (1893–1918)

56. MINI-ANTHOLOGY

continued

THE CHARGE OF THE LIGHT BRIGADE

I

Half a league, half a league,
  Half a league onward,
All in the valley of Death
  Rode the six hundred.
'Forward, the Light Brigade!
Charge for the guns!' he said:
Into the valley of Death
  Rode the six hundred.

II

'Forward, the Light Brigade!'
Was there a man dismay'd?
Not tho' the soldier knew
  Some one had blunder'd:
Their's not to make reply,
Their's not to reason why,
Their's but to do and die:
Into the valley of Death
  Rode the six hundred.

III

Cannon to right of them,
Cannon to left of them,
Cannon in front of them
  Volley'd and thunder'd;
Storm'd at with shot and shell,
Boldly they rode and well,
Into the jaws of Death,
Into the mouth of Hell
  Rode the six hundred.

IV

Flash'd all their sabres bare,
Flash'd as they turn'd in air
Sabring the gunners there,
Charging an army, while
  All the world wonder'd:
Plunged in the battery-smoke
Right thro' the line they broke;
Cossack and Russian
Reel'd from the sabre-stroke
  Shatter'd and sundre'd.
Then they rode back, but not,
  Not the six hundred.

V

Cannon to right of them,
Cannon to left of them,
Cannon behind them
  Volley'd and thunder'd;
Storm'd at with shot and shell,
While horse and hero fell,
They that had fought so well
Came thro' the jaws of Death
Back from the mouth of Hell,
All that was left of them
  Left of six hundred.

VI

When can their glory fade?
O the wild charge they made!
  All the world wonder'd.
Honour the charge they made!
Honour the Light Brigade,
  Noble six hundred!

Alfred, Lord Tennyson (1809–1892)

57. SUBJECT AND THEME

SUBJECT

Write a summary of the subject matter of the poem.

THEME

Identify the main theme and explain what the poet has to say about it.

58. VERSE FORM

FORM	EXAMPLE
BALLAD FORM Alternate lines of 4 stresses and 3 stresses, second and fourth lines rhyme (a b c b). One of the simplest rhyming forms, this is often used to tell a story.	
BLANK VERSE Continuous lines of poetry with a regular rhythm (usually iambic pentameter) but no rhyme. Blank verse is often used for serious and philosophical writing as it allows the poet more freedom to express complex ideas.	
COUPLETS Pairs or rhyming lines written as continuous poetry or grouped into stanzas. Usually four or five stress lines. Four-stress couplets are one of the commonest verse forms and are used to express a wide range of ideas. Five-stress couplets usually have a more serious effect.	
FREE VERSE No regular pattern of rhythm and rhyme. Line breaks are the main method of giving emphasis. Free verse is used by most modern poets for serious and philosophical writing, as it allows the poet more freedom to express complex ideas.	
SONNET Fourteen rhyming iambic pentameters. Various rhyme schemes have been used. This form is usually chosen to express a single deeply felt idea or emotion.	
STANZA Commonly known as a 'verse' of poetry. Stanzas can be from two lines long to twenty or more. They are constructed of patterns of rhyme. Some of the rhyme patterns have specific names, e.g. 'Ottava Rima'. Generally, the longer the stanza, the more serious the effect.	

How to write about verse forms (example from Pope's 'An Essay on Criticism')

DESCRIBE THE VERSE FORM	EXPLAIN WHAT EFFECT IT HAS
'An Essay on Criticism' is written in five-stress (iambic pentameter) couplets.	The long five-stress line suits the serious subject matter, and Pope uses different rhythms to reinforce the points he makes. The rhymes clinch each point.

59. FIGURES OF SPEECH

A figure of speech is saying something in a way that is different to plain, literal expression.

FIGURE OF SPEECH	EXAMPLE
ALLUSION A reference to a well-known person or thing, e.g. 'as vulnerable as Marilyn Monroe'. This example shows that allusions only work if the reader knows something about the person or thing alluded to.	
IMAGERY A blanket term which includes all figures of speech which are 'word pictures', particularly *simile* and *metaphor* (see below).	
IRONY Expressing something by saying the opposite, e.g. saying 'You're a big help!' to someone who breaks a dish while helping to wash up.	
METAPHOR A direct comparison, e.g. 'A black hole'; 'My hands are ice'. An **extended metaphor** develops a metaphor with more ideas from the same comparison, e.g. '. . . and my fingers are icicles.'	
PERSONIFICATION Describing an object as though it had human qualities (see Table below).	
SIMILE A comparison using 'like' or 'as', e.g. 'My hands are as cold as ice', 'Flight 19 disappeared as though it had gone to Mars.'	
SYMBOL Something that stands for something else, e.g. a skull can be used as a symbol for death or a heart for love, etc.	

How to write about figures of speech (example from Donne's 'Death Be Not Proud')

INTRODUCTORY SENTENCE USING THE CORRECT TERM	AN EXPLANATION OF HOW THE WRITER USES THE FIGURE OF SPEECH	AN ANALYSIS OF WHAT EFFECT IT HAS
The poet, Donne, uses *personification* to describe death: 'Death, be not proud, though some have called thee . . . dreadful . . .'	He says that death has the human quality of pride.	The effect of this is to make death seem less fearful. By giving it human qualities, Donne makes us feel we can fight back.

60. DICTION

Diction is the poet's choice of words.

TYPE OF WORDS	EXAMPLES FROM _____
ADJECTIVES/ADVERBS Adjectives describe nouns, adverbs describe verbs	
VERBS The action words in sentences	
ARCHAIC Old words not in common use today	
INTERESTING/UNUSUAL Any word that stands out in any way	
DIALECT Words which represent a regional or ethnic variety of English	
SLANG Non-standard English used in cultural subgroups	
ALLITERATION Two or more words in the same line begin with the same sound	
ONOMATOPOEIA The sounds of words suggests the meaning	

How to write about diction (example from 'Cargoes' by John Masefield)

DESCRIBE THE POET'S DICTION	EXPLAIN WHAT EFFECT IT HAS
In the first two stanzas, Masefield uses many interesting and unusual words, e.g. 'quinquereme', 'moidores', and verbs such as 'rowing' and 'dipping' to describe the motion of the ships. In the last verse the diction is plain, e.g. words such as 'coaster' and the verb 'butting'.	The interesting and unusual words emphasise the strange, beautiful and exotic cargoes. The verbs suggest an elegant motion. This contrasts with the dull, cheap cargoes of the modern ship, and the verb 'butting' suggests its clumsy motion.

61. TONE AND MOOD

TONE AND MOOD in _____

TONE

◆ What is the poet's attitude to his or her subject?

◆ Which words/phrases/figures of speech reveal his or her attitude?

MOOD

◆ What emotions are created in the reader?

◆ What words/phrases/figures of speech does the poet use to create these feelings?

◆ How do you feel about the poem?

62. POETRY ANALYSER

SUBJECT AND THEME

VERSE FORM

FIGURES OF SPEECH

DICTION

TONE AND MOOD

INTERPRETATION

63. GENERAL ASSIGNMENTS

Speaking and listening

Imagine Job Davies (the character in the poem 'Lore' by R. S. Thomas) meets a modern farmer, who tries to persuade him to give up his old-fashioned methods in favour of modern mechanised farming, GM foods, and the Common Agricultural Policy. Improvise what they would say to each other.

Use Toolkit Resource 20, 'Drama Techniques', to explore the poems in a range of different ways.

Roger McGough wrote that 'Poets get their poems into the Top 20'. Make a top 20 of all the poems you have studied recently, giving reasons for the three highest- and three lowest-placed poems.

Reading

Use the techniques in this unit to help you study a range of other poems.

Choose another poet from *A Choice of Poets* for detailed study.

Writing

Imagine Shelley's traveller told him about the Pyramids, Stonehenge or some other ancient monument. What might he have written? Write a poem or a diary entry. Try to include a thought-provoking ending.

Rewrite one of the extracts from Wordsworth's 'Prelude' (I or II) as a modern diary entry. Write a brief commentary on the differences in language and style.

Reread 'Westminster Bridge' by Wordsworth, then write a description of a view of modern London.

Write a plan of how you would make a short film about one of the poems.

Write a literary essay about a poem written by yourself or a friend.

The wider curriculum

Find a short encyclopedia or reference book article on the subject matter of some of the poems – e.g. death, London, tiger, tractor, Westminster Bridge, World War I – then compare the language, style, amount of factual information and emotional impact of the article with the poem.

Spiritual, moral, ethical, social and cultural issues

Write and perform a script for a radio or TV documentary about the suffering on the streets of London today, e.g. drug addicts, muggings, 'cardboard city', comparing them with the sufferings described in Blake's poem, 'London'.

ICT

Use an online rhyming dictionary (see www.rhyme.com) and thesaurus (see www.plumbdesign.com/thesaurus/index.html/) to help with the development of your own poetry.

Try an online automatic poetry-writing programme (see www.burningpress.org/toolbox/).

64. ENGLISH LITERATURE EXAMINATION-STYLE QUESTIONS

Foundation tier

Blake's poem 'The Tiger' is more about God than a description of a tiger. Do you agree?

In your answer, you should:

◆ say whether you agree with the statement and why
◆ explore words and phrases which refer to the creator of the tiger
◆ discuss what the tiger shows us about the nature of God.

Write about two of the poems that specially interested you. You should write about:

◆ the ideas expressed by the poems
◆ the way the poet uses language
◆ your personal response.

Write about one of the following in any two poems: places, nature, people, childhood. You should write about:

◆ what the poet says about his subject
◆ how he uses language to describe it effectively.

Higher tier

Reread 'Holy Thursday'. What does William Blake say about poverty in this poem? How does he say it so that it comes across with maximum effect? What does he say about poverty in his other poems?

Reread Blake's 'London' and 'Westminster Bridge' by Wordsworth and, with close reference to the words of the poems, compare and contrast the way the two poets see London.

Wordsworth wrote that 'Poetry is the spontaneous overflow of powerful feelings.' Explore the feelings in the poems of Wordsworth or any other poet you have studied.

By referring to at least one poem by each poet, examine how Blake and Wordsworth present the power of nature in their poetry.

Show how Robert Frost and R. S. Thomas make poetry out of ordinary everyday experiences. Refer in detail to at least two poems by each poet.

The experience of the Welsh farm worker seems tougher than that of his American counterpart. Discuss with detailed reference to at least one poem by R. S. Thomas and one poem by Robert Frost.

Read the extract from Pope's 'An Essay on Criticism' then say how he would respond to two of the poems you have read.

UNIT 7: *CHINESE CINDERELLA*

RESOURCES: *Chinese Cinderella* by Adeline Yen Mah, ISBN 0–141–30487–1

BOARD: Edexcel terminal examination; coursework, all boards

RANGE: Prose text from a different culture or tradition

AO	TEACHING SEQUENCE	RESOURCES	OUTCOMES
AO2i	Pre-reading: historical and geographical background	Book: *Historical Note*, pp. 230–232, Internet, library	Understanding of the context of the book
AO2i **AO3 i–iii**	Working in groups of four, students read and discuss key readings in class; each student takes notes on an aspect of the book Personal writing in response to each key reading	65, 'Eight Key Readings' 66, 'Responding to the Readings' 67, 'Adeline Yen Mah' 68, 'Other Characters' 69, 'Themes' 70, 'Culture'	Understanding of characters, themes and culture Essay or presentation on an aspect of the book Personal response to the book
AO2i	(Optional) Read about Chinese astrology and relate it to own character and the characters in the book	71, 'Chinese Astrology'	Deeper understanding of Chinese culture Written analysis of own character or character from book
AO2i	(Optional) Read some of Confucius' 'Analects' and relate them to own culture and the issues in the book	72, 'Sayings of Confucius'	Deeper understanding of Chinese culture Written analysis of an issue from the book in the light of Confucius' sayings
Various	One or more General Assignments	73, 'General Assignments'	As appropriate
LIT AO 1–4	If the text is being studied for the English literature examination, use these questions for practice and revision	74, 'English Literature Examination-Style Questions' Toolkit 11, 'Literary Essay Template'	One or more literary essays using notes made in previous lessons

Introduction

This is the true story of Adeline Yen Mah's childhood in China and the abuse she suffers from her father and stepmother. After her mother dies giving birth to her, Adeline's family calls her 'bad luck'. When her father remarries, she and her brothers and sisters have to take second place to the two new children. As the youngest, she is the 'Cinderella' of the whole family. However, she is supported by Aunt Baba and grandfather Ye Ye at home, and by her teachers and friends at school. Finally, with the help of her 'fairy godmother' – her intelligence – she triumphs. She wins an international writing competition that makes her father proud of her and persuades him to agree to her dearest wish: to be sent to university in England.

Students will be deeply moved by this well-written story of personal triumph over the odds, and will hopefully be inspired to write about their own lives, which this unit encourages them to do in parallel with studying the text.

Notes on the Resources

65. EIGHT KEY READINGS

 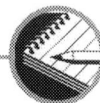

AIM: read and respond to the book

Reading

Students work in groups of four throughout the unit. Each student is responsible for making notes on one of the following aspects of the book. This should be done a bit at a time, as the reading progresses, using the following resource sheets:

■   67, 'Adeline Yen Mah'
■   68, 'Other Characters'
■   69, 'Themes'
■   70, 'Culture'.

Students should be strongly advised to read the whole book in their own time at home. The key readings will be done in class and will be the focus of detailed study.

The process is as follows:

The key readings are done in class. Following each reading, groups of students discuss the questions on Resource 66, 'Responding to the Readings', make notes on the resource sheet for which they are responsible, and do the personal writing task.

The intervening chapters should be read in class, within groups, or for homework, students making notes on the resource sheet for which they are responsible.

When reading is completed, groups could reform so that all the students working on a particular resource sheet have a session together to compare notes (groups could be subdivided to keep numbers in each group manageable).

Students then rejoin their original groups and present an overview of their topic.

Writing

Finally, students write an essay or prepare a presentation on their topic. Essays should be duplicated and shared among the group, the aim being that all students get to know about all topics.

66. RESPONDING TO THE READINGS

AIM: deepen understanding of book through discussion; relate the book to own life through personal writing

After each key reading, students use questions from the resource sheet as a basis for discussion of what they have just read. Discussion questions are followed by a prompt for personal writing. These written responses can later be collated, redrafted and developed to form an autobiography.

67. ADELINE YEN MAH

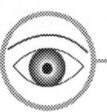 

AIM: detailed knowledge of the main character

The table on the resource sheet has been designed to help students focus on the strongly contrasting positive and negative influences in Adeline Yen Mah's life. This will work best if it is completed as the reading progresses. Encourage students to include page numbers for future reference and useful quotations.

68. OTHER CHARACTERS

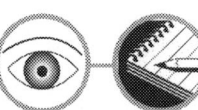

AIM: knowledge of the other main characters

This resource covers the other main characters in the book. Students could also include a list of minor characters, with brief notes on their role in the book (write the list on the back of the resource sheet). Students should include page numbers for future reference and useful quotations.

69. THEMES

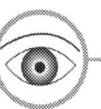 

AIM: show insight into issues raised (themes)

This resource sheet should be allocated to one of the abler students in the group as themes are by their nature more abstract than characters, and it is correspondingly harder to make notes on them. Encourage students to include page numbers and useful quotations.

70. CULTURE

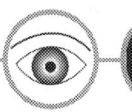 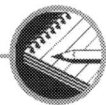

AIM: understand cultural differences

Students should note that some of the important information for this topic is not in the eight key readings in Resource 65. For example, they will need to read Chapter 12 ('Big Sister's Wedding') to find out about marriage customs, and the Author's Note (pp. xi–xiii), Chapter 16, ('Hong Kong'), pages 288 and 299 to find out about the Chinese language and writing system.

71. CHINESE ASTROLOGY

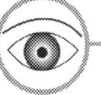  

AIM: explore aspects of Chinese culture

This resource can be used as follows.

Read and discuss the Chinese horoscope. An interesting way to do this is to compare the character types with the Western horoscope. A summary of Western astrological zodiac signs can be found at www.astrology-numerology.com

Relate the characters in the book to the different character types in the Chinese horoscope as far as possible.

72. SAYINGS OF CONFUCIUS

AIM: explore aspects of Chinese culture

The following background information will help to set the sayings in context.

Confucius founded one of the three main schools of Chinese philosophy. He was born in the Chinese state of Lu in 551 BC. His name is a Westernised version of 'Kong Qiu-zi'. In his lifetime he was not very successful, but after his death (497 BC) Confucianism became the most important influence on Chinese culture. His philosophy emphasises the importance of ritual, order in relationships (particularly family relationships) and the individual's relationship with the State. Also important is the concept of *jen*, which can be translated as 'humanity', 'benevolence' or 'goodness', and how each individual can develop into *the Superior Man* – a person who has made good progress in the Way (Tao) of self-development.

The resource contains a short selection of Confucius' 'Analects' and can be used as follows.

Read and discuss the sayings, comparing them with the values of other cultures, particularly traditional Christian values, and with current liberal values.

Discuss how the sayings can help the reader to understand the issues in the book – for example, the emphasis placed on obedience to the father.

73. GENERAL ASSIGNMENTS

AIM: explore the book from a wider range of perspectives

The resource sheet provides a list of suggestions for responding to the book from a wider range of perspectives. The activities are particularly suited to coursework, but can also be used as supporting exercises for an examination text. Toolkit Resources – for example, Toolkit Resource 17, 'Forms of Writing' – can be used to support several of the assignments on this resource.

74. ENGLISH LITERATURE EXAMINATION-STYLE QUESTIONS

AIM: prepare and practise for examination

These questions can be used for practice by students who are preparing the text for the Edexcel English literature examination. Foundation-tier students may find it helpful to use Toolkit Resource 11, 'Literary Essay Template', as a support for their writing.

65. EIGHT KEY READINGS

You are strongly advised to read the whole book in your own time at home. The following key readings will be done in class and will be the focus of detailed study.

Dedication, Preface and Chapters 1–3 ('Top of the Class', 'A Tianjin Family' and 'Nai Nai's Bound Feet').

Adeline Yen Mah explains why she wrote the book and introduces us to her family – the Yen family. This consists of five children (including Adeline Yen Mah) from her father's first wife and two children from his second wife, Niang. Grandfather, Ye Ye, Grandmother, Nai Nai, and Aunt Baba also live with them.

Chapter 6 – 'First Day at School'

Her first day at school. Nobody comes to pick her up at the end of the day. She tries to find her own way home but gets lost. Luckily she remembers her telephone number.

Chapter 8 – 'Tram Fare'

The children are expected to walk to school even though it is some distance away. Big Sister asks for tram fare and father finds out that Ye Ye has been giving them the money. Niang insists that if they all apologise they will be given the tram fare. Only Adeline Yen Mah holds out because of 'loyalty, fair play and a sense of obligation'.

Chapter 10 – 'Shanghai School Days'

Adeline Yen Mah makes friends with Wu Chun-mei. She is good at sport and shares Adeline Yen Mah's interest in books. She lends her *A Little Princess* by Frances Hodgson Burnett. The book makes such an impression on Adeline Yen Mah that she copies it out by hand. She comes top of the class again and wins a children's writing competition.

Chapter 11 – 'PLT'

The children are given a baby duckling each. Adeline Yen Mah gets the scrawniest. She calls it Precious Little Treasure (PLT) and loves and cares for it so well that it soon becomes as strong as the others. Father wants to test Jackie's obedience on one of the ducklings and PLT is brought by Big Brother. The obedience test fails and PLT is injured and later dies.

Chapter 14 – 'Class President'

Adeline Yen Mah is elected class president. A crowd of friends come to her house to celebrate and give her presents. Niang slaps Adeline Yen Mah and tells her to send them away. Father makes her throw the gifts in the bin. She is told she will be sent away to an orphanage at Tianjin.

Chapter 18 – 'Miserable Sunday'

Soon after being sent to Tianjin, Adeline Yen Mah's aunt Reine Schilling (Niang's older sister) takes her to Hong Kong to escape the Communist Chinese. Here she attends boarding school. This chapter describes how lonely she feels on Sundays, when all the other children wear nice clothes, get eggs (sent by relatives) for breakfast and receive visits.

Chapter 21 – 'Play Writing Competition' and 'Postscript'

Adeline Yen Mah has to stay at boarding school during the holidays because she has nowhere else to go. She decides to enter a play-writing competition. She wins the competition and for once her father is proud of her – so proud that he agrees to send her to university in England, which for Adeline Yen Mah is a dream come true. The postscript tells of her success and happiness in England and, later, America.

66. RESPONDING TO THE READINGS

Dedication, Preface and Chapters 1–3 ('Top of the Class', 'A Tianjin Family' and 'Nai Nai's Bound Feet').

Describe Adeline Yen Mah's family. How are the children from Father's two different wives treated? How does this compare with the folk-tale *Cinderella* referred to in the title of the book? What do we learn about the treatment of women in China (particularly in the past) from the opening three Chapters?

Write background information about your own family.

Chapter 6 – 'First Day at School'

What is Adeline Yen Mah's biggest problem during her first day at school and how does she solve it?

Write about your first day at school.

Chapter 8 – 'Tram Fare'

Why are Niang and Father angry about the children accepting their tram fare from Ye Ye? What does Niang demand as a solution to the problem? Why does Adeline Yen Mah refuse to give and what does this show about her character?

Write about a time when you acted because of a sense of loyalty or fair play.

Chapter 10 – 'Shanghai School Days'

How did Adeline Yen Mah and Wu Chun-mei become friends and what did they have in common? What nasty trick did Third Brother play on Adeline Yen Mah? Why was she particularly upset over the incident?

Write about your experiences at school. Has anyone every played a nasty trick on you? How did you react?

Chapter 11 – 'PLT'

Why does Adeline Yen Mah love her duckling so much? How does this affect her attitude to duck as food? How does Third Brother show his care and support for Adeline Yen Mah after the PLT's death?

Describe any pet that you have had, or would like to have.

Chapter 14 – 'Class President'

What does being elected class president do for Adeline Yen Mah's self-esteem? Describe what happens when her friends come to her house to celebrate. Give your opinion of the way Niang and Father behave. How does it make Adeline Yen Mah feel?

Write about a time when you received a prize or honour of some kind and/or write about your friends, and whether they are accepted by your family.

Chapter 18 – 'Miserable Sunday'

Make a list of the ways in which Adeline Yen Mah feels different. How does she feel about this? How does she try to hide her embarrassment?

Write about a time that you feel you have been left out or have been embarrassed about being different from others.

Chapter 21 – 'Play Writing Competition' and 'Postscript'

How does the short story competition change Adeline Yen Mah's life? What do you think would have happened to her if she had not won the short story competition?

Describe your dream. How do you think you could make it come true?

67. ADELINE YEN MAH

◆ As you read the book, make notes on the character of Adeline Yen Mah, particularly on the positive and negative influences that affected her life. Include quotations from the text in your notes.

PERSONALITY AND APPEARANCE

NEGATIVE INFLUENCES	POSITIVE INFLUENCES

◆ Now write an essay or prepare a presentation on the character of Adeline Yen Mah.

68. OTHER CHARACTERS

◆ As you read the book, make notes on the following characters. Include quotations from the text in your notes.

AUNT BA BA

BROTHERS AND SISTERS

FATHER

NIANG

YE YE

◆ Now write an essay or prepare a presentation on one of the characters.

69. THEMES

◆ As you read the book, make notes on the following themes. Include quotations from the text in your notes.

COURAGE AND PERSEVERANCE
FAMILY RELATIONSHIPS
LONELINESS/REJECTION
SELF-ESTEEM
THE POWER OF STORIES

◆ Now write an essay or prepare a presentation on one of the themes.

70. CULTURE

◆ As you read the book, make notes on the following aspects of Chinese culture. Include evidence from the text in your notes.

CLOTHING
CUSTOMS
FAMILY
LANGUAGE
MARRIAGE
RELIGION

◆ Now write an essay or prepare a presentation on Chinese culture.

71. CHINESE ASTROLOGY

The Rat

Rat people are charming and ambitious. They are always busy and seldom able to relax fully. If not, they get bored easily or get bad tempered. They enjoy going to parties or having a quick round of chat. Rats like to reach their goals by fair play. They are shrewd and not easily fooled.

The Ox

The Ox person is not happy with change and prefers conformity and convention. Ox people love the traditional value of hard work and a stable family life. Ox people enjoy material things and they are more than prepared to work hard to acquire a lifestyle that suits them.

The Tiger

The tiger is highly regarded in China, with almost magical powers to keep thieves and ghosts at bay. A Tiger person is 'born to command and not to obey'. Tigers are charismatic and dynamic. They are courageous and respected even by those who oppose them.

The Rabbit

A Rabbit person is peace-loving, usually kind, sweet and popular with a well-ordered life. Rabbits are not weak, they merely avoid a fight and have great diplomatic and negotiating skills. They prefer to spend their time at home with their family rather than going out for entertainment. Rabbits are a symbol of longevity and often live to a ripe old age.

The Dragon

The Dragon is the symbol of ancient China. There are many folk tales about dragons. The Dragon is revered with status equal to the Chinese Emperor whose throne is the Dragon and only he can wear the Dragon robe. The Dragon year is popular as every Chinese parent hopes for a Dragon child. A Dragon person is interesting and has lots of charisma.

The Snake

In the Chinese Horoscope, the Snake is not a symbol of evil as in other cultures. Snake people are intelligent, talented, determined and great organisers. They are philosophical and good thinkers.

The Horse

A Horse person is generally popular and the heart and soul of every party. In ancient China, the Horse symbolises freedom and a distinguished career. People born under this sign are lively, cheerful and sociable.

The Ram

The Ram is a symbol of social success and a good career in China. Generally, Ram people are elegant, charming and creative. However, they are the most moody amongst all of the Chinese Horoscope signs. Rams are very romantic, gentle, caring and endearing but a bit bossy.

The Monkey

Monkeys are intelligent, quick-witted and resourceful. Monkeys are fun loving, full of energy, imagination and ideas. A Monkey person is clever, cunning, agile and lively. Monkeys are good problem solvers.

The Rooster

Roosters have a keen sense of observation and like to be noticed and flattered. It is not easy to fool a Rooster and they make good trouble shooters. They are conscious of their appearance and what they wear.

The Dog

The Dog is a symbol of loyalty and wisdom for the Chinese. It is one of the most likeable signs of the Chinese Horoscope. The Dog values honour and enjoys helping other people. A Dog person is loyal, honest and affectionate and has a deep sense of justice and fair play.

The Pig

The Pig stands for wealth, family and prosperity, happiness and good luck. Pigs are considered the 'jewels' of the Chinese Horoscope as they are honest, upright and thus very popular. Pig people are open and straightforward. They do not know how to be devious or underhand but are honest and trustworthy.

72. SAYINGS OF CONFUCIUS

1. *Confucius said*: 'A young man should serve his parents at home and be respectful to elders outside his home. He should be earnest and truthful, loving all, but become intimate with jen*. After doing this, if he has energy to spare, he can study literature and the arts.'

2. *Confucius said*: 'When the Superior Man† eats he does not try to stuff himself; at rest he does not seek perfect comfort; he is diligent in his work and careful in speech.'

3. *Confucius said*: 'The 300 verses of the Book of Odes can be summed up in a single phrase: "Don't think in an evil way."'

4. *Confucius said*: 'See a person's means [of getting things]. Observe his motives. Examine that in which he rests. How can a person conceal his character?'

5. *Confucius said*: 'The Superior Man is not a utensil.'

6. *Tzu Kung asked about the character of the Superior Man. Confucius said*: 'First he practises what he preaches and then he follows it.'

7. *Confucius said*: 'The Superior Man is all-embracing and not partial. The inferior man is partial and not all-embracing.'

8. *Confucius said*: 'To study and not think is a waste. To think and not study is dangerous.'

9. *Confucius said*: 'Yu, shall I teach you about knowledge? What you know, you know, what you don't know, you don't know. This is knowledge.'

10. *Confucius said*: 'If a person lacks trustworthiness, I don't know what he or she can be good for. When a pin is missing from the yoke-bar of a large wagon, or from the collar-bar of a small wagon, how can it go?'

11. *Confucius said*: 'If you see what is right and fail to act on it, you lack courage.'

12. *Confucius said*: 'If you lack jen you can't handle long periods of difficulty or long periods of comfortability. Jen men are comfortable in jen. The wise take advantage of jen.'

13. *Confucius said*: 'If you are really committed to jen, you will have no evil in you.'

14. *Confucius said*: 'Riches and honours are what all men desire. But if they cannot be attained in accordance with the Tao they should not be kept. Poverty and low status are what all men hate. But if they cannot be avoided while staying in accordance with the Tao, you should not avoid them. If a Superior Man departs from jen, how can he be worthy of that name? A Superior Man never leaves jen for even the time of a single meal. In moments of haste he acts according to it. In times of difficulty or confusion he acts according to it.'

15. *Confucius said*: 'When the Superior Man deals with the world he is not prejudiced for or against anything. He does what is Right.'

jen – humanity, benevolence, goodness
†*the Superior Man* – a person who has made good progress in the Way (Tao) of self-development

73. GENERAL ASSIGNMENTS

Speaking and listening

'Hot-seat' Niang or Father and interrogate them about why they treated Adeline Yen Mah as they did.

Role-play the conversation that might take place if Adeline Yen Mah phoned 'Childline'.

Discuss how Adeline Yen Mah's life might have been even worse if she had not been so successful at school.

Reading

'This fairy-tale of seven-year-old motherless Sara Crewe, who started life as an heiress, turned overnight into a peniless servant girl and eventually changed her life through her own efforts, gripped my imagination as no other book had ever done before' (page 69). Read *A Little Princess* by Frances Hodgson Burnett and discuss why it inspired Adeline Yen Mah so much.

Writing

Bring together your personal responses to each of the 'Eight Key Readings' (see Resource 65) and develop them into your own autobiography.

Rewrite or act out a scene from the book as it might take place in a modern British or American family. Explore how a Western youngster would respond to such treatment.

Find your animal in Chinese astrology by visiting http://chinese.astrology.com. Simply type in your date of birth and it will tell you your animal and give you information about it. Write a response to this information. Do you think it is a good description of your personality? Is it more or less accurate than the description given in the Western zodiac?

The wider curriculum

Beginning with the 'Historical Note' on page 230 of the book, find out more about the geography, history and politics of China.

Spiritual, moral, ethical, social and cultural issues

Ye Ye is a Buddhist. Find out about Buddhism in the library or by visiting www.buddhanet.net/ and clicking on 'Basic Buddhism Guide'.

Find out about the United Nations Declaration of the Rights of the Child and discuss how far Father and Niang have breached these rights.

Find out more about the Chinese New Year.

74. ENGLISH LITERATURE EXAMINATION-STYLE QUESTIONS

Foundation tier

Describe the problems that Adeline Yen Mah faced in her life and explain how she overcame them. In your answer, you should:

◆ explain the family situation, particularly her relationship with her stepmother
◆ describe some of the things she had to suffer
◆ show how she was supported by Aunt Baba, Ye Ye, and pupils and teachers at school
◆ show how she overcame her problems partly through her own courage and determination.

If anything, Niang's treatment of Adeline Yen Mah is even worse than the stepmother's treatment of Cinderella in the fairytale. Discuss this statement by referring to:

◆ the character of Niang
◆ specific details of how she treated Adeline Yen Mah
◆ comparison with the fairytale *Cinderella*.

Write about one of the following themes in *Chinese Cinderella*: courage and honour, family and relationships, loneliness, self-esteem.

Explore the differences between your own culture and Chinese culture by focusing on any *two* of the following: school, marriage, family relationships, language and writing, religion.

Higher tier

'Everything is ugly. I loathe myself' (p. 215). Describe the events in Adeline Yen Mah's life that made her say this about herself. Explain how she fought back.

'I love my school. There I have friends! There I have fun! We sit together and discuss books and things. My friends respect me. My teachers like me. They've nominated me for class president!' (p. 122). Show how Adeline Yen Mah's education was one of the most important things in helping her to build up her self-esteem.

'She slapped me with the back of her hand against my other cheek. "Show-off! I'll teach you to be so sneaky!" she screamed loudly. "Go downstairs this minute and tell your hooligan friends to get out! They are not welcome!"' (p. 128). Describe Niang's treatment of Adeline Yen Mah and how it made her feel. How did she fight back?

In the Preface, Adeline Yen Mah writes that: 'In one way or another, every one of us has been shaped and moulded by the stories we have read and absorbed in the past.' Explore how stories helped to shape her life.

'To those who were neglected and unloved as children, I have a particular message. In spite of what your abusers would have had you believe, please be convinced that each of you has within you something precious and unique' (p. ix). Explain how this book might help and inspire neglected and unloved children.

UNIT 8: THE ASTROLOGY PROJECT

RESOURCES: Photocopiable resources in unit and Toolkit – no additional resources required

BOARD: All boards for coursework

RANGE: Non-fiction

AO	TEACHING SEQUENCE	RESOURCES	OUTCOMES
A02i	Revise summary skills using Toolkit Resource 19. Students read and discuss 'Diana's Stargazer'; use questions on Resource 79 and vocabulary and summary questions to make a written comprehension paper (optional)	Toolkit 19, 'Reference Skills' 75, 'Diana's Stargazer' 79, 'Questions Based on the Texts'	Discussion Written comprehension (optional) Improved summary skills
A02i	Students read and discuss 'Moonlight Fit'; use questions on Resource 79 and vocabulary and summary questions to make a written comprehension paper (optional)	76, 'Moonlight Fit' 79, 'Questions Based on the Texts'	Discussion Written comprehension (optional) Improved summary skills
A02i	Explain how to distinguish between fact, opinion and reasoned argument using Toolkit Resource 18. Students read and discuss 'Letter to the Editor'; use questions on Resource 79 and vocabulary and other questions to make a written comprehension paper (optional)	Toolkit 18, 'Fact and Opinion' 77, 'Letter to the Editor' 79, 'Questions Based on the Texts'	Discussion Written comprehension (optional) An increased ability to recognise fact, opinion and reasoned argument
A02i	Explain how to analyse an argument using Toolkit Resource 10. Students read and discuss 'Astrology'; use questions on Resource 79 and vocabulary to make a written comprehension paper (optional)	Toolkit 10, 'Types of Argument' 78, 'Astrology' 79, 'Questions Based on the Texts'	Discussion Written comprehension (optional) An increased ability to analyse an argument
Various	With teacher guidance, students choose one or more of the tasks on Resource 80, 'General Assignments'	80, 'General Assignments' Toolkit 19, 'Reference Skills' 75, 'Diana's Stargazer' 76, 'Moonlight Fit' 78, 'Astrology'	One or more General Assignments An increased ability to select, collate and cross-reference texts

Introduction

This selection of texts provides opportunities for students to practise all of the reading objectives. Each of the texts can be used separately as comprehension exercises using the questions on Resource 79, 'Questions Based on the Texts', but they can also be used together to practise AO2iv, which refers to skills of selection, collation and cross-referencing. Note that, unless students really need lots of comprehension practice, it would be better to set a written comprehension on just one or two of the texts rather than all four. The additional vocabulary questions can be covered orally. However, it is important that at least one of the summary exercises is attempted, as the ability to summarise – though not tested separately on current GCSE papers – is nevertheless an important analytical skill.

Notes on the Resources

75. DIANA'S STARGAZER

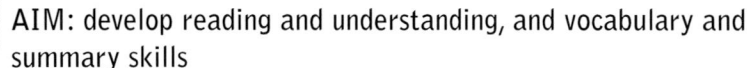

AIM: develop reading and understanding, and vocabulary and summary skills

Use Toolkit Resource 19, 'Reference Skills', to revise key summary skills. These may be found in the second box on the resource sheet.

Students read the article and then discuss the questions on Resource 79, 'Questions Based on the Texts', in pairs or small groups. This can be followed by a written comprehension, which could also include the following:

■ Define the following words and phrases as they are used in the text:
'clandestine' (col. 1, para. 9)   'intuition' (col. 2, para. 5)
'I felt we clicked instantly' (col. 2, para. 3)   'psychotherapy' (col. 5, para. 9)
'excruciating' (col. 2, para. 4)   'beaten her demons' (col. 6, para. 4)

■ Practice in summary writing.

Write a summary of the text in approximately 100 words. Use Resource 19, 'Reference Skills', box two, to help you.

76. MOONLIGHT FIT

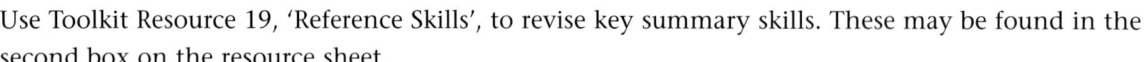

AIM: develop reading and understanding, and vocabulary and summary skills

Use Toolkit Resource 19, 'Reference Skills', box two, to revise key summary skills.

Students read the article and then discuss the questions on Resource 79, 'Questions Based on the Texts', in pairs or small groups. This can be followed by a written comprehension, which could also include the following:

■ Define the following words and phrases as they are used in the text:
'affected' (col. 1, para. 1)   'psychotic disorders' (col. 2, para. 4)
'profound effect' (col. 1, para. 3)   'concurs' (col. 2, para. 5)
'unequivocal' (col. 1, para. 4)   'surmise' (col. 4, para. 3)
'hyperactive' (col. 2, para. 3)

■ Practise in selective summary writing:
Write an 80-word summary of the scientific evidence presented in the article.
or
Write an 80-word summary of the legendary and mythical references in the article.
Use Toolkit Resource 19, 'Reference Skills', box two, to help you.

77. LETTER TO THE EDITOR

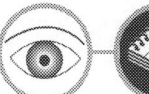

AIM: reading and understanding; distinguishing between fact, opinion and reasoned judgement

Use Toolkit Resource 18, 'Fact and Opinion', to explain the differences between fact, opinion and reasoned judgement. Students will find it helpful to refer to this resource when answering question 3.

Students read the letter and then discuss the questions on Resource 79, 'Questions Based on the Texts', in pairs or small groups. This can be followed by a written comprehension, which could also include the following:

■ Define the following words and phrases as they are used in the text:

'pernicious' (para. 1)　　　　　　　　　'predicted dire consequences' (para. 2)

'erroneous' (para. 1)　　　　　　　　　'affairs of the heart' (para. 2)

'astrophysics' (para. 1)　　　　　　　　'emotionally scarred for life' (para. 2)

■ Using the letter as a model, write a letter to a newspaper expressing an opinion about an issue that concerns you.

78. ASTROLOGY

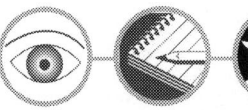

AIM: reading and understanding; following an argument; vocabulary skills

Use Toolkit Resource 10, 'Types of Argument', to review the types of argument used in a persuasive text. Students will find it helpful to refer to this resource when answering question 2.

Students read the article and then discuss the questions on Resource 79, 'Questions Based on the Texts', in pairs or small groups. This can be followed by a written comprehension, which could also include the following.

■ Define the following words and phrases as they are used in the text:

'zodiac' (para. 1)　　　　　　　　　　'constellations are arbitrary concepts' (para. 3)

'predestined' (para. 1)　　　　　　　　'close proximity' (para. 5)

'phenomenon' (para. 6)　　　　　　　　'precession of the equinoxes' (para. 6)

'countless' (para. 8)

79. QUESTIONS BASED ON THE TEXTS

AIM: to explore the texts and deepen understanding; develop written comprehension skills (optional)

Use the questions on Resource 79 as a basis for discussion or written comprehensions (optional).

80. GENERAL ASSIGNMENTS

AIM: select and collate material from different sources

All the written tasks on this resource sheet require students to select and collate material from different sources, and some of them require the use of references and cross-references. There are also several General Assignments, which explore the texts from a wider range of perspectives. All students should choose at least *one* written task. Another written task or general assignment is optional. Prepare for the written tasks as follows:

■ Use Toolkit Resource 19, 'Reference Skills', to explain the skills that will be needed.

■ Help students to choose one or more suitable tasks from the foundation- or higher-tier section as appropriate.

75. DIANA'S STARGAZER

Diana's

DEBBIE FRANK was Princess Diana's personal astrologer. For eight years until she died, they were in regular contact and became close friends. Debbie still misses her, especially, she says, 'her wonderful laugh'. As we all know, Diana cried as often as she laughed and when her tears were flowing, Debbie was the person to whom she often turned. Debbie's warm, compassionate manner and her intimate knowledge of the stars seemed to provide Diana with just the right brand of celestial comfort.

Debbie – star sign Scorpio with seven planets in water signs – will be providing personal, tailor-made horoscopes *free* for Daily Mail readers.

She's an ideal choice. Debbie has an unusual and fascinating attitude to astrology. 'I see it as a kind of psychology,' she explains. 'My main aim is to help people understand themselves rather than predict what will happen to them.

'Knowing your chart and the position of your Sun and Moon signs helps you understand yourself and attract the best of what is meant for you.

'Sometimes I call myself a celestial map reader. I plot someone's stars, show them that they are at a particular spot, tell them what their journey through the next few months will be like and help prevent them taking a wrong turning. I cover love, relationships, work and even moving home.

'No one can stop certain things happening, but it helps if you understand what is going on. I believe that astrology can make a difference to people's lives.'

Her new-age attitude to the planets obviously endeared her to Diana, whose star sign was the emotional, home-loving Cancer. The two met in 1989 – one of the most traumatic years of Diana's life. Diana was 28, a radiant beauty but feeling ugly and desperately unhappy inside.

Andrew Morton's devastating book *Diana: Her True Story* had yet to be published and the public still believed she and Charles had a fairy-tale marriage.

Diana, of course, knew otherwise. Charles's on-off romance with Camilla was firmly back on that year and the two had even managed to sneak a clandestine romantic two-day cruise off the Turkish coast. Diana was devastated when she found out.

■ **She so wanted to have a daughter ... but Charles refused to sleep with her**

■ **She never liked Princess Anne and had no time for Cherie Blair either**

■ **I didn't see Diana's death in the stars. I wish I could have saved her**

At the time, she didn't know what to do or where to turn. A friend, Mara Berni, who owns Diana's favourite restaurant San Lorenzo, in Knightsbridge, suggested Diana call Debbie.

Debbie, 41, remembers it well. 'It was February 2 when she rang. She just said, "It's Diana here, a friend of Mara's."

'She then said: "Can you help me?" She started to talk. We were roughly the same age and I felt we clicked instantly. I also quickly realised that she was in terrible emotional pain.

'She told me she found Charles's relationship with Camilla excruciating. And that she couldn't bear to live a lie. After we'd talked for a while, I said I would look at her astrological chart in detail. She told me the exact time and date of her birth, and when we next spoke on the telephone, I told her I could see her current troubles in her chart. It seemed to give her some relief.'

It was the start of a firm friendship and it is a great tribute to Debbie's intuition and sensitivity that unlike most of those Diana brought in and then pushed out of her ever-changing circle, she never fell out with Debbie.

'Diana then began calling me as often as three times a day,' Debbie remembers, 'and I became her astrological counsellor. She badly needed someone to listen to her and I was always there for her.

'After a while, the phone calls settled down to about one a week. Every couple of months she would invite me for a lovely lunch at Kensington Palace.

There was usually just the two of us and we would have fish or seafood with perhaps some wonderfully fresh green beans tied up in a parcel. This would be followed by a sorbet decorated with fresh flowers or a chocolate dessert and then delicious, fresh ginger tea.'

Their lunches, Debbie admits, were spent mainly talking about Diana. 'We were friends on her terms at the pace she wanted, which was fine by me. I never tried to push the relationship. We were very close but I never forgot that I was her astrologer.'

Debbie, who is divorced, is pretty, with thick, dark hair, soft features and a warm and welcoming smile. We talked in front of the fire in her cosy coach house in South London. The remains of a vast candle gently burned in the hearth, filling the primrose-coloured room with a heavenly scent of warm vanilla.

'It was a present from Diana,' she told me when I commented on the candle's beautiful smell. 'I don't light it often because I don't want to use it up.'

75. DIANA'S STARGAZER

continued

Stargazer

Working on Diana's chart gave Debbie a searing insight into her complex nature. 'I could see she'd had a complicated childhood and that her emotional instability was directly connected to her mother.

'She always had a feeling of waiting. I traced this back to when she was five and watched her mother pack her evening dresses into her car. She was leaving home but Diana told me she said to her: "Darling, I'll come back." So Diana sat for ages on the steps of their home waiting for her to return, but she never did.

'Being an abandoned little girl was the source of her original pain. She was very damaged by it and never quite got rid of it. In fact, she repeated the story of how her mother left her at our final lunch together, in July, 1997, a month before she died. It set a pattern for her future love life. Just as she had waited for her mother, she thought in the early years of her marriage that if she sat tight, Charles would come back and love her again.

'She certainly loved him and tried hard to get him back. She wanted to have another child with him, particularly a little girl, but he didn't want another child.'

Did Charles refuse to sleep with Diana? 'Yes,' Debbie says quietly.

Soon after they met, Diana asked Debbie to prepare detailed astrological charts for the queen, Prince Charles, and her sons William and Harry.

Contrary to a lot of recent comments, Diana did get on with the Queen,' Debbie insists. 'She was never once

disrespectful about her. Instead, Diana wanted to try to understand the Queen, and particularly what went wrong with her relationship with Charles, and how that, in turn, affected Charles's relationship with Diana.

'It was all there in the stars and we discussed it a lot. The queen is a typical Taurean, constant, persistent and down to earth. Whereas Diana was a very emotional water sign, Cancer, so it was difficult for one to understand the other.

'Charles is a Scorpio, a sign which is usually very compatible with Cancerians. But he has his moon in Taurus, the same sign as his mother. This signifies a contradiction between the mind and the heart, which is why he has had so much trouble coming to terms with his relationship with Camilla.

'Ironically, Camilla's birth sign is also Cancer. But she and Diana are very different. Camilla's planets are all positioned in areas that show she wants to be behind the scenes, which is why her relationship with Charles works well.'

Over the years, Diana and Debbie discussed the star signs of most of the members of the Royal Family. But never Princess Anne.

'Diana wasn't remotely interested in doing so. She and Anne didn't have a relationship mainly because Anne isn't at all sensitive.

'In the early days, Diana got on best with Princess Margaret – they both loved the Arts, and Margaret had also been a bit of a rebel – but they didn't remain close. The Royal Family close ranks when there is trouble.'

Debbie insists that although Diana was fascinated by the stars she didn't let them control her. She enjoyed the fun aspect of astrology, too, and often asked Debbie to tell her what it revealed about some of the world leaders she met. 'She asked me to do Bill Clinton and Nelson Mandela's charts, and we enjoyed talking about them.

Debbie gradually became increasingly important in Diana's life. It was Debbie who convinced Diana to have psychotherapy to help her cope with her eating disorder, bulimia nervosa. Shortly afterwards she started seeing therapist Susie Orbach.

Although Diana eventually managed to control the illness, Debbie feels she never quite got over it. 'There were still times when it re-occurred, usually when she had a problem with a relationship with a man. But it was nothing like it was at its height.'

Debbie was her most supportive during 1992 when Diana and Charles separated, a trauma that Debbie foresaw in her charts. 'There was a crisis due to Pluto, the planet of total transformation. I could see she was in a black hole, but getting through it would give her a tremendous awareness.'

Far more significant and heartwarming in Debbie's opinion, was that in the last couple of years of her life Diana began to relax. She even started to drink a little. 'When I first knew her she wouldn't touch alcohol at all, but by the end of her life she would have a glass of wine with a meal, which I saw as a very good sign.'

She seemed to have finally beaten her demons just before she died. 'The Diana I saw in her last months was such a different Diana from the one I first knew. It was quite remarkable.

'When I met her, she felt a victim and powerless to do or change anything. Towards the end of her life she had made peace with herself and felt that everything that had happened to her was for a reason and had taught her so much.

'She felt her own suffering had helped her to relate to people. Also that the level of pain she had experienced could enable her to really do something in the world.

'Nor did she regret marrying Charles. She was convinced it was the right thing to have done, even if it turned out wrong. She felt divorcing him, too, was the natural course of events.'

Debbie's last meal with Diana took place on July 30, a month before she died. Debbie remembers it well. 'She had just come back from dress designer Gianni Versace's funeral and looked amazing in one of his pink dresses.

While you can see difficult times ahead, you cannot see death in the starts,' says Debbie. 'Thank goodness for that. It would be just too dreadful to know when everyone was going to die.

'There was, however, an eclipse in Diana's chart at the time she died, which if I had been a medieval astrologer I would have interpreted as the end of an era.

'Instead, I interpreted it as her going through a psychological death and rebirth, which as also true.'

Angela Levin
Daily Mail, 12 July 2002

76. MOONLIGHT FIT

THE WAY WE BEHAVE – IN MADNESS OR . . .

Are we all prone . . .

All water on the earth is pulled by the moon, and humans and animals are made up of more than 90 per cent water. Of course we're going to be affected: our inner tides, as it were, rise higher at the time of a new moon.

'It's no coincidence that women's menstrual cycles are 28 days, exactly the same length of time between full moons; and farmers have always known that you get better results from your crops if you plant and harvest according to the phases of the moon.

'People have known of the moon's profound effect on us for years `– the truth is that people just go pottier around the full moon; even the words lunacy and lunatic are derived from lunar.'

But this 'pottiness' is not confined to dark tales of vampires and werewolves. There are very real examples of increased violence under the light of a full moon. A scientific study of prisoners at the maximum security wing of Armley jail, in Leeds, showed an unequivocal rise in violence during the days either side of a full moon.

The study of all 1,200 inmates over three months was carried out by officer Claire Smith, who recorded every violent incident, as well as asking prisoners to keep 'mood diaries'.

She found there were as many as five violent incidents a day around a full moon – far more than at other times of the month.

'This has proved a definite link between the moon and behaviour,' she says. 'If the moon controls the tides, what is it doing to us? I have been amazed by the response. We were even contacted by parents whose children became hyperactive at the time of a full moon.'

The 28-day lunar cycle also coincides with increased mental disturbance. 'It is a generally accepted fact among mental health carers that patients with psychotic disorders present more extreme symptoms at the time of a full moon,' says former psychiatric nurse Mark Radcliffe.

Vanessa Kyle, a casualty nurse, concurs: 'We experience a dramatic rise in the number of disturbed patients requiring treatment on the night of a full moon. It is a well-known phenomenon.'

Richard Allport, a vet in Potters Bar, Hertfordshire, has found that epileptic fits among domestic animals tend to increase around a full moon.

'There's no doubt in my mind that there's a link there,' he says. 'I have one patient, a dog who has epilepsy which seems almost to be triggered by the full moon. Ironically, I'm treating him with a homeopathic remedy called Lunar.

'Though I really only deal with dogs and cats, I've heard tales of all creatures being affected, even parasitic activity, especially on the Continent.

'The effect of the full moon is something that binds both humans and animals – we're all touched by it in some way.'

So, could it be that the fear and importance that man has always attached to the phases of the moon may have had some basis in scientific fact after all; that the old wives tales of animal madness and bloodthirsty killers stalking their prey under the light of the full moon, may not just be something with which to frighten the children once a month?

Jack the Ripper claimed two of his victims under a full moon and, in Argentina, tradition has it that every seventh son will turn into a 'lobizon' or werewolf at midnight once every 28 days, returning to human form at dawn. Juan Peron, the former Argentine president, even decreed compulsory baptism for every seventh son as a precautionary measure.

---

10 THINGS YOU DIDN'T KNOW ABOUT FULL MOONS

- Robert Louis Stevenson's Dr Jekyll and Mr Hyde was based on the true story of Charles Hyde's chilling series of full moon murders in the late 1880's.

- According to scientists at Georgia State University, there is a reported eight per cent increase in average meal sizes on the day of the full moon, and a 25 per cent rise in drinking rates.

- Women who have already had children are significantly more likely to give birth on the day of a full moon. In the South Pacific, meanwhile, the Palolo worm mates only once a year under a full moon in late October.

- Households make more calls and log on to the Internet more frequently in the days leading up to a full moon, according to BT, supporting the belief that there is a build-up of creative and emotional energy around at this time.

- The full moon has provided many a traveller with a good party. The hippy-inspired Full Moon Parties are held on various tropical beaches around the world, the most famous being at Ko Pha-Ngan in Thailand.

- The most significant Buddah celebration happens every May on the night of the full moon.

- In 1974, 16 people were killed in Cambodia when soldiers fired guns at what they thought was a monkey eating the full moon. It was, in fact, a lunar eclipse.

- Forensic psychiatry studies show that people who behave dangerously are more agitated during a full moon. One example is Christopher Gore who, in 1992, killed his parents and two others on full moon nights.

- Russian researchers found an increase in epileptic seizures during the period of the full moon, which they attributed to the moon's magnetic effects.

- A research team at Leeds University discovered that GP visits rose by 3.6 per cent six days after the full moon. This is the equivalent of doctors making 30,000 extra visits nationally per lunar cycle.

76. MOONLIGHT FIT

continued

... IN AGGRESSION – IS LINKED TO THE LUNAR CYCLE

... to a moonlight fit?

Why vampires and werewolves like to howl in the night

When science and folklore collide, there is usually a degree of truth behind the myths.

Astronomer Donald Maycock says that while such theorising on the effects of the moon upon earth's inhabitants is interesting, it is 'not really astronomy – more like something to approach from a biological or evolutionary viewpoint.

'For example, I have heard theories that, as human evolution can be traced all the way back to a time when we were organisms living in the sea anyway, one might surmise that we have this deeply ingrained evolutionary instinct to be governed by the tides. But, of course, it's not scientifically provable.'

As an astrologer, whose whole belief system revolves around the effect of astronomical bodies upon us, Jonathan Cainer insists that the moon is central to human and animal behaviour.

'The phases of the moon are the essence of astrology,' he says. 'It's the first thing an astrologer looks at when drawing a forecast.

'Though it's primarily associated with negativity – madness and vampires and so on – I would say it's a case simply of more happening when the moon is full. There's more activity, more going on when our inner tide is being pulled like that.'

There are other, rather more dull, theories. In the days before street lights, for example, more would happen on nights when the moon was full, simply because those were the only nights in which one could see.

The increase in activity was as banal and explainable as the decrease in activity on days when it was pouring with rain, for example. Jack the Ripper may have preferred a full moon simply because, in the thick fog of Victorian London, such light made it easier to stalk and slay his victims.

And yet, even 32 years after man first walked on the moon, there are still aspects of our closest astronomical neighbour hidden to scientists. 'We're very interested in something called Transient Lunar Phenomena,' says Maycock.

'People have seen what look like changes of colour around the moon and nobody is really sure what it is. It could

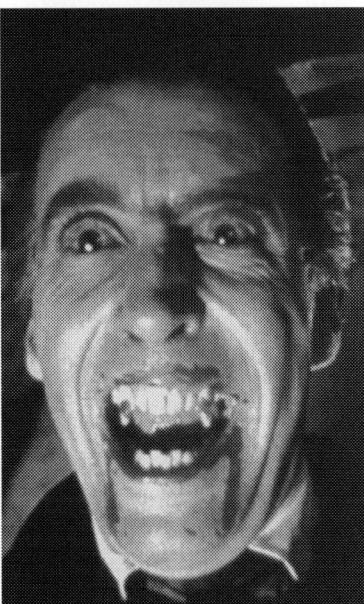

The full moon has always played a central role in mythology and folklore. Under its eerie glow, witches flee, lunatics are set loose, werewolves howl in the night and vampires creep around in search of a delicate neck on which to feast.

Since the late eighteenth century, horror novels have played on these myths and,

more recently, the full moon has become a popular motif in films. Bram Stoker used the light of the full moon to illuminate many of Dracula's feeding frenzies and *An American Werewolf in London* and *Teenwolf* are just two of the many films in which men change to blood-hungry werewolves when the moon is full.

In medieval Europe, the clergy and their faithful regarded werewolves as dangerous fact, and the last religious study to treat them as real was written by the clerical scholar Montague Summers as late as 1961. He wrote: 'A werewolf is a human being, man, woman or child (more often the first), who either voluntarily or involuntarily changes into the apparent shape of a wolf, and who is then possessed of all the characteristics, the foul appetites, ferocity, cunning, the brute strength, and swiftness of that animal.'

even be gases escaping from the interior.'

And then there are 'moonquakes', where the conjunction of the earth, sun and full moon can literally move mountains.

'There's no doubt that just as the moon has a tidal pull on us, so we do on it,' continues Maycock. 'These "moonquakes" are caused by the tidal movement of rock brought about by our gravitational pull.

'The Apollo missions left seismometers [used to measure earthquakes] up there and they have measured over 3,000 quakes a year over the last 30 years or so.

'And for exactly the same reasons the moon affects us, so the earth and the sun exert the greatest pull on the moon every 28 days – every time there's a full moon.'

Daily Express, 30 January 2001

77. LETTER TO THE EDITOR

Dear Sir,

I am a science teacher and I am writing to complain about the pernicious effect on my pupils of your newspaper's obsession with astrology. Not only do you publish a daily horoscope, but you have recently run a special offer on a detailed personal horoscope by your resident astrologer. My concern is that astrology is based on an erroneous model of the universe and thus confuses pupils who are trying to learn complex scientific theories of astrophysics. I also believe that astrology can be positively dangerous. It claims to be able to predict the future, and this can cause serious psychological problems.

Let me give you an example. One of my pupils took up your horoscope offer, and soon after receiving her detailed personal horoscope asked me what 'retrograde' meant. I explained that it was an outdated idea that a planet could move backwards. She then asked me if I thought it would affect her love life (apparently her horoscope had said that Venus was retrograde and predicted dire consequences in all affairs of the heart). She looked so unhappy about it that I was very much afraid that she would be emotionally scarred for life.

Indeed, I was so shocked that she could believe in this rubbish that I decided to devote a whole lesson to the subject. I drew a diagram of the universe as described by Ptolemy in the second century AD and explained that this was the universe that astrologers believe in. The diagram had the Earth at its centre. The Earth is surrounded by seven planets including the sun and the moon. Beyond the planets are the 'fixed stars'. Some of these stars are particularly important because they form a belt of constellations through which the planets appear to move. Of course, with the Earth instead of the sun at the centre, the planetary movements appear rather strange, as at certain points they seem to move backwards.

I am sorry to say that my pupils paid more attention to the lesson in susperstition that they have ever paid to my serious science lessons. Be that as it may, I then went on to show how modern science, beginning with Copernicus in 1530, has since shown the Ptolemaic model of the universe to be nonsense. If astrology is based on an erroneous model of the universe, it must also be nonsense.

I think, therefore, that it would be highly desirable to stop polluting young minds with astrology and publish some real science instead. For example, you could begin with an article on Newton's Theory of Universal Gravitation, and replace the horoscope with the Periodic Table. A series of articles on famous scientists might also be interesting.

Finally, I think you should sack your resident astrologer and replace him with a resident scientist – I might even apply for the job myself!

Yours,

I. Boreham

78. ASTROLOGY

http://new-age_nonsense

The Truth About Astrology

Ancient peoples, gazing at the stars, noticed that some were 'fixed' and others were 'wanderers' (the planets). They noticed that groups of fixed stars (constellations) suggested pictures, for example, of a hunter (Orion), a scorpion (Scorpio) or a bear (Ursa Major). Some of the constellations were particularly important because they formed a belt through which the wandering stars (the planets) seemed to move. These are the constellations that form the Zodiac – the twelve constellations used in Astrology: Aries, Taurus, Gemini, Cancer, Leo, Virgo, Libra, Scorpio, Sagittarius, Capricorn, Aquarius, Pisces. The wandering stars were thought to be gods and were named after Roman gods and goddesses: Mercury,

MENU
The Truth About Alien Abductions
The Truth About Aromatherapy
The Truth About Astral Projection
The Truth About Levitation
The Truth About Near-Death Experiences
The Truth About Palmistry

Venus, Mars, Jupiter, Saturn. To these were added the sun and the moon making the seven traditional 'planets' of Astrology. Ancient peoples believed that the position of the seven planets in the Zodiac at the time of a person's birth was significant as it could be used to predict character and foretell the future. The most important of the planets was the sun, so if the sun was in Aries at the time of a person's birth, that person was an Aries. The predictions of character and fate (a person's predestined life pattern) were made by imaginative interpretations based on the pictures made by the constellations and the attributes of the god associated with each planet. Thus, Leos are often said to be proud and to make good leaders, attributes that are clearly influenced by the idea of the lion as 'the king of beasts'. Another example is that people with the planet Mars in an important position are said to make good soldiers. Mars, of course, was the Roman god of war.

This is the basis of the astrological system that is still used today – and astrology has never been more popular. Most magazines and newspapers include horoscopes and millions of people, including some politicians, use them regularly. Astrology's current popularity has many reasons, but two are particularly important: the decline of belief in traditional religions has left an aching void that people are trying to fill; and astrology has a scientific and mathematical basis that appeals to the modern mind. Despite this, as I hope to show in this article, astrology is nothing more than a lingering superstition that cannot stand up to close scrutiny.

To begin with, constellations are arbitrary concepts. The patterns of stars that we see from Earth would look different from other points in space since they are separated by hundreds of light years. The pictures that people see in constellations are different. For example, in the constellation Ursa Major, people have seen a bear, a plough and a big dipper. The Chinese have imagined a completely different set of images. Am I really expected to believe that a person will be 'bullish' just because a pattern of stars looked a bit like a bull to a Babylonian shepherd a few thousand years ago?

The associations of the planets are also arbitrary. The planet Venus can easily be associated with love when it shines poetically at dusk as 'the evening star', but the reality of a searing hell with a surface temperature of over 400 degrees Celsius is enough to dispel any notions of romance.

78. ASTROLOGY

continued

Astrologers argue that Astrology can be proved scientifically. They point to the influence of the moon upon the tides and suggest that, as 70% of our body chemistry is water, then the moon is bound to affect us. There is no evidence for this and if the moon, with its close proximity to earth cannot affect us, how can we be affected by a star which is hundreds of light years away? They also point to statistical evidence. For example, in a study of 1000 people, 232 were in occupations associated with their zodiac sign as opposed to the 120 that would occur by chance. Even if those figures are correct, they don't exactly inspire me with the confidence to go to an astrologer for careers advice! To be able to calculate the position of planets was a major achievement for the ancients and this scientific and mathematical basis can give a spurious authenticity to astrology. Calculating an individual horoscope involves plotting the position of each of the planets relative to the time and place that an individual was born. This can now be done on a computer, but it used to be done by hand with the help of tables called 'Sidereal Tables'.

However, if you examine the result of all this fancy mathematics, you will find that it is based on an illusion. The test is simple. Compare the night sky with a natal chart of a child who has just been born. If the natal chart says that Mars is in the constellation of Aquarius, you should find it there – but you won't. The reason for this is a phenomenon called the precession of the equinoxes.

The Earth's axis is not fixed in space but moves backward one degree every 72 years. At this rate, each of the 12 signs of the zodiac takes about 2100 years to pass through. The result is that the signs of the zodiac are not where astrologers say they are (based on calculations made by the Babylonians 2000 years ago). In fact, they are approximately one whole zodiac sign behind. This means that I am not an Aquarius after all, I'm a Capricorn – but, hang on, I don't want to be a Capricorn! Capricorns are a miserable, pessimistic lot! Don't worry, reply the astrologers, you're still 'really' an Aquarius – help, I'm confused!

If this is a bit confusing, there is another, much more obvious, flaw in the 'science' of astrology. A glance at any 'natal' chart will show that the 'planets' (including the sun and moon) revolve around the earth. Since Copernicus (1473–1543), we have known that the sun is at the centre of the solar system, and if there is any lingering doubt about it, we have seen it for ourselves through the eyes of countless astronauts. The model of the universe on which astrology is based is wrong, and if your model is wrong, your results will be wrong. It is a bit like trying to perform a heart transplant with a medieval diagram of the human body.

For hundreds of years scientists and philosophers have rejected astrology as nonsense. The classic work against astrology is Louvain's 'Dissertation' (1945) in which he presents similar arguments to those given above, but in much more detail. It would be interesting to quote some of Louvain's conclusions here. However, I have chosen instead the conclusions of a more recent scientist, Dr David Whitehouse, because his humour provides a more effective riposte to the ridiculous claims of the astrologers than any number of reasoned arguments:

When I look at the evidence that astrology works I come away very unimpressed. Just because science can't explain everything doesn't mean that it has not explained astrology. Because we cannot explain why some things work, like some drugs, does not mean that astrology works in an as yet undiscovered way. Some things are just plain wrong. Thor is not the god of thunder, the earth isn't the centre of the universe and there are not fairies at the bottom of my garden.

79. QUESTIONS BASED ON THE TEXTS

Diana's stargazer

1. What is 'unusual and fascinating' about Debbie's approach to astrology?
2. What was the source of Diana's pain?
3. How was Debbie able to predict a trauma in Diana's life?
4. How did astrology help Diana to understand her relationships?
5. According to Debbie, why did she fail to predict Diana's death?
6. How does the page layout add to the impact of the article? Consider the effect of headline and subheadings, photographs, other features of design.

Moonlight fit

1. What is the evidence that the moon affects human behaviour? Try to find at least five points.
2. What 'rather more dull' theory offers an alternative explanation of human behaviour on the nights of the full moon?
3. What is Donald Maycock's profession? How does this affect your view of the scientific validity of his arguments?
4. How are the two inset boxes used to make the article more interesting? How relevant to the main argument is the information in these boxes?
5. In what other ways has the author tried to 'sensationalise' the article?
6. Explain the effect of the different sizes and types of font used in the article.

Letter to the editor

1. What is the science teacher complaining about?
2. What reasons does he give for his complaint?
3. How do you think the newspaper's readership would react to his ideas for replacing the astrology column?
4. Highlight *facts* in one colour, *opinions* in another and *reasoned arguments* in another. Use Resource 18, 'Fact and Opinion', to help you.

Astrology

1. What arguments does the author give against the validity of astrology?
2. Use Resource 10, 'Types of Argument', to help you evaluate the arguments in this text.
3. Find and quote examples of the author's use of humour, and discuss the extent to which this makes the article more effective.
4. This website is soon to be published as a book. What will be the main differences in layout and organisation?

80. GENERAL ASSIGNMENTS

Speaking and listening

Write and deliver a debate speech for the motion, 'This house believes that astrology is superstitious nonsense.' Refer to your sources as appropriate.

◆ Begin with a brief explanation of astrology (see Resource 78, 'Astrology').
◆ Take the most effective arguments from 'Astrology' and express them in your own words. (Quote facts and figures, names, sources, etc. to give authenticity.)
◆ Show that the astrologer's model of the universe is out of date (see Resource 77, 'Letter to the Editor').
◆ Show how 'Diana's Stargazer', Debbie Frank – though she gave Diana psychological support – was unable to make any accurate or useful predictions about her life (Resource 75).
◆ Choose a 'punchy' argument from 'Astrology' to conclude.

Write and deliver a debate speech against the motion in a similar way.

Reading

Research astrology in the library and on the Internet. Try to find out if there is any scientific basis for astrology.

Writing

Foundation tier

What can we learn about astrotherapy by collating information from 'Diana's Stargazer' and 'Astrology' (Resources 75 and 78)?

Write the editor's reply to Resource 77, 'Letter to the Editor'. Focus on what you think readers enjoy, and refer to the two newspaper articles in this unit as examples.

Higher tier

If we compare information from 'Moonlight Fit' with 'Astrology' (Resources 76 and 78), what contradictions and correspondences do we find, with reference to the effect of the moon on living things? Both articles claim to be scientifically based. Which do you think is the most credible and why?

Write an article in which you argue for the validity of astrology. Include cross-references in your article.

◆ Begin with a brief explanation of astrology (see 'Astrology').
◆ Adapt some of the information from 'Astrology'. (Some of the evidence against astrology can be turned around to argue *for* it. Quote facts and figures, names, sources, etc. to give authenticity.)
◆ Use some of the evidence from 'Moonlight Fit'. (Quote facts and figures, names, sources, etc. to give authenticity.)
◆ Refer to 'Diana's Stargazer' (Resource 75) to show how astrology actually helped Diana to cope with her problems.

The wider curriculum

Ask your science teacher what his or her views are on astrology. Make notes on his or her response.

Spiritual, moral, ethical, social and cultural issues

How would the belief that your fate was predetermined in the stars affect the way you lived your life? What spiritual, moral, ethical, social and cultural issues does this belief raise?

ICT

Visit www.ouroboros.com. This site will calculate a chart based on your birth data and give you a complete interpretation for free. Do this for the whole class, then discuss the accuracy of the results.

UNIT 9: *METROPOLIS*

RESOURCES: *Metropolis,* any version, though the latest reconstruction (2003) has tracked down fully three quarters of the original, with the missing scenes covered by descriptive inter-titles (the Giorgio Moroder version (1984) is also recommended, with a pop-style soundtrack that will appeal to young people)
BOARD: Any for English coursework
RANGE: Media

AO	TEACHING SEQUENCE	RESOURCES	OUTCOMES
A02iv	Pre-viewing activity: research social class, particularly Marx's views on class	Library, Internet	Understanding of the theory underlying the main theme of class conflict
A02i	Show the first 11 minutes of the film (up to the explosion of the machine) and discuss first impressions of the film and what it is about	Film, *Metropolis*	Adjustment to the cinematic techniques of the 1920s
A02i	Students work in groups of 4, with each student making notes on a different aspect of the film Restart the film just before the vision of Moloch	81, 'Setting and Plot' 82, 'Characters' 83, 'Christian References' 84, 'Production Techniques'	Knowledge of the setting, plot and techniques used in the film Notes on resource sheets
A02i	Stop film just before the false Maria speaks to the workers Students discuss the film so far, catch up on their resource sheets, and discuss what will happen next	81, 'Setting and Plot' 82, 'Characters' 83, 'Christian References' 84, 'Production Techniques'	Knowledge of the setting, plot and techniques used in the film Notes on resource sheets
A02i A01ii	Show the film to the end Students finish making notes on their resource sheets and then report back to other members of the group Discuss the ending – how will *Metropolis* change?	81, 'Setting and Plot' 82, 'Characters' 83, 'Christian References' 84, 'Production Techniques'	Knowledge of the setting, plot and techniques used in the film Completed resource sheets
A02i	Working in pairs, students use the resource sheet to discuss the two main themes and write an essay about one of them	85, 'Themes'	Knowledge of the two main themes through discussion and analysis of one in depth in writing
A02i A03 i–iii	Students read Resource 86, '*Metropolis* Review', followed by discussion and/or comprehension (Resource 87) Write own review of film	86, '*Metropolis* Review' 87, '*Metropolis* Review Comprehension' Toolkit 15, 'Film Review'	Wider understanding of the director, the film and how it was made Written comprehension (optional) Own review of film
Various	Students choose one or more activities from Resource 88, 'General Assignments'	88, 'General Assignments'	One or more general assignments

Introduction

Metropolis, directed by Fritz Lang, 1926, is the seminal science fiction film. It tells the story of a future city in which the rich elite live lives of pleasure while the workers work for ten hours a day on underground machines. A working girl, Maria, tries to help them and she inspires Freder – son of the Lord of Metropolis, Joh Fredersen* – to help. However, a mad scientist (Rotwang) makes a robot in her image which leads the workers to rebel. The machines are stopped and their underground city is flooded, but Maria has escaped in time to save the children. At the end of the film, the Lord of Metropolis and the workers are reconciled.

Although made so long ago, this film has immediate appeal, and most GCSE students will find it interesting and enjoyable.

*Title cards and reviews sometimes give his name as John, but we can see from his name on the invitation from Rotwang towards the end of the film that his name is spelled 'Joh'.

Notes on the Resources

81. SETTING AND PLOT

AIM: detailed knowledge of setting and plot

Students could begin making notes on setting after watching the opening sequence (the first ten minutes or so) as this shows us most of what we need to know, though they will need to add to their notes later to include information about the different levels, Rotwang's house, the catacombs and the cathedral.

The best way to summarise the plot is to make notes after each viewing. Note that Resource 86 contains a summary of the plot – there is also one at the beginning of these notes – and either can be used for revision. The only things that may be hard to remember after one viewing are the names of the characters. Students will find the main characters listed on Resource 82.

82. CHARACTERS

AIM: knowledge of main characters

In a silent film like *Metropolis*, there is little opportunity for character development with the result that most characters are simple or even merely stereotypes. For example, Rotwang is the stereotypical mad scientist. However, students should make notes on the characters' role in the film, their personality (and in the case of Freder and Joh Fredersen) how they develop through the film.

83. CHRISTIAN REFERENCES

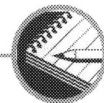

AIM: understand how allusions are used to develop the themes of the film

There are several scenes in the film which have strong Christian associations. Students should describe these scenes and then explain their significance. Explain to students that, in literary terms, a reference to something outside the text is called an *allusion*. These allusions help to develop the themes of the film. Briefly the significance of each is as follows:

Vision of Moloch

In the Bible, Moloch was appeased with human sacrifice. The way the workers have to suffer and die to operate the machines is equivalent to human sacrifice – that is to say, it is morally wrong.

The tower of Babel

In the film, the story is used to convey a different message than the Bible story. In the Bible, God punishes the pride of the Babylonians for building their tower by confusing their languages. In the film, the story is used to introduce the idea of a mediator between the workers and the ruling elite.

Christ on the cross

For a brief moment, Freder slumps with exhaustion with his hands extended on the hands of the machine. This position and the cry to his father echo Christ on the cross. The parallel is that the 'son' has come down from the father and has taken on human suffering.

Seven deadly sins

These symbolise the sins that are at work in *Metropolis*:

- *pride* – in the building of *Metropolis* and Rotwang's fiendish inventions
- *covetousness* ⎫
- *envy* ⎬ when the worst feelings of the workers are aroused by the false Maria
- *anger* ⎭
- *lust* – when the false Maria dances almost naked for the crowd
- *gluttony* – in the rich elite's enjoyment of the good things of life
- *sloth* – in the way the rich elite enjoy a life of idleness while the workers work ten hours a day.

Ask students if they notice any other Christian references in the film. They may notice:

The crosses behind Maria

This shows that the meeting is more than just political. It has a religious dimension. Maria's message also has a mystical, semi-religious element because she advises that the workers wait for a 'mediator'.

The cathedral

This acts as a haunting backdrop to the final scenes of the film. At one point, some workers are seen in the nave as though they are attending (or have just attended) a service.

The flood

This reference is not as specific as the ones on the resource sheet. There is no equivalent to the animals entering the ark. However, Noah's flood symbolises a general clearing away of evil, and the flood in *Metropolis* acts in the same way.

The idea of a prophet and a saviour

In the New Testament, John the Baptist prophesied and Christ came as a saviour. Freder, though not quite a saviour, is a mediator.

84. PRODUCTION TECHNIQUES

AIM: comment on the techniques which are used to make the film, and compare with modern film techniques

Camera techniques

Students could use Toolkit Resource 16, 'Film Techniques', alongside this resource, as it gives some idea of the much wider range of modern film techniques. In *Metropolis*, most shots are still. Panning is little used (there are some examples when Rotwang chases Maria) and there is no use of zoom at all. However, the camera angles are varied and interesting, and skilful editing gives a sense of movement.

Special effects

Of course, the special effects are nothing like the computer-generated effects of today, but they are very effective nonetheless. Noteworthy are the opening sequence in which different machines are superimposed; the explosion of the machine; the cross-fade between the plan of the catacombs and the workers marching along the tunnels; the change from the robot to Maria; and the flood sequence near the end of the film.

Acting

The acting is very stylised compared to today's 'realistic' school of acting. This is partly to compensate for the lack of sound (gestures taking the place of words). There are also several striking 'tableaux' in which postures are struck to make a memorable still scene – for example, when Rotwang strikes a pose with the robot behind him, or when the architects pose on either side of a model of the Tower of Babel.

Sound

A good soundtrack can bring the film to life. Though students will probably prefer the 'pop' soundtrack of the Giorgio Moroder version (1984), the author's favourite is the 1998 soundtrack by Peter Osborne which, through repetitive phrases and rhythms, successfully evokes the idea of an industrial city of the future.

85. THEMES

AIM: show insight into issues raised (themes)

The resource sheet contains a series of bullet points on each of the two main themes. These bullet points can be used as a focus for discussion and writing: when developing each point, encourage students to 'quote' specific moments from the film very much in the way that they would use quotations in an essay on a novel or a play. They should also refer to Resources 81, 82, 83 and 84 completed earlier in the unit – for example, referring to one of the Christian references to support a point about a theme.

86. *METROPOLIS* REVIEW

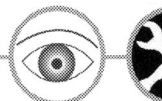

AIM: find out about the background of the film and read a good model of review writing

This excellent review by Roger Ebert is worth reading even if it is not intended that students will do the comprehension based on it. It gives valuable background information on the director, Fritz Lang, and the making and history of the film, as well as its immense influence on later films.

After reading the review, students could write their own review of the film. Foundation-tier students would benefit from using Toolkit Resource 15, 'Film Review', as a guide.

87. *METROPOLIS* REVIEW COMPREHENSION

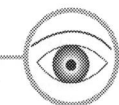

AIM: develop ability to understand texts

English departments have their own procedures for marking comprehension exercises. One approach is to give an overall grade for the whole comprehension; another is to allocate specific marks for each question. The important thing is that students know what to expect.

Suggested marking scheme

In question 1, the single words could be given 1 mark and the phrases 2 marks. In the higher-tier questions, 3 marks could be awarded. Questions 2 to 7 have two parts each, so a mark out of 4 (two marks for each part) would allow sufficient scope to differentiate between answers (higher-tier questions could be marked out of 6).

88. GENERAL ASSIGNMENTS

AIM: explore the film from a wider range of perspectives

The resource sheet provides a list of suggestions for responding to the film from a wider range of perspectives. One of the most valuable is making your own short film about the future, as the best way to learn about film techniques and increase appreciation of the way famous directors use them is to try it for oneself. All that is needed is a video camera – a resource that is available in most schools. Ideally, this will be a digital video camera that can be linked to a computer for editing. The set can be any bleak modernist building (most comprehensive schools are ideal!). Students could experiment with a silent version of the film, which could be set to music by GCSE Music students. The film can be shown at an annual event, such as an arts fair or open evening.

81. SETTING AND PLOT

As you watch the film, make notes on the setting and plot in the boxes below.

SETTING
Describe Metropolis (a city of 2026). Explain the different levels and what be found on them. Write about what the city reminds you of. Can you trace any influences in later films?

PLOT
Write a brief summary of the plot (names of characters can be found on Resource 82, 'Characters').

82. CHARACTERS

Write brief notes on each of the following characters and their role in the film.

MARIA

JOH FREDERSEN

FREDER

JOSEPH

ROTWANG

THE ROBOT

THE WORKERS

83. CHRISTIAN REFERENCES

Watch the scene in which each of these Christian references occurs, then briefly describe what happens. Explain what Fritz Lang was trying to communicate by making the reference.

VISION OF MOLOCH
Moloch was a pagan god at the hilled site of Topheth who demanded human sacrifice (see 2 Kings 23:10).

THE TOWER OF BABEL
A huge tower built in the land of Shinar in Babylon some time after the flood. God saw it as the product of human pride and destroyed it (see Genesis 11:1–9).

CHRIST ON THE CROSS
Watch carefully when Freder is working the machine. Note that when Christ was on the cross he cried out, 'Father forgive them, for they know not what they do.'

SEVEN DEADLY SINS
These are: pride, covetousness (wanting something that belongs to someone else), lust, envy, gluttony, anger and sloth. Which of these sins have been committed in this film?

84. PRODUCTION TECHNIQUES

As you watch the film, make notes on the film techniques below.

CAMERA TECHNIQUES
Study the way the film is shot and edited, and compare it with a modern film. What differences do you notice?

SPECIAL EFFECTS
Describe some of the special effects in the film and compare them with today's special effects.

ACTING
Closely observe the way the actors act and compare this with a modern film. Can you think of a reason for the differences in acting technique?

SOUND
Metropolis is a silent film. The original soundtrack would have been improvised at the piano or theatre organ. Comment on the film score of the version you are watching. How effectively does it reflect the action?

---

85. THEMES

Discuss the bullet points in each of the boxes, then choose one of the themes to write about.

THE CLASS STRUGGLE

◆ Describe the conditions of the two classes (working class and upper class) in Metropolis.

◆ Explain how Freder finds out about the conditions of the working class through Maria.

◆ Describe Maria, and explain her message to the workers about the way to solve their problem. Their needs are never expressed. What changes do you think they want?

◆ Show how Joh Fredersen tries to maintain the status quo and recruits Rotwang to help him.

◆ How are the class differences resolved at the end of the film? They shake hands, but what kind of future do you think they will agree upon?

◆ Briefly explain Marx's theory of class and relate it to the ideas in the film.

◆ How far is the future predicted in the film coming true, i.e. are the classes getting further apart or closer together? What is happening to traditional working-class jobs?

TECHNOLOGY GONE BAD

◆ Explain how Metropolis (the technological city of the future) works. Explain the different levels, and what the machinery does.

◆ Describe how this technology has actually enslaved the majority of people (the workers) rather than improved their life.

◆ Explain Rotwang's vision of the future.

◆ Describe what happens when the workers stop operating the machines.

◆ What improvements do you think will happen after the reconciliation at the end of the film?

◆ Relate this theme to technology in modern life. Can you think of examples where technology has led to more work rather than more leisure?

86. *METROPOLIS* REVIEW

Stirred by the visionary power of *Dark City*, I revisited Fritz Lang's *Metropolis* and once again fell under its eerie spell. The movie has a plot that defies common sense, but its very discontinuity is a strength. It makes *Metropolis* hallucinatory – a nightmare without the reassurance of a steadying story line. Few films have ever been more visually exhilarating.

Generally considered the first great science-fiction film, *Metropolis* (1926) fixed for the rest of the century the image of a futuristic city as a hell of scientific progress and human despair. From this film, in various ways, descended not only *Dark City* but *Blade Runner, The Fifth Element, Alphaville, Escape From L.A., Gattaca*, and Batman's Gotham City. The laboratory of its evil genius, Rotwang, created the visual look of mad scientists for decades to come, especially after it was mirrored in *Bride of Frankenstein* (1935). And the device of the 'false Maria', the robot who looks like a human being, inspired the 'Replicants' of *Blade Runner*. Even Rotwang's artificial hand was given homage in *Dr. Strangelove*.

What many of these movies have in common is a loner hero who discovers the inner workings of the future society, penetrating the system that would control the population. Even Batman's villains are the descendants of Rotwang, giggling as they pull the levers that will enforce their will. The buried message is powerful: science and industry will become the weapons of demagogues.

Metropolis employed vast sets, 25,000 extras and astonishing special effects to create two worlds: the great city of Metropolis, with its stadiums, skyscrapers and expressways in the sky, and the subterranean workers' city, where the clock face shows 10 hours to cram another day into the workweek. Lang's film is the summit of German Expressionism, the combination of stylized sets, dramatic camera angles, bold shadows and frankly artificial theatrics.

The production itself made even Stanley Kubrick's mania for control look benign. According to Patrick McGilligan's book *Fritz Lang: The Nature of the Beast*, the extras were hurled into violent mob scenes, made to stand for hours in cold water and handled more like props than human beings. The heroine was made to jump from high places, and when she was burned at a stake, Lang used real flames. The irony was that Lang's directorial style was not unlike the approach of the villain in his film.

The story tells of a great city whose two halves – the pampered citizens of the surface and the slaves of the depths – are ignorant of one another. The city is run by the ruthless Joh Fredersen (Alfred Abel), a businessman-dictator. His son Freder (Gustav Froehlich) is in the Pleasure Gardens one day when Maria (Brigitte Helm), a woman from the subterranean city, brings a group of workers' children to the surface. Freder, struck by Maria's beauty and astonished to learn of the life led by the workers, seeks out the demented genius Rotwang (Rudolf Klein-Rogge), who knows the secrets of the lower world.

What follows is Freder's descent into the depths and his attempts to help the workers, who are rallied by the revolutionary Maria. Meanwhile, Rotwang devises a robot, captures the real Maria, and transfers her face to the robot – so that the workers, still following Maria, can be fooled and controlled. (The electrical arcs, bubbling beakers, glowing rings of light and mad scientist props in the transformation sequence have influenced a thousand films.)

Lang develops this story with scenes of astonishing originality. Consider the first glimpse of the underground power plant, with workers straining to move heavy dial hands back and forth. What they're doing makes no logical sense, but visually the connection is obvious: they are controlled like hands on a clock. And when the machinery explodes, Freder has a vision in which the machinery turns into an obscene devouring monster.

Other dramatic visual sequences: a chase scene in the darkened catacombs, with the real Maria pursued by Rotwang (the beam of his light is like a club to bludgeon her). The image of the Tower of Babel as Maria addresses the workers. Their faces, arrayed in darkness from the top to the bottom of the screen. The doors in Rotwang's house, opening and closing on their own. The lascivious dance of the false Maria, as the workers

86. *METROPOLIS* REVIEW

continued

look on, the screen filled with large, wet, staring eyeballs. The flood of the lower city and the undulating arms of the children flocking to Maria to be saved.

The gaps and logical puzzles of the story (some caused by clumsy re-editing after the film left Lang's hands) are swept away by this torrent of images. 'To enjoy the film, the viewer must observe but never think,' the critic Arthur Lennig said, and Pauline Kael contrasted its 'moments of almost incredible beauty and power' with 'absurd ineptitudes.' Even when the plot seems adrift, the movie itself never lacks confidence: the city and system are so overpowering they dwarf any merely logical problems. Although Lang saw his movie as anti-authoritarian, the Nazis liked it enough to offer him control of their film industry (he fled to America instead). Some of the ideas in *Metropolis* seem echoed in Leni Riefenstahl's pro-Hitler *Triumph of the Will* (1935) – where, of course, they have lost their irony.

Much of what we see in *Metropolis* doesn't exist except in visual trickery. The special effects were the work of Eugene Schuefftan, who later worked in Hollywood as the cinematographer of *Lilith* and *The Hustler*. According to Magill's *Survey of Cinema*, his photographic system "allowed people and miniature sets to be combined in a single shot, through the use of mirrors, rather than laboratory work." Other effects were created in the camera by cinematographer Karl Freund.

The result was astonishing for its time. Without all of the digital tricks of today, *Metropolis* fills the imagination. Today the effects look like effects, but that's their appeal. Looking at the original *King Kong* not long ago, I found that its effects, primitive by modern standards, gained a certain weird effectiveness. Because they looked strange and unworldly compared to the slick, utterly convincing effects that are now possible, they were more evocative: the effects in movies like *Jurassic Park* and *Titanic* are done so well, by comparison, that we simply think we are looking at real things, which is not quite the same kind of fun.

Metropolis has not existed for years in the version that Lang completed. It was chopped by distributors, censors and exhibitors, key footage was lost, and only by referring to the novelization of the story by Thea von Harbou can various story gaps be explained. In 1984 a reconstructed version was released, adding footage gathered from Germany and Australia to existing prints, and that version, produced by Giorgio Moroder, was color tinted 'according to Lang's original intentions' and given an MTV-style musical score. This is the version most often seen today.

Purists quite reasonably object to it, but one can turn off the sound and dial down the color to create a silent black-and-white print. I am not crazy about the soundtrack, but in watching the Moroder version I enjoyed the tinting and felt that Lang's vision was so powerful it swept aside the quibbles: it's better to see this well-restored print with all the available footage than to stand entirely on principle.

Metropolis does what many great films do, creating a time, place and characters so striking that they become part of our arsenal of images for imagining the world. The ideas of *Metropolis* have been so often absorbed into popular culture that its horrific future city is almost a given (when Albert Brooks dared to create an alternative utopian future in 1991 with *Defending Your Life*, it seemed wrong, somehow, without Satanic urban hellscapes). Lang filmed for nearly a year, driven by obsession, often cruel to his colleagues, a perfectionist madman, and the result is one of those seminal films without which the others cannot be fully appreciated.

Metropolis

Maria: Brigitte Helm
Joh Fredersen: Alfred Abel
Freder: Gustav Froehlich
Rotwang: Rudolf Klein-Rogge
Grot: Heinrich George

Directed by Fritz Lang. Written by Lang and Thea von Harbou, based on her novel. No MPAA rating (no objectionable material for mature audiences).

© 2003 Hodder & Stoughton
Copying permitted in purchasing institute only

87. *METROPOLIS* REVIEW COMPREHENSION

1. In your own words, give the meaning of the following words and phrases *as they are used in the review.*

All students

◆ 'demagogues' (para. 3)
◆ 'pampered' (para. 6)
◆ 'undulating' (para. 9)
◆ 'its very discontinuity is a strength' (para. 1)
◆ 'visually exhilarating' (para. 1).

Higher tier

◆ 'a hell of scientific progress and human despair' (para. 2)
◆ 'The production itself made even Stanley Kubrick's mania for control look benign' (para. 5)
◆ 'they become part of our arsenal of images for imagining the world' (para. 15).

All students

2. What does Roger Ebert like about the film? What do you like or dislike about it?
3. How has the film influenced modern film-makers? Can you think of any other influences?
4. Which visual sequence does Ebert like best, and why? Comment on some different sequences which (in your opinion) were equally effective.
5. Summarise what we learn about the director Fritz Lang and the history of the film.

Higher tier

6. Pauline Kael contrasted its 'moments of almost incredible beauty and power' with 'absurd ineptitudes'. Explain what is meant by 'absurd ineptitudes', and give examples of both aspects of the film.
7. 'Although Lang saw his movie as anti-authoritarian, the Nazis liked it'. In what sense is *Metropolis* 'anti-authoritarian'. If it is anti-authoritarian, why do you think the Nazis liked it?

88. GENERAL ASSIGNMENTS

Speaking and listening

Mime – in groups of around 6 to 8, practise the 'Metropolis walk' (watch the workers in the first 5 minutes of the film). Then, stage a 'Metropolis walkabout' around the school. Prepare an answer to the following question: 'Why are you walking like that?' The answer could be a comment on issues such as the National Curriculum turning education into a production line, etc.

The dialogue in *Metropolis* is summarised in a few short sentences on title cards. Choose a scene and re-enact it, filling in the dialogue by improvisation. (*Note*: don't try to lip-read from the film unless you speak German!)

Reading

Research the genre of science fiction. Make a list of science fiction classics in fiction, film and TV.

Read *The Time Machine* by H. G. Wells and compare it with *Metropolis*. *The Time Machine* also explores class differences in a future society.

Writing

Plan a film set in the future to explore your ideas about social class. For example, the working class disappear altogether in a world where all work is done by machines. The world could be a Utopia of endless leisure or a hell of mass unemployment and poverty.

Write 'An Engineer's Guide to Metropolis' in which you say what kind of machines the workers work on and the kind of work they have to do. Try to explain all the technical features you see in the film, such as a huge machine at the beginning where part of a crankshaft can be seen. What does this machine do? What do the workers have to do to operate it?

The wider curriculum

Explore images of future cities. Paint or draw your own idea of a city of the future.

The planes and cars in *Metropolis* don't seem to have progressed as much as the architecture. Design a plane and a car for the year 2026.

Make your own short film about the future.

Spiritual, moral, ethical, social and cultural issues

The film is based on a Marxist analysis of the class struggle, though with a simpler resolution than Marx envisaged. How relevant do you think this view of class is in the modern world?

Explore the role of women in *Metropolis*. Why is the 'prophet' figure a woman (Maria)? Why is the robot a woman? Why do we not see the women workers until the end of the film?

ICT

Plan a computer game based on the film *Metropolis*.

UNIT 10: TEENAGE REBELLION

RESOURCES: *Rebel Without a Cause*, Nicholas Ray, 1955

Internet to access and play the recommended 1960s songs

BOARD: Any for English coursework

RANGE: Media

AO	TEACHING SEQUENCE	RESOURCES	OUTCOMES
PART 1: *REBEL WITHOUT A CAUSE*			
A02 iv	Pre-viewing: research the background to the film	89, 'Background and Discussion'	Better understanding of context
A02i	Begin viewing the film; after the first viewing, students examine the 'Rap Rebel' screenplay to see how a screenplay is set out; students write their own screenplay or a continuation of 'Rap Rebel'	90, 'Screenplay: Rap Rebel' Film: 'Rebel Without a Cause'	Screenplay of a short scene or a continuation of 'Rap Rebel'
A02i A01ii	Students continue to view the film, viewing followed by discussion At some point during viewing, students study film techniques using Toolkit Resource 16	89, 'Background and Discussion' Toolkit 16, 'Film Techniques'	Analysis of types of shot
A02 i	When viewing is complete, students read and discuss the extract from the synopsis by Tim Dirks	91, 'Synopsis of *Rebel Without a Cause*'	Reading and discussion Use the full synopsis as a basis for essay writing or film review (higher tier)
A02i A03i–iii	Students write an essay on the character of Jim Stark	92, 'Essay on Jim Stark'	Essay on the character of Jim Stark
A02i A03 i–iii	Students write an essay on the theme of teenage rebellion in *Rebel Without a Cause* or *Rebel Without a Cause* and Songs of the Sixties (if the latter, the essay should be deferred until part 2 has been completed)	93, 'Teenage Rebellion'	Essay on teenage rebellion
A03 i–iii	Write a film review of *Rebel Without a Cause*	Toolkit 15, 'Film Review'	Film review
PART 2: SONGS OF THE SIXTIES			
A02i A01ii	Students listen to the songs while reading the lyrics, then in small groups discuss them using the questions on Resource 95 as a starting point	95, 'Songs of the Sixties Questions'	Discussion
A03 i–iii	Students choose one or more of the tasks for written assignment	95, 'Songs of the Sixties Questions'	One or more written assignments
Various	One or more General Assignments	96, 'General Assignments'	As appropriate

Introduction

Rebel Without a Cause was based on an actual case study of a delinquent, teenage psychopath. It is considered Hollywood's best 1950s film of rebellious and restless youth. The film begins with Jim, Judy and Plato at the police station for various offences. Next day Jim starts his first day at Dawson High. This includes a trip to the Planetarium, where Buzz and his gang decide to 'bring him down'. Buzz challenges him by slashing his car tyre. They fight with knives. Jim wins. Buzz challenges Jim to a 'chickie run'. At the chickie run, Buzz's sleeve gets caught in the car door and he dies. Jim goes home and tries to get his father to understand and help (the detailed synopsis on Resource 91 takes up the story at this point). Buzz's gang members are pursuing him and Judy and they hide in the old mansion with Plato. Plato shoots one of the gang members when they break into the mansion, and flees to the Planetarium as police arrive. Jim persuades him to come out, but he is frightened by a light, runs and is shot dead by the police. Jim and his father are reconciled at the end of the film.

In part 2 of the unit, the theme of teenagers and teenage rebellion is explored in songs of the 1960s.

Notes on the Resources

Part 1: Rebel Without a Cause

89. BACKGROUND AND DISCUSSION

AIM: find out about the background to the film and develop understanding of the unfolding plot, characters and themes through discussion

Before viewing the film, students should undertake some background research. A range of suggested topics is given on the resource sheet. These could be divided amongst students, who could research their topic in the library and on the Internet and then report back to the rest of the class.

Show the film in several sessions. How long this will take depends on the length of the English periods, but allow at least 10 minutes for discussion at the end of each session – longer for sessions where there is an additional activity (see below). The discussion questions on the resource sheet can be used as a starting point.

After the first viewing, introduce Resource 90, 'Screenplay', which is the first two pages of the screenplay for *Rebel Without a Cause*.

After a later viewing, introduce Toolkit Resource 16, 'Film Techniques'. Replay a short section of the film and ask students to look for and discuss examples of different types of shot. Then choose a 1-minute sequence from a 10-minute scene. Show the whole scene to establish the context for the sequence, then replay it several times as students discuss the sequence and then write about it.

90. SCREENPLAY: RAP BEBEL

AIM: understand the conventions of screenplays

Students read the screenplay and discuss how it differs from play scripts. (The main difference is that a screenplay contains information about camera shots and sound). The next step is to discuss the situation in this screenplay and how it might develop. Finally, students should write a continuation, remembering to include instructions for camera shots and sound.

Students who are interested in this and would like to make their screenplays as much as possible like the real thing will find many examples online. For example, they can access the screenplay of *Rebel Without A Cause* at: www.scenariomag.com/current/rebel.html.

91. SYNOPSIS OF *REBEL WITHOUT A CAUSE*

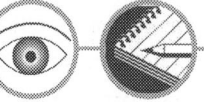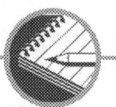

AIM: consolidate knowledge of plot, characters and themes of the film; read a model of a good film review

One of the problems of studying a film is that it is much harder to work with than a book – especially if students don't have their own copies! Students can be encouraged to acquire their own copies of the film on video or DVD (it is available for less than £10). Note that *Rebel Without A Cause* is regularly shown on TV, especially on TCM. Another solution is to use a detailed synopsis. Resource 91 contains an extract from an excellent synopsis by Tim Dirks, which also contains analysis and review. The full text can be found at www.filmsite.org/rebel.html. This text is worthy of detailed study in itself and it is worth requesting permission from the author to print out the whole synopsis for use in class. Note that this will come to around 16–18 A4 sheets.

Students read and discuss the synopsis (either the full version or the extract) and use it as a 'text' when writing about the film. The synopsis describes key visual moments and also includes extensive sequences of dialogue, both of which can be used as evidence when writing essays and reviews.

Higher-tier students could be asked to write about the film, e.g. the essay on Jim Stark (see Resource 92) and the essay on teenage rebellion (see Resource 93), using the full synopsis as a basis rather than the prompts and quotations in these resources.

Writing

Finally, the review itself can be used as a model for writing a review about any film, especially for higher-tier students (foundation-tier students could write reviews based on the template on Toolkit Resource 15, 'Film Review').

92. ESSAY ON JIM STARK

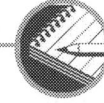

AIM: understand and write about the character of Jim

Give out Resource 92, 'Essay on Jim Stark', and discuss each section in detail in preparation for writing the essay. If necessary, refer to Toolkit Resource 11, 'Literary Essay Template', which will give help on the different ways of using evidence from a text.

Some groups of students would benefit from a 'guided writing' approach to the essay. To do this, discuss each paragraph in turn and then ask students to write a rough draft of the paragraph. The discussion ideas will be fresh in their mind, and they can be supported as they write (see Introduction for more information).

Higher-tier students should be encouraged to adapt the paragraph plan freely and find additional quotations as evidence. Alternatively, they could work directly from the full synopsis of the film (see Resource 91).

As a follow-up, students could also be asked to write a similar essay on the character of Judy.

93. TEENAGE REBELLION

AIM: understand and write about the theme of teenage rebellion; develop the skill of writing an essay that refers to two or more texts

This template can be used to write about teenage rebellion in the film, or in the film and the songs (in part 2 of this unit). If it is to be used for the latter, the task will need to be held over until part 2 has been completed.

Begin by discussing the concept of rebellion. The OED gives this definition of the word: 'Organised armed resistance to the ruler or government of one's country. Open or determined defiance of, or resistance to, any authority or controlling power.'

- Thus, most rebellion has a political motive, so what are modern teenagers rebelling against?
- Discuss examples of teenage rebellion in the last half-century.
- What form does teenage rebellion take today?
- What are the teenagers in *Rebel Without a Cause* rebelling against? What does the title of the film suggest about Jim's rebellion?

Give out Resource 93, 'Teenage Rebellion', and discuss each section in detail in preparation for writing the essay. The two-column format has been designed to help students with the structure of an essay that refers to more than one text.

Some groups of students would benefit from a 'guided writing' approach to the essay. To do this, discuss each paragraph in turn and then ask students to write a rough draft of the paragraph. The discussion ideas will be fresh in their mind, and they can be supported as they write (see Introduction for more information).

Higher-tier students should be encouraged to adapt the paragraph plan freely and perhaps refer to a wider range of films and songs.

Part 2: Songs of the Sixties

94. SONGS OF THE SIXTIES

AIM: explore the theme of teenagers and teenage rebellion in songs

This two-page resource includes four classic songs about teenagers and teenage rebellion in the 1960s. The songs can be found at Real Audio Favourites 1960–1969 http://www.foxlink.net/~bobnbren/1960s.html and P3 directory – Oldie Downloads http://www.canehdian.com/mp3/downloads/oldies.html. Most GCSE classes will contain at least one student who is an expert at downloading music files, so the task can easily be delegated. At the same time, students could also be asked to find some modern songs about teenage rebellion.

95. SONGS OF THE SIXTIES QUESTIONS

AIM: explore the songs through a wide range of approaches

Working in groups of 3 to 6, students discuss the questions on the resource sheet, then work individually on one or more written tasks with the guidance of the teacher. Note that the written tasks are arranged in approximate order of difficulty, so that foundation-tier students should be choosing from the top of the list and higher-tier students from towards the bottom.

96. GENERAL ASSIGNMENTS

AIM: explore the film from a wider range of perspectives

The resource sheet provides a list of suggestions for responding to the film from a wider range of perspectives.

89. BACKGROUND AND DISCUSSION

BACKGROUND

Before watching the film, find out about the following.

◆ James Dean's biography – see www.JamesDean.com, the official James Dean website.

◆ 1955 (and the 1950s generally). What was life like for the average person? What was in the news? What kind of cars did they drive? What did they wear, etc?

◆ Rock and Roll. Collect some rock and roll song lyrics and write about them.

◆ See *The Blackboard Jungle* and find out what an urban city school was like in the USA in 1955.

◆ CinemaScope® and why it was so important to the movie industry in the 1950s.

◆ The terms 'rebel', 'alienation', and the term and concept of the teenager.

DISCUSSION

After each viewing, discuss the following questions (as appropriate).

◆ What are your first impressions of Jim and his family?

◆ What is Judy's problem?

◆ What is Plato's problem?

◆ Why do you think Judy's behaviour to Jim changes when the gang appears?

◆ Do you think Jim's parents are good parents?

◆ What does Jim most dislike about his father?

◆ Why does Plato hero-worship Jim?

◆ Why do you think Buzz wants to pick a fight?

◆ What should Jim have done when Buzz slashed his car tyres?

◆ When Jim finds out what a chickie/chicken run is, he is clearly worried and tries to get his father's advice. Do you think he should have gone ahead, backed out or told the police?

◆ What is Jim's idea of 'being a man'?

◆ How is this brought out in the family argument that follows the chickie run?

◆ What does Judy like about Jim?

◆ What kind of manhood does Jim represent, and what is your opinion of this?

◆ How do you relate to Jim and Judy?

◆ What have Jim and Judy learned by the end of the film?

90. SCREENPLAY: RAP REBEL

A SCHOOL OFFICE – ESTABLISHING SHOT

Through the window of the office the houses of a run down council estate can be seen. The sky is grey and all the colours are muted to emphasise the bleakness of the scene. A Careers Officer is interviewing Dan. Dan sits slumped in his chair in an attitude that conveys his alienation from everything to do with school.

CAREERS OFFICER So, Dan, what kind of...er...career...had you in mind?

DAN Dunno.

CAREERS OFFICER Well, on the basis of your school reports, I'm afraid there's not much open to you... though you could always get a job at the local supermarket. They're looking for shelf-stackers right now, I believe.

CLOSE UP Dan looks up, not at the Careers Officer, but past him, through the open window. As the camera follows his gaze, the image blurs to:

FANTASY SEQUENCE Black and white images of shelf stackers dressed like the workers in *Metropolis* and moving in a similar mechanical fashion. The effect is emphasised by a rhythmic minimalist music score.

FADE TO Dan as he blinks back to reality.

CAREERS OFFICER (realising that Dan does not exactly relish the idea of stacking shelves) Well, you can't expect much with no qualifications.

DAN Well, Striker an't got none as 'e's got a Beamer!

CAREERS OFFICER (looking confused) Striker? Beamer?

DAN Yeh. Josh Strike his real name is. Beamer – a BMW.

CAREERS OFFICER Oh, and what does Mr Strike do?

DAN He's a gangsta...

FANTASY SEQUENCE Rich colour, pounding dance music. Dan is driving a BMW convertible with a beautiful girl leaning on his arm. People in the street look at him with respect as he drives past.

FADE TO Dan smiling.

CLOSE UP Careers Officer looking anxious.

CAREERS OFFICER Dan, Dan, don't fall into that trap. There must be something you can do, something that you're good at, that you could do for a living.

DAN Dunno. Rap. I like rap. I write rap. I...

90. SCREENPLAY: RAP REBEL

continued

CLOSE UP of Careers Officer's face, He looks surprised.

CAREERS OFFICER Rap – that's a kind of poetry isn't it? Does your English teacher know that you write...er...poetry...rap?

DAN Nah. He keeps going on about Shakespeare and all that stuff.

FANTASY SEQUENCE An English lesson. The teacher is reading a Shakespeare sonnet. The sound is muffled so the words cannot be clearly heard. Camera pans to Dan staring out of the window and looking bored.

CAREERS OFFICER I'll have a word with him myself. Perhaps he can help you.

DAN nods agreement but we can see that he very much doubts it.

CAREERS OFFICER Well, your interest in poetry is something to build on – but I can't see a job in it. Have you any other interests or hobbies?

DAN DJ.

CAREERS OFFICER I beg your pardon?

DAN DJ – Disk Jockey.

CLOSE UP of Careers Officer's face. He is looking pleased.

CAREERS OFFICER Ah! There we have it! Did you know you can do a course at the local FE College in DJ Studies? It's a BTEC – worth two A levels. Of course you'll have to get some GCSEs to get in – a C in English and a couple of Cs or Ds in some other subjects should be enough. Not impossible, if you're prepared to work.

CLOSE UP of Dan looking amazed.

DAN You mean I can study DJ-ing – and get qualifications!

FANTASY SEQUENCE Dan sees himself at the decks in a sophisticated modern night-club. A group of teenage girls are gazing at him in adoration. The scene is accompanied by pounding dance music.

FADE TO Dan smiling.

CAREERS OFFICER So you'd like to have a go?

CLOSE UP of Dan as he wrestles with this surprising new information.

DAN Yeh, I'd like to have a go, but there's just one thing – I don't want the other kids to know – I mean, poetry, qualifications – they'd think I'd gone soft. I'm supposed to be a rap rebel!

90. SCREENPLAY: RAP REBEL

91. SYNOPSIS OF *REBEL WITHOUT A CAUSE*

DETAILED SYNOPSIS OF PART OF FILM

(from just after the chickie run to the love scene in the old mansion).

When Jim enters the house, in a memorable image signifying the anxiety and overheated condition he finds himself in, Jim drinks milk directly from the bottle, and then puts the cold glass on his forehead and cheek to cool himself. He finds his father downstairs, complacently asleep (literally and morally) in front of the television – all the stations have gone off the air and only static is visible. Jim lies backwards on the red living room couch with his head dangling off the front end. When his mother approaches from upstairs, the camera revolves an entire 180 degrees counter-clockwise to reflect his point of view. His mother asks if he is all right.

In a memorable speech at the start of an emotionally-climactic scene, he tells his parents that he needs a 'direct answer' this time, because he is 'in trouble.' He explains how he protected his honor in a game of chicken and must come to terms with the part he played in Buzz's death.

Dad, I said it was a matter of honor, remember? They called me chicken. You know, chicken? I had to go because if I didn't I'd never be able to face those kids again. I got in one of those cars, and Buzz, that – Buzz, one of those kids – he got in the other car, and we had to drive fast and then jump, see, before the car came to the end of the bluff, and I got out OK, and Buzz didn't and, uh, killed him . . . I can't – I can't keep it to myself anymore.

Obviously, both parents want to discourage him from calling the police and not confess his role in the incident, but he wants them to confirm that he should go to the police. Jim implicates his parents as partly to blame: 'You're involved in this just like I am.' Jim is determined to be honest and report the tragic accident to the police, but his concerned father doesn't want him to get involved: 'Did anyone see you there? Did anyone see your license plate?' His domineering mother wonders whether the other boys will go to the police. Exasperated with them, he repeats over and over again his frustration with their solution. He is determined to be honest, if only with himself:

Jim: It doesn't matter. It doesn't matter. It doesn't matter. It doesn't matter. It doesn't matter. It doesn't matter.
Jim's mother: Why should you be the only one involved?
Jim's father: Far be it from me to tell you what to do . . .
Jim's mother: Oh, are you going to preach? Do we have to listen to a sermon now?
Jim's father: Well, I'm only trying to tell him what you mean. You can't be

91. SYNOPSIS OF *REBEL WITHOUT A CAUSE*

continued

idealistic all your life, Jim.
Jim: Except to yourself.
Jim's father: Nobody thanks you for sticking your neck out.
Jim: Except – except to yourself.
Jim's father: Wait a minute.
Jim: Except to yourself.

His parents believe there will be too much negative publicity, but he won't allow them to be objective or dispassionate:

But I am involved. We are all involved. Mom, a boy, a kid was killed tonight. I don't see how I can get out of that by pretending that it didn't happen. His weak-willed, indecisive father cannot offer support: 'But you know that you did the wrong thing. That's the main thing, isn't it?' Jim wants to tell the truth to the authorities as his father had instructed him, but his mother suggests that he just not 'volunteer' the information. Jim doesn't want to live that way and 'tell a little white lie.' Supposedly, according to his father, he will learn when he gets older. Then his mother suggests that they move away again to get away from the problem. Jim objects to that idea: 'You're not tearing me loose again.'

A terrific domestic family argument ensues on the family stairs – a symbolic location for matters of indecisiveness and crisis. Jim confronts his irresponsible mother and father:

Jim: You are not going to use me as an excuse again.
Jim's mother: I don't.
Jim: Every time you can't face yourself, you blame it on me.
Jim's mother: That is not true!
Jim: You say it's because of me. You say it's because of the neighborhood.
Jim's mother: No!
Jim: You use every other phony excuse. Mom, I, just once, I want to do something right, and I don't want you to run away from me again. Dad?
Jim's father: This is all going too fast for me.
Jim: You better give me something. You better give me something fast.
Jim's mother: (addressing him as a juvenile) Jimmy, you're very young. A foolish decision now could wreck your whole life. In ten years, you'll never know this even happened.
Jim: Dad, answer her. Tell her. Ten years. Dad, let me hear you answer her. Dad, Dad, stand up for me.

But his father is powerless and impotent, his head buried in his hands. Jim lunges, pulls his father from his chair and stands him up, drags him into the living room, knocks him down over another chair and chokes him until his mother pulls on him to stop. At the porch doors, he viciously kicks a hole in a portrait painting that stands on the floor – a symbol of his contempt for his parents and for their decorative pretense.

Created in 1996–2002 © by Tim Dirks. All rights reserved.
(Read the full review at www.filmsite.org/rebel.html)

92. ESSAY ON JIM STARK

Use this paragraph plan and list of quotations to help you to write an essay on Jim Stark.

SUGGESTED PLAN

Paragraph 1: Briefly explain who Jim Stark is and give a description of his appearance.

Paragraph 2: Explain Jim's problem. Begin by explaining the problems in his parents' relationship and the poor role model provided by his hen-pecked father. You could refer to the scene where his father is on his knees wearing an apron. Show how this makes him determined never to be called 'chicken'. Explain that this family situation is basically what Jim is rebelling against.

Paragraph 3: Explain how he deals with Buzz's gang. Show how he tries to avoid violence, but gets drawn into it. Discuss the 'chickie run'. What is Buzz trying to prove? Why does Jim agree to it?

Paragraph 4: Describe his relationship with Judy. How does she treat him at first? Why does she treat him this way? What does she come to like about him?

Paragraph 5: What does Jim learn through the tragic events at the end of the film? How does this help him to grow up and get on better with his parents?

Paragraph 6: Write a personal response to the character of Jim. Did you find the character's problems convincing? Are there similar problems for teenagers today? How did you relate to the character of Jim? In what sense is he a rebel?

USEFUL QUOTATIONS

Jim: You're tearing me apart! . . . You say one thing, he says another, and everybody changes back again.

Jim: How can a guy grow up in a circus like that? . . . Boy, if, if I had one day when, when I didn't have to be all confused, and didn't have to feel that I was ashamed of everything . . . If I felt that I belonged someplace, you know, then . . .

Jim: Is that meaning me? Is that meaning me? . . . Chicken?

Jim: What can you do when you have to be a man? . . . Now you give me a direct answer! Are you gonna keep me from going?

Jim: Dad, I've never done anything right. I've been going round with my head in a sling for years.

Jim: But I am involved. We are all involved. Mom, a boy, a kid was killed tonight. I don't see how I can get out of that by pretending that it didn't happen.

Judy: Is this what it's like to love somebody?
Jim: I don't know.
Judy: What kind of a person do you think a girl wants?
Jim: A man.
Judy: Yes. But a man who can be gentle and sweet . . .

---

93. TEENAGE REBELLION

Use this paragraph plan and list of quotations to help you to write an essay on teenage rebellion. Use column one only if you are basing your answer on *Rebel Without a Cause.* Use ideas from column two if you wish to include the 1960s Songs in your essay.

Paragraph 1: Briefly discuss the concept of teenage rebellion by comparing it with the basic concept of rebellion, which is 'organised armed resistance to the ruler of a country'. Refer to the ideas raised in the introductory discussion.	
Paragraph 2: Briefly introduce the film and the main characters, and describe the comfortable middle-class lifestyle against which all the young people are rebelling. Explore Jim and Judy's parents' desire for respectability and traditional values.	Add to *Paragraph 2* a brief explanation of how teenage rebellion is expressed in the songs, particularly 'He's a Rebel' and 'Leader of the Pack'.
Paragraph 3: Explore how these acts of rebellion backfire and lead to two unnecessary deaths.	Add to *Paragraph 3* an exploration of how Jimmy's rebelliousness led to his death in 'Leader of the Pack', and the consequences of the night of love in 'Will You Love Me Tomorrow'.
Paragraph 4: Explain why at the end of the film Jim and Judy are ready to cease being rebels and reintegrate into society.	Add to *Paragraph 4* a discussion of how far this is true of all rebels. For example, will the boy in 'He's a Rebel' ever fit in? Do you think most teenagers grow out of it?
Paragraph 5: Compare the teenage rebellion in the film with teenage rebellion today. Do teenagers rebel against the same things? Is teenage rebellion more or less serious today than is portrayed in the film. Again, ideas from the introductory discussion will help you.	

USEFUL QUOTATIONS

It is said that when James Dean was asked what he was rebelling against, he replied, 'What have you got?'

Judy: I don't think, I know. He looks at me like I was the ugliest thing in the world. He doesn't like my friends. He doesn't like one thing about me. He called me – he called me a dirty tramp, my own father.

Jim: Somebody ought to put poison in her Epsom salts. (*referring to his mother*)

Plato: What does he know about man alone?

Judy's mother: She'll outgrow it dear, it's just the age . . . It's just the age when nothing fits.

Jim: Why do we do this?
Buzz: You gotta do something, now dontya?

(See also the quotations on Resource 92, 'Essay on Jim Stark'.)

94. SONGS OF THE SIXTIES

Teenagers and teenage rebellion in four classic songs of the 1960s

A TEENAGER IN LOVE

Each night I ask the stars up above
Why must I be a teenager in love
Why must I be a teenager in love
Put me in your milling machine,
I never thought you could act so mean
Now I'm wondering what to do,
To see if you could love me too
Each night I ask, the stars up above
Why must I be a teenager in love
Why must I be a teenager in love

Each night I ask the stars up above
Why must I be a teenager in love
Why must I be a teenager in love
Though my knees are getting weak,
And my brain is getting flatter
Something is near, to tell me it's been badder
I don't know just what to do,
To see if you could love me too
Each night I ask the stars up above
Why must I be a teenager in love
Why must I be a teenager in love

Dion DiMucci (1959)

WILL YOU LOVE ME TOMORROW

Tonight you're mine, completely. You give your love so sweetly.
Tonight the light of love is in your eyes.
Will you still love me tomorrow?

Is this a lasting treasure, or just a moment's pleasure?
Can I believe the magic of your sighs?
Will you still love me tomorrow?

Tonight with words unspoken, you've said that I'm the only one.
But will my heart be broken when night meets the morning sun?

I'd like to know that your love is one I can be sure of.
So tell me now and I won't ask again.
Will you still love me tomorrow?
Will you still love me tomorrow?

Sung by the Shirelles (1961)

94. SONGS OF THE SIXTIES

continued

HE'S A REBEL

See the way he walks down the street
Watch the way he shuffles his feet
My, he holds his head up high
When he goes walking by
He's my guy

When he holds my hand I'm so proud
'Cause he's not just one of the crowd
My baby, oh he's the one
To try the things they've never done
Just because of that they say

Chorus

He's a rebel and he'll never ever be any good
He's a rebel and he'll never ever be understood
And just because he doesn't do what everybody else does
That's no reason why I can't give him all my love
He is always good to me, always treats me tenderly
'Cause he's not a rebel, no no no
He's not a rebel, no no no, to me

Instrumental

If they don't like him that way, they won't like me after today
I'll be standing right by his side, when they say

Repeat Chorus

Sung by The Crystals, 1962

94. SONGS OF THE SIXTIES

continued

LEADER OF THE PACK

Is she really going out with him?
Well, there she is. Let's ask her.
Betty, is that Jimmy's ring you're wearing?
Mm-hmm
Gee, it must be great riding with him
Is he picking you up after school today?
Uh-uh
By the way, where'd you meet him?

I met him at the candy store
He turned around and smiled at me
You get the picture? (yes, we see)
That's when I fell for (the leader of the pack)

My folks were always putting him down (down, down)
They said he came from the wrong side of town
(whatcha mean when ya say that he came from the wrong side of town?)
They told me he was bad
But I knew he was sad
That's why I fell for (the leader of the pack)

One day my dad said, 'Find someone new'
I had to tell my Jimmy we're through
(whatcha mean when ya say that ya better go find somebody new?)
He stood there and asked me why
But all I could do was cry
I'm sorry I hurt you (the leader of the pack)

[spoken]
He sort of smiled and kissed me goodbye
The tears were beginning to show
As he drove away on that rainy night
I begged him to go slow
But whether he heard, I'll never know

Look out! Look out! Look out! Look out!

I felt so helpless, what could I do?
Remembering all the things we'd been through
In school they all stop and stare
I can't hide the tears, but I don't care
I'll never forget him (the leader of the pack)

The leader of the pack – now he's gone
The leader of the pack – now he's gone
The leader of the pack – now he's gone
The leader of the pack – now he's gone

Sung by the Shangri-La's, 1964

95. SONGS OF THE SIXTIES QUESTIONS

- Which of these song lyrics (i.e. words only) do you think are the best-written, and why?

- The first song expresses the agony of the boy's doubt about whether the girl loves him in return. Role-play the dialogue that might take place when he finally plucks up courage to speak to her.

- The second song expresses a girl's thoughts and feelings about her decision to make love with her boyfriend. What are her doubts and worries? Is this issue still relevant today? What advice would you give to the girl?

- What is Jimmy in 'Leader of the Pack' rebelling against? How does he express his rebellion? What is he rebelling against when he is killed?

- Two of the songs tell stories. Choose one of them and retell the story as a short story with dialogue or a newspaper article.

- 'He's a Rebel' doesn't give us much information about what he actually does that is rebellious. Write a continuation in prose or verse which gives more information about the rebel and his relationship with the girl.

- 'Leader of the Pack' has been described as 'a mini-opera for teens', but at three minutes long it makes a very short opera. Write a plan explaining how you would extend it into a full-length musical. Comment on the music you would include, the special effects and, above all, how you would expand the story. Write one scene in detail.

- Examine the verse for one of the songs. Do this by marking the stressed syllables in each line with an accent mark (/) and by noting the rhyme schemes using letters of the alphabet. How do the verse forms compare with those of poetry?

Follow-up

- Find examples of modern songs about teenage love and rebellion, examine them in the same way, and compare them with these 1960s songs, e.g. is it tougher being a teen in the twenty-first century?

96. GENERAL ASSIGNMENTS

Speaking and listening

Role-play what would happen if there was a police inquiry about the shooting of Plato.

In schools where there is a video camera and some basic editing facilities, students should be encouraged to make a short film of their own about teenage rebellion.

Plan a musical, or scene from a musical about teenage rebellion. Include ideas from the film, using your own ideas. Combine 1960s songs with modern songs for the music.

Reading

Watch other films about this issue from the same period, e.g. *The Wild Bunch* starring Marlon Brando, or *The Blackboard Jungle*. Alternatively, choose a recent film that deals with this theme.

Writing

When James Dean was asked what he was rebelling against, he replied, 'What've you got?' How far is the rebellion of the teenagers in the film a result of real social problems, or is it merely the fashion of the time?

Write Jim Stark's diary from the point of meeting Buzz's gang up to the end of the chicken run.

Imagine Buzz does not get killed on the chicken run. Write a synopsis (similar to the synopsis above) of how the story might develop.

Write a scene from a film script of your own film about teenage rebellion set in the twenty-first century. Write your ideas about how the film should be directed. If you have artistic ability, sketch some storyboard sequences for the film. If you are musical, sketch ideas for a score.

Try writing some additional verses to the 1960s songs, or writing your own songs about rebellion.

The wider curriculum

Listen to 'Leader of the Pack'. This song tells a sad story of teenage rebellion. Take the idea in the song and develop it in some way. For example,

◆ Write a brief for a pop video – include storyboard if possible

◆ Turn the song into a story

◆ Develop the song into a film like *Rebel Without a Cause* and write a full script for one of the scenes.

Explore the art and iconography associated with James Dean.

Spiritual, moral, ethical, social and cultural issues

'What can you do when you have to be a man?' Trace Jim's exploration of what it means to be a man. Do you think he achieves this by the end of the film?

How many of the social problems are commonplace in the UK and Europe today? Do you think these problems are the result of too much affluence, American culture, the 1960s liberal revolution, or other factors?

ICT

Search the Internet for information about James Dean. There are plenty of good sites. Begin with the official James Dean website, at www.JamesDean.com

European dimension

Make a list of the consumer goods enjoyed by the Stark family and find out what consumer goods a typical European family might have had in 1955. Try to explain the difference in standard of living. Is the gap between standards of living as wide today?

UNIT 11: THE ADVERTISING PROJECT

> **RESOURCES:** Photocopiable resources in unit and a selection of car advertisements from magazines
>
> **BOARD:** AQA coursework (A), prereleased news item (B); Edexcel unprepared (A), coursework (B), OCR unit 1; WJEC paper 2.
>
> **RANGE:** Media

AO	TEACHING SEQUENCE	RESOURCES	OUTCOMES
AO2iv	Students find out about advertising	Library, Internet (see Introduction for suggested websites)	Knowledge of background issues relating to advertising
AO2 i–iii	Higher-tier students read Resource 97, 'What Value is There in Studying Advertisements?' (optional) All students read Resource 98, 'The Rhetoric of the Image' Higher-tier students supplement the reading with further research	97, 'What Value is There in Studying Advertisements?' 98, 'The Rhetoric of the Image' Website: see teacher's notes	Understanding of the key issues in advertising (higher tier, optional) Understand how to write about an advertisement
AO2v AO3 i–iii	Students use Resource 99, 'Advertisement Analysis Template' to make notes on and write about one or more car advertisements	99, 'Advertisement Analysis Template' Own choice of car advertisements from magazines or TV (or use resource sheets below)	Essay on a car advertisement
AO2 i–v AO3 i–iii	Students answer an examination-style question on one or more car advertisements Higher-tier students write an essay based on Resource 97, 'What Value is There in Studying Advertisements?' (optional)	One or more of: 100, 'Alfa 147' 101, 'BMW 318i ES' 102, 'Seat Toledo' 103, 'MG Magnette' 105, 'Questions for Discussion and Writing'	Examination-style essay on a car advertisement Essay on advertising using examples from car advertisements (higher-tier, optional)
AO3 i–iii **AO1 i–iii**	Working in groups, students prepare an advertising campaign for a car Students present the advertising campaign	104, 'Design Brief and Presentation' Powerpoint, OHP, video (optional)	A4 car advertisement and/or storyboard for TV advertisement

Introduction

This unit is based on car advertisements, though it could be easily adapted to focus on another topic. Another alternative is to have different groups looking at advertisements for different types of product. Before starting, each group should collect several examples of advertisements from different magazines. It would also be helpful to carry out some background research on advertising. Here are a few starting points.

Research

History of advertising at www.hatads.org.uk

History of Jaguar car advertisements at www.mcload.com/Personal%20Site/jaguar_ads.html

Advertising Standards Authority website at www.asa.org.uk

Guinness World Records book, or website at www.guinnessworldrecords.com

TV advertising

If required, an extra dimension could be added to this unit by including car advertising on TV. This would involve recording a number of contrasting car advertisements. The teachers notes below suggest when and how these recordings could be used.

Notes on the Resources

97. WHAT VALUE IS THERE IN STUDYING ADVERTISEMENTS?

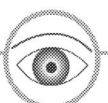   

AIM: understand the key issues in advertising

Reading

This article is an excellent introduction to the study of advertising. As this is an academic article, which includes some difficult vocabulary and concepts, it is best suited to higher-tier students only. Foundation-tier students should begin with the following lesson.

Discussion

Students read the article and discuss it. Some questions to focus discussion may be found on Resource 105, 'Questions for Discussion and Writing'.

Writing

When students have studied several car advertisements, they can then do the written task on Resource 105, 'Questions for Discussion and Writing'. This is basically to rewrite Helen Ingham's essay in their own words, using car advertisements as examples.

98. THE RHETORIC OF THE IMAGE

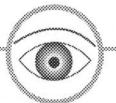  

AIM: understand how to write about an advertisement

'The Rhetoric of the Image' is an example of how to write about an advertisement. The ideas are taken from Roland Barthes' classic study, *The Rhetoric of the Image* (1977). This semiotic analysis is far too complex to use in its original form (an abstract of the study may be found at http://mh.cla.umn.edu/edibld4.html) However, the basic ideas have been represented in the same format as Resource 99, 'Advertisement Analysis Template'. Higher-tier students could explore the meaning of the following semiological terms and use them in their analyses.

- *sign* – something that stands for something else; it has two aspects: the signifier, which is the sign itself, and the signified, which is what it stands for
- *denotation* – the basic meaning of a word or image
- *connotation* – the associations of the word or image

Research

To understand the above terms in context, students could read *Semiotics for Beginners* by Daniel Chandler at www.aber.ac.uk/media/Documents/S4B/semiotic.html, particularly the introduction and the last chapter, 'DIY Semiotic Analysis'. Note also that Pre-1914 Literature Toolkit Resource 5, 'Critical Approaches 4: Semiotics', provides a much simplified template for a semiological (means the same as semiotic) analysis of any text, written or visual.

Reading and discussion

Working in pairs, students read and discuss 'The Rhetoric of the Image'. In particular, they should note how every detail is significant, and how the associations are just as important as the basic objects (or, in semiotic-speak, how the connotative meaning of signs is just as important as the denotative meaning). This resource sheet can be used as a model when students write their own analyses of advertisements.

99. ADVERTISEMENT ANALYSIS TEMPLATE

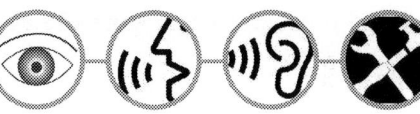

AIM: understand and write about the linguistic, structural and presentational devices in an advertisement using a template for support

Reading and note-making

This template can be used with any type of advertisement. Students make notes on the template as they discuss an advertisement in pairs or small groups. The notes can then be used as the outline for an essay. Resource 98, 'The Rhetoric of the Image', can be used as a model. The resource includes suggestions for writing about TV advertising. Note that students may need to refer to Toolkit Resource 16, 'Film Techniques', to help them identify different camera angles and editing technques.

Higher-tier students could use Literature Toolkit Resource 5, 'Critical Approaches 4: Semiotics' in combination with this resource to produce a more academic analysis. Note that, in order to use this resource effectively, they will need some understanding of the basics of semiotics (see Resource 98).

100. ALFA 147

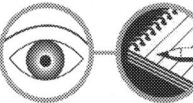

AIM: understand and evaluate how advertisers use linguistic, structural and presentational devices to achieve their effects

Reading

This advertisement appeared on the inside front page of *Weekend* magazine (a *Daily Mail* Saturday supplement) on 27 July 2002. Full-page (tabloid) and full-colour, it can be used with Resource 99, 'Advertisement Analysis Template', as a supplement to (or an alternative to) working on own advertisements.

The advertisement article can be turned into a formal exercise for GCSE coursework or examination practice (check latest specifications) by using the article with Resource 105, 'Questions for Discussion and Writing'.

101. BMW 318i ES

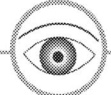

AIM: understand that some advertisers use simpler and more factual forms of advertising

Reading

This advertisement appeared on page 52 of the *Luton/Dunstable on Sunday* on 19 January 2003. Half-page (tabloid), it is included for purposes of comparison, as this is a 'bread and butter' advertisement paid for by a dealer rather than the manufacturer. As such, it gives a straightforward picture of the car with no other figures or objects, along with detailed technical and financial information. Use Resource 99, 'Advertisement Analysis Template', to make notes on the advertisement, and then compare it with the Alfa 147 advertisement in Resource 100.

The advertisement article can be turned into a formal exercise for GCSE coursework or examination practice (check latest specifications) by using the article with Resource 105, 'Questions for Discussion and Writing'.

102. SEAT TOLEDO

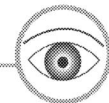

AIM: understand and evaluate how advertisers use linguistic, structural and presentational devices to achieve their effects

Reading

This advertisement appeared on the back cover of *What Car? Awards 2002* magazine. Full-page (A4) and full-colour, it can be used with Resource 99, 'Advertisement Analysis Template', as a supplement to (or alternative to) working on own.

The advertisement article can be turned into a formal exercise for GCSE coursework or examination practice (check latest specifications) by using the article with Resource 105, 'Questions for Discussion and Writing'.

103. MG MAGNETTE

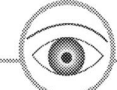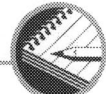

AIM: understand and evaluate how the use of linguistic, structural and presentational devices has changed over time

Reading

This advertisement from the early 1960s is included for purposes of comparison. The speech bubble and text show a rather crude appeal to snobbishness. Many of today's advertisements also appeal to people's snobbishness, but in more subtle ways. Use Resource 99, 'Advertisement Analysis Template', to make notes on the advertisement, and then compare it with the Alfa 147 advertisement in Resource 100, or any other car advertisement that makes an appeal to people's snobbishness.

The advertisement article can be turned into a formal exercise for GCSE coursework or examination practice (check latest specifications) by using the article with Resource 105, 'Questions for Discussion and Writing'.

104. DESIGN BRIEF AND PRESENTATION

AIM: deepen understanding of the way in which advertisers use linguistic, structural and presentational devices; to achieve their effects by designing own advertisements

Students work in small groups of 3 or 4 to design an advertisement and an advertising campaign, and prepare a presentation to the manufacturer. Before beginning, decide whether the campaign will be for magazines, TV, or both. If TV is included, students will need to prepare a storyboard. A storyboard is a series of sketches showing the main camera shots. See Toolkit Resource 16, 'Film Techniques' for a description of the main types of camera shot. Students should then work through the following stages:

Brainstorming

Explore ideas with particular reference to the 'What You Need to Do' section of the resource sheet.

Rough drafts of ideas

Jot down draft text and slogans, make rough sketches of layout and/or storyboard.

Preparation of final version

A good final version can be made without artistic skills. The illustration on the resource sheet can be cut out, and this can be combined with images (e.g. background or figures) cut from magazines (a technique called *montage*). Text can be written on a computer using appropriate fonts, then printed out and pasted onto the advertisement. The end result will give a good idea of the intended advertisement. A storyboard can be prepared in a similar way.

Preparing a presentation

The presentation should be about the whole advertising campaign. This should include the advertisement, the slogan, the magazines the advertisement will be placed in and for how long. There are a number of ways in which this can be presented:

- *Powerpoint* (or similar program) – The final version can be scanned and placed on a Powerpoint slide. This can be linked to a number of other slides, which highlight the main features of the advertising campaign.
- *OHT* – As above, but using overhead projector slides.
- *Show and tell* – Old-fashioned, but works even during a power-cut! It also has the advantage of requiring no additional preparation. If this method is to be used, it would be a good idea to prepare the advertisements on A3 or even A2 paper.
- *Video* – If school resources allow, it may even be possible to make the actual *video* of the planned TV advertisement.

One final touch could be a panel of pupils who represent the manufacturer. They could choose between the different presentations and say which advertising campaign they think is most effective and why.

105. QUESTIONS FOR DISCUSSION AND WRITING

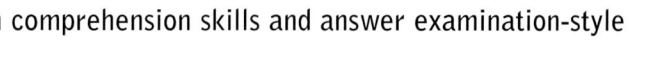

AIM: to develop written comprehension skills and answer examination-style essay questions

The questions on this resource sheet should be used with the appropriate resources. Note that, though the questions on the car advertisements have been divided into two tiers, the most effective approach is for all students to examine and discuss all four advertisements, and then to choose a writing task from the appropriate section.

106. GENERAL ASSIGNMENTS

AIM: explore the resources from a wider range of perspectives

The resource sheet provides a list of suggestions for exploring more widely.

97. WHAT VALUE IS THERE IN STUDYING ADVERTISEMENTS?

'Pervading all the media, but limited to none, advertising forms a vast superstructure with an apparently autonomous existence, and an immense influence' (Williamson, 1991: 11).

Few would question the enormity of the advertising 'machine' that runs within our society. Therefore, in asking what value there is in studying it, we are also asking what value it has within our society, and as such, the impact and influence that it has on our lives.

It can be argued that the main function of advertising is to sell us, the consumers, products. But how do they achieve this? One might argue that advertising simply serves to inform us of the choices that we have as consumers, and leaves us to make rational decisions based on what we need. This is somewhat problematic; for example, how can we define a need in comparison to a want? Many of the products we buy, we do not *need*, in so far as we are perfectly able to live without them. One might ask, therefore, what the reason is for buying a specific product, be it shampoo or a new car. Indeed, many car ads portrayed on television say little, if anything about the car's capabilities, instead showing an individual driving fast around steep mountain roads etc. Through examples such as these car adverts, it is obvious that many advertisers do not rely on rationalism and information to sell their products. Furthermore, as Myers argues, advertising does not allow us to make any real choices between products. Indeed, our 'choice' frequently consists of different brands manufactured by the same company, or being distorted by a form of advertising reliant on frustration or other negative feelings in order to sell its products. So therefore, what exactly are we buying into when we consume products, and perhaps more importantly, why?

In answering these questions, we need to focus upon how we make sense of the adverts we see, how the advertisers reach us and persuade us, and the complexity involved in this process. In watching an advert on television, or looking at one in a magazine, we do not simply come under some hypnotic 'spell' resulting in an unquenchable desire to buy a new type of toilet roll etc. simply because the advert states that it's the answer to all our problems. Adverts are generally far more complex: furthermore, so are we.

Depending upon the media used, adverts generally consist of images, text and sound. Each of these aspects are encoded with various meanings and messages, some of which are associated with the particular product the advertisement is trying to sell, and some of which are associated with its image. The phrase 'a picture can speak a thousand words' is far from untrue.

As for us, far from being passive, we actively, although perhaps subconsciously, construct meaning according to our knowledge of the world and our experience in it, building associations with concepts presented to us within a given advertisement.

Within such a context then, advertisements are largely created to appeal to the irrational aspects of our psyche; using emotional appeals, playing on our fears, our need to belong; and in doing so, offer us their product as an answer. This theory has been supported by a great deal of research, which has found relatively few purchases to be made by rational choice. Indeed, how can 'rational' choices be made between those goods which have the same use values, for example, different brands of toothbrush? We can see from examples such as car ads, how advertisements have become less concerned with communicating essential information with regard to the product in question, and more involved with manipulating attitudes and social values.

Owing to the fact that different brands of a product are not necessarily so different in content, the advertisers must market the product in such a way as to persuade the consumer to buy it. Indeed, Packard found that advertisers are given clues via our 'subconscious needs, yearnings and cravings'. Furthermore, once advertisers have identified our psychological needs, they can design an appeal focused towards it and based upon the product. Packard went on to identify a number of psychological appeals that are utilised in adverts, some of which will be highlighted now.

Firstly, he found that adverts sell a 'reassurance of worth'. Using the example of the housewife in the 1950s, he notes how adverts would sell them pride in their designated 'role' according to how 'white their whites were' or how clean their house was etc. Today, however, owing to the great changes that have taken place; i.e. women moving out more into the workforce, such selling tactics do not necessarily play on affirming a particular role that the consumer has, instead, encouraging a self-indulgence because 'you're worth it'; more as a person than simply a functional role.

The flip-side to this particular method of advertising is one that Packard did not cite, but one which has become a standard approach for some types of product; that is to play on our guilt, fear, and insecurities. These can include anxieties regarding looks, age, loss of respect and status, and so on. The anxieties of consumers, especially with regard to physical appearance, have been 'homed-in' on. The product in question tends to be held up as a cure for physical sensitivities; for example acne. Focusing on presenting the product as a cure for one's skin complaint also tends to present it as a cure for one's isolation, shame,

97. WHAT VALUE IS THERE IN STUDYING ADVERTISEMENTS?

continued

feelings of unattractiveness etc. The majority of adverts used to promote acne creams have tended to follow the same format: Girl/boy has spots and is isolated, and after using the product, has baby-like skin, and a much improved social life as a result of being a more 'attractive' person.

Some advertisers even go to lengths to reinforce this. Brierly cites the example of *Ryvita*, whose main selling point is that it 'helps you win the inch war'. It reminds women that they need to lose weight in order to achieve the 'ideal' 24-inch waistline, as indicated by a measuring tape on the packet. With such appeals, the consumer is made to feel guilty concurrently for not 'measuring up' and at the same time, is offered a solution in the form of *Ryvita*. In realistic terms, however, we are generally aware that we are not going to gain the 'perfect' figure by simply eating *Ryvita*. In such a way, therefore, adverts offer us solutions, while simultaneously separating us from them, in order to continue to sell their product ...

Packard found that, particularly in men, there is an inherent desire for power. Indeed, advertisers have tapped into these motives and exploited them. Such a selling point has obviously been aimed mainly at men, with products such as cars, chocolate (*Yorkie Bars*), deodorant (*Lynx*) and so on. As an appeal, the use of the 'powerful man' has been applied in contexts such as power over the environment, physical power, and power over women. Increasingly, however, the power appeal has also been used in ads aimed at women; yet these tend to be within a more traditionally feminine context. For example, a girlfriend getting revenge on her boyfriend for criticising her driving (*Fiat Punto*). The eighties saw the birth of women in advertising displaying the same aggressive qualities of power traditionally associated with masculinity. For example, a *Clarks* advert portrayed women getting revenge on men by performing such actions as stapling the boss' tie to his desk, or pouring dinner over the head of an unfaithful partner. However, such portrayals proved unsuccessful as they tended to be associated with radical feminism and 'man-haters', the result of which was rejection by the majority of female consumers ...

The advertising machine is not without its critics; indeed, it is not short of them: the majority of which are concerned about the negative effects that advertising might have in our society. Many see the advertising industry as decadent and corrupt. Some criticise it for inspiring 'irrationality of emotion'. Raymond Williams has been cited as arguing that advertising 'plays a role in the destruction of a decadent society' where it is 'no longer just a way of selling goods, but a true part of the culture of a confused society' (Myers). Some argue that perhaps were we not seduced by the glamorous world of advertising, we would make more rational decisions regarding the products we buy.

However, the reason that advertisers have to 'induce' us to purchase their product is because the use of a rationalist approach tends not to sell the product in sufficient quantity. Dyer cites Leavis, who drew attention to what he considered to be the 'numbing effect' that adverts have on people's critical responses to their environment. Many agree with this school of thought, pointing out how advertising can lead to apathy and 'one-dimensional thought' (The Frankfurt School of Thought & Herbert Marcuse). However, it is very possible that such arguments are aimed at creating moral panics and finding a scapegoat for all of society's ills, which has not been unusual with any kind of medium.

However, there is concern for the extent to which advertising can attempt to dehumanise people, compensating for, and concealing the deficiencies we have in our lives. Indeed, the promises advertisements make, Dyer argues, 'can keep people from knowing what the root causes of social and personal problems are, and from knowing what they really want'. To an extent, this is undoubtedly true, given the examples of how adverts use their consumers' guilt and fear in order to sell a product; moreover, we have seen how some may even instigate and sustain those feelings.

Through studying advertisements, and the various aspects of how they work, we are able to look at them with open eyes and an open mind, being able to see the 'hows' and 'whys' of adverts appealing to us as they do. We are also more likely to be aware of our own reactions to adverts; why we find some appealing, yet others not: taking a critical stance. On a wider scale, we can also appreciate the role it plays in the economy, and the processes which take place in order for adverts to reach us.

Perhaps one of the most interesting reasons for studying adverts is to appreciate them as a form of art. On a single page of paper, or in thirty seconds of our viewing time, an advert has to be created to make an impact. Being consciously aware of the meanings and connotations within an advert, helps to make us more aware of how we interpret them, how we think, and how we take an active role in forming 'meaning' in adverts.

In conclusion then, we can argue that the value in studying advertisements gives us a greater awareness and understanding; not only of the marketing machine, but also of ourselves.

Helen Ingham

(edited – read the full article online at www.aber.ac.uk/media/Students/h2i9403.html)

98. THE RHETORIC OF THE IMAGE

BASIC INFORMATION

This is a French advertisement of the mid-1970s for Panzani food products. It was chosen because it is the subject of Roland Barthes' classic analysis of an advertisement *The Rhetoric of the Image*, 1977. The ideas below are based on Barthes' analysis.

IMAGES

The advertisement shows two packets of pasta, a can of sauce, a sachet of Parmesan cheese, some tomatoes, onions and peppers falling from a string bag. The image of the products falling from a bag suggests that the buyer has just returned from the market. This in turn suggests the freshness of the products, though a glance at their packaging reveals that they are factory-produced. The presence of the fresh vegetables reinforces the idea of freshness. The image also suggests the idea of traditional shopping in which products are chosen with care from different shops or stalls, rather than the hasty stocking-up of a visit to the supermarket.

WORDS

'Panzani' is the name of the firm, but it signifies 'Italianicity' to the French reader. Close inspection of the product labels shows that Panzani is actually a French firm (Parthenay, France) – so why does it have an Italian-sounding name? The answer lies in the products. Pasta and associated products originate in Italy, so the target audience would assume that an Italian product would be of better quality and more 'genuine'. The only other text is 'Pâtes – Sauce – Parmesan à l'Italienne de luxe' ('Pasta – Sauce – Parmesan in deluxe Italian style'). This shows the range of products on offer and reinforces the idea that they are Italian and of good quality.

TARGET GROUP

The target group is the French homemaker. Part of French culture is the value placed on good food and, as a result, traditional shops and markets still survive. This advertisement is based on an appeal to those values.

PERSUASION

By a process of association, the advertisement tells us that Panzani products are natural and fresh, and that they are Italian – none of which is true. This is done by suggestion not deliberate deception. Indeed, the reader can quite easily find this out by looking at the packaging (plastic packets, tin can) and the labelling.

EVALUATION

The advertisement would probably be successful in appealing to its target audience, though it would be less successful in a modern British context because of the differences between French and British culture with regard to food and shopping (see Target Group above).

99. ADVERTISEMENT ANALYSIS TEMPLATE

BASIC INFORMATION

Give details about the product, and the magazine or TV 'slot' (channel and time) in which it is advertised.

IMAGES

Describe in detail everything you can see, then comment on the associations of the images, i.e. what do they remind you of, what feelings do they evoke? Look for the product's brand name and logo and note where they are positioned in the advertisement. In TV ads, consider camera angles and editing.

WORDS

Look for the slogan, the supporting text and the small print. Consider how much factual information about the product is included. In TV ads, consider sound effects and music.

TARGET GROUP

Consider price range of the product and the way it is advertised. Give your opinion about the target group of the advertisement, e.g. young people, families, executives, men, women.

PERSUASION

How does the advertisement try to persuade the target group? For example, does it appeal to their need to be different, to be the envy of their friends, to feel successful, to be respected, to feel pride, etc. What other techniques are used to persuade, e.g. humour, unusual images, statistics, performance figures, list of extras, price figures.

EVALUATION

In your opinion, how successful is the advertisement? Did it catch your eye? Did it contain helpful information? Do you think it would appeal to the target group?

100. ALFA 147

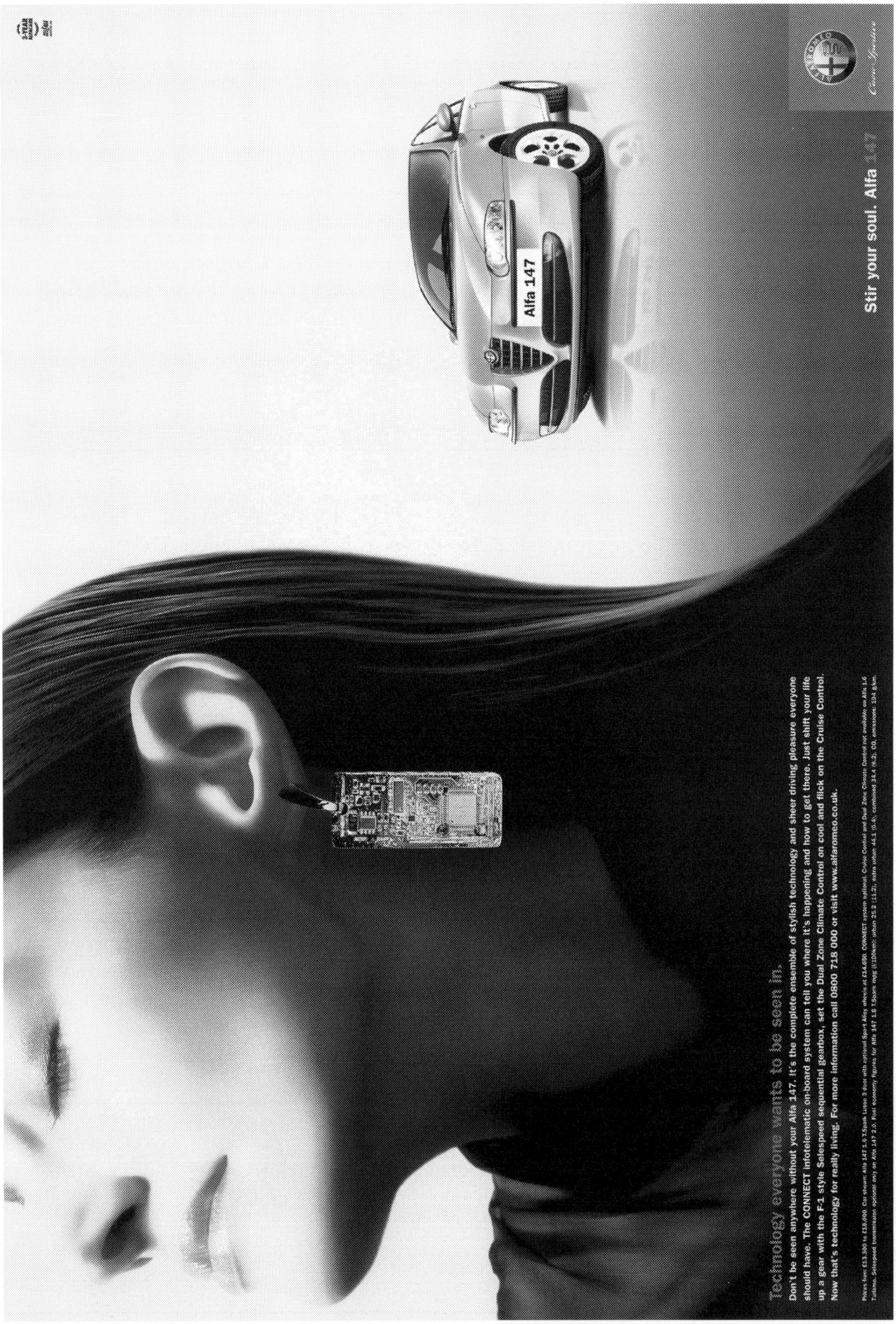
Alfa 147
Stir your soul. Alfa 147
Technology everyone wants to be seen in.
Don't be seen anywhere without your Alfa 147. It's the complete ensemble of stylish technology and sheer driving pleasure everyone should have. The CONNECT infotelematic on-board system can tell you where it's happening and how to get there. Just shift your life up a gear with the F-1 style Selespeed sequential gearbox, set the Dual Zone Climate Control on cool and flick on the Cruise Control. Now that's technology for really living. For more information call 0800 718 000 or visit www.alfaromeo.co.uk.

101. BMW 318i ES

The BMW 3 Series

318i ES Saloon

The Ultimate Driving Machine

**It's not just the suspension that's low.
The BMW 318i ES. Only £19,995**

The ES 'Edition Sport', is a new range of performance orientated models from BMW. For example, the 318 ES Saloon comes equipped with, ●16" alloy wheels ●Leather sports steering wheel ● Cornering Brake Control ● CD player ● Air conditioning ● Car key memory ● ABS Dynamic Traction Control ● 143 bhp Valvetronic engine ● Sports suspension, for a lower centre of gravity.

The other models in the ES range are the 320d ES Saloon at £20,995, the 318i ES Touring at £20,750 and the 320d ES Touring at £21,750.

Call us today for further information or to arrange a test drive*.

Specialist Cars

76 - 88 Marsh Road Luton 01582 576622 www.specialistcarsbmw.co.uk

£299 pcm 5.4% APR+ £2,990 deposit

(plus acceptance fee and optional final payment).

*Subject to availability and at participating dealers only. Finance example is based on a 36 month BMW Financial Services Select Personal Contract Purchase agreement for a BMW 318i ES Saloon with a mileage of 10,000 per annum (30,000 in total). On the road cash price £19,995 is based on the manufacturers recommended retail price and includes 3 year BMW Dealer Warranty, BMW Emergency Service, 12 months Road Fund Licence, First Vehicle Registration Fee of £25, delivery, number plates and VAT. Deposit of £2,990 followed by 35 monthly payments of £299. A £95 acceptance fee is payable with the first monthly payment. One final payment of £8,424.48 plus a £25 purchase fee is optional to purchase the vehicle. Total amount payable is £21,999.48. APR 5.4%. Deposit must not exceed 30% of the vehicle's on the road cash price. Excess mileage will be charged at 10p per mile (inc VAT). If the vehicle is returned it must be returned in good condition otherwise further charges will be incurred. All finance is subject to status and available to over 18s in the UK only (excluding the Channel Islands). Guarantees and indemnities may be required. Written quotations are available on request. Prices are correct at time of going to print and are subject to change without notice. *Test drive subject to applicant status and availability. The Official Fuel Economy Figures range for 3 Series: Extra Urban 64.2-32.1 mpg (4.4-8.8l/100km) Urban 37.2-15.8 mpg (7.6-17.9l/100km). Combined 51.4-23.3 mpg (5.5-12.1l/100km). CO2 emissions 148-292 g/km.

102. SEAT TOLEDO

Relationship saving device.

How many times do you and your loved one argue in the car over map reading or choice of music - to name a couple? Probably it's a case of, "If I had a penny..." We've all been there.

SEAT, not quite in the form of Cupid, has come up with a clever solution to in-car bickering - satellite navigation. This is fitted as standard to all V5's available for £16,995 on the road*, it will talk you through getting from A to B and automatically recalculate your route if you need to take a detour.

Toledo 2.3 V5 £16,995*
on the road

- Combined fuel consumption of 32.1 mpg**
- Cruise control
- Electronic climate control
- CD autochanger
- ABS
- Electric windows
- Front windscreen wipers with rain sensor
- Combined leather and alcantara seats

- CO_2 emissions at 211g/km†
- Front sports seats
- Electronic differential system
- Traction control
- Driver's, front passenger's and front side airbags
- 170bhp
- Heated electrically adjustable door mirrors with electric folding facility

Call today to find your local SEAT Dealer
and put a little bit of harmony back in your motoring.

0500 22 22 22
or visit
www.seat.co.uk

SEAT
auto emoción

103. MG MAGNETTE

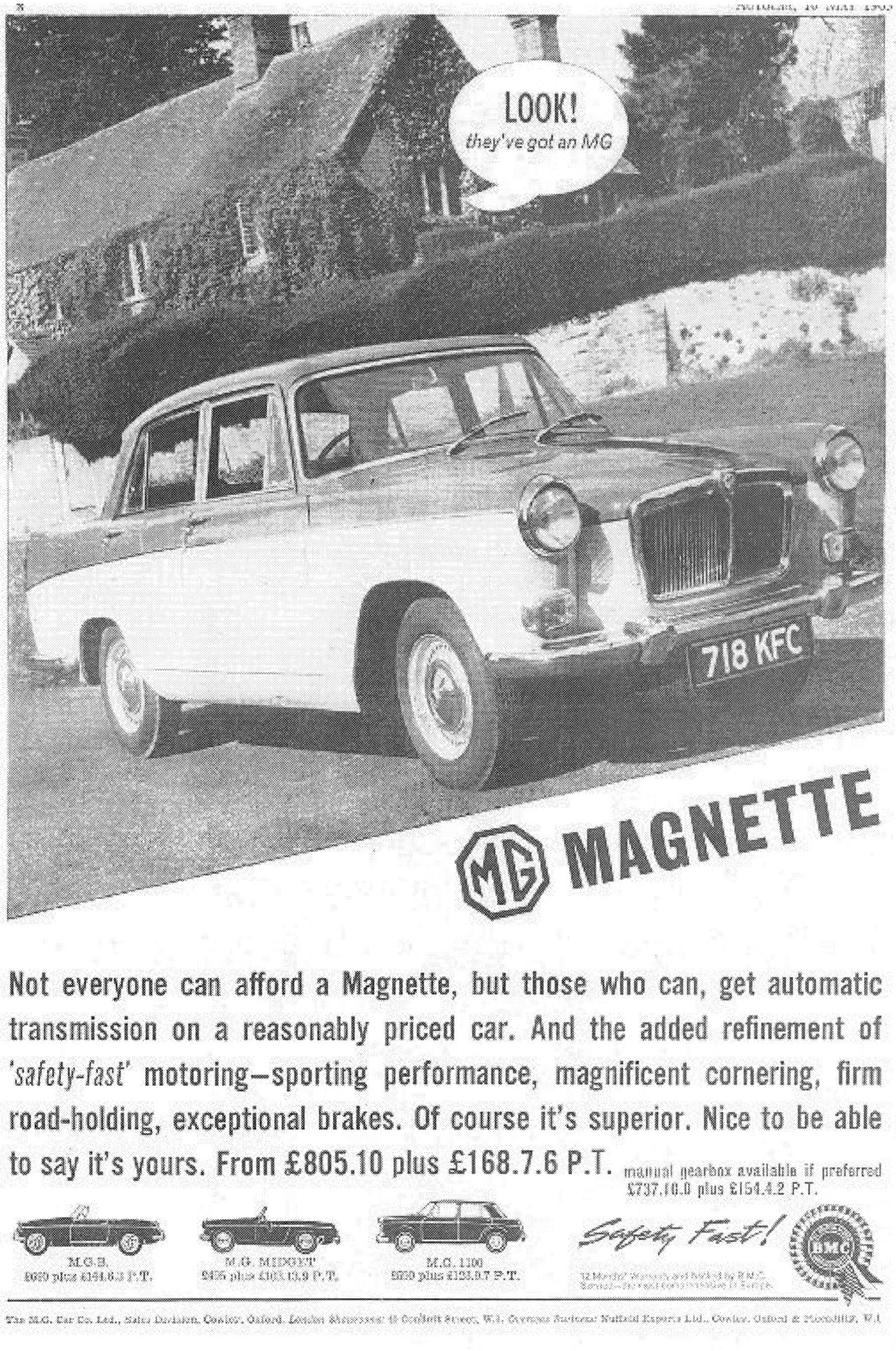

Not everyone can afford a Magnette, but those who can, get automatic transmission on a reasonably priced car. And the added refinement of *'safety-fast'* motoring—sporting performance, magnificent cornering, firm road-holding, exceptional brakes. Of course it's superior. Nice to be able to say it's yours. From £805.10 plus £168.7.6 P.T. manual gearbox available if preferred £737.10.0 plus £154.4.2 P.T.

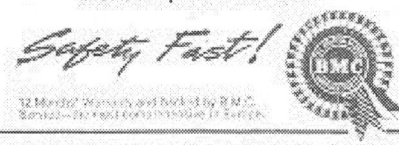

104. DESIGN BRIEF AND PRESENTATION

Design an advertising campaign which may include:

◆ an A4 page advertisement for magazines
◆ a 60-second TV advertisment.

The manufacturer's design team has supplied you with a specification, complete with notes on how this car compares with other cars. Your job is to make the most of its strong points, and disguise its weak points.

THE CAR

SPECIFICATION

◆ 0–60 in 20 seconds (rather slow compared to most full-sized cars)
◆ 60mpg (much higher than full-sized cars)
◆ adjustable steering wheel (standard on most cars)
◆ boot capacity: 374 litres (as much luggage space as a standard hatchback)
◆ driver and passenger airbags (standard on most cars)
◆ electric windows (standard on most cars except basic models)
◆ engine: 498cc (very small by comparison with full-sized cars)
◆ length: 2300mm (approx. half the length of a standard saloon car)
◆ max. speed: 70 mph (slower than almost any full-sized car)
◆ RDS stereo radio/CD player (the CD player can still be considered a luxury extra)
◆ remote-control central locking (standard on most cars except basic models)
◆ two seats (can be a serious limitation)
◆ price: £6999, delivery, number plates and metallic paint extra (approximately 20 different models of four-seat hatchbacks can be bought for this price or less).

WHAT YOU NEED TO DO:

◆ think of a catchy name for the car
◆ think of a suitable slogan to help to sell the car
◆ decide which features of the specification you will emphasise – think of the advantages of the design concept and emphasise these
◆ decide what kind of setting will you choose for the car, and what kind of people you will show with it
◆ (for a magazine) decide on the page layout
◆ (for a TV ad) decide on the sequence of events.

105. QUESTIONS FOR DISCUSSION AND WRITING

Discussion

What value is there in studying advertisements?

◆ What is the difference between a want and a need?

◆ How do advertisers persuade us to buy a specific product?

◆ What kind of 'psychological appeals' do advertisers use to sell products?

◆ Helen Ingham refers to some specific advertisements. Can you think of other advertisements which use the same 'psychological appeals'?

◆ What criticisms have been made of the advertising industry?

◆ Give your opinion about Dyer's statement that 'advertising can keep people from knowing what the root causes of social and personal problems are, and from knowing what they really want'.

◆ Why does Helen Ingham believe that advertising is worth studying? Do you agree?

Writing

Pick out the main points in Helen Ingham's article and show how they apply to car advertisements.

Foundation tier

Alfa 147

How does this advertisement seek to persuade its target audience? In your answer, you should write about:

◆ the two main images – the woman and the car

◆ the slogan, the main text and the small print

◆ the balance between emotional appeal and practical information

◆ the appeal of the advertisement to its target audience.

BMW 318i ES

This is a 'bread and butter' advertisement paid for by a dealer rather than the manufacturer. It has a simple image and occupies half of a tabloid page only. Compare it with the Alfa advertisement with reference to:

◆ the design

◆ the amount of practical, technical and financial information given

◆ the overall impact and appeal to the target audience.

Higher tier

Seat Toledo

How does this advertisement differ from most other car advertisements, and why do you think the advertising agency decided to advertise the car in this way? Do you think it is successful?

MG Magnette

In the 1950s and 1960s, advertisements were simpler and less subtle in their appeal to emotions. Discuss this statement with reference to the MG Magnette advertisement and any modern car advertisement.

106. GENERAL ASSIGNMENTS

Speaking and listening

Plan and record radio advertisements for each of the cars in the unit.

Discuss or debate one of the following:

◆ The car is bad for the environment, therefore car advertising, like tobacco advertising, should be strictly controlled.

◆ A car is as much a fashion item as a pair of shoes.

◆ Your Top Ten of the world's best cars.

Role-play the haggling process for a second-hand Mondeo. Before beginning, you will need to decide the details, e.g. age, condition, price (look in a car magazine for accurate details).

Reading

Read reviews of cars in different car magazines.

Watch *Top Gear* and compare the way cars are reviewed with reviews in car magazines.

Watch a range of TV advertisements for cars and analyse them in the same way you analysed the magazine advertisements.

Study the advertising of another product, e.g. holidays, cosmetics, medicines.

Writing

Write a review of your favourite car or other product.

Write the script for a two-minute TV advertisement for any product.

Design your ideal car and write an explanation of why it is ideal.

The wider curriculum

Find out about the pollution caused by car exhaust fumes in science. Find out about alternative means of propulsion.

Find out about the history of the motor car and car advertising.

Spiritual, moral, ethical, social and cultural issues

A tiny fraction of the world's population has the luxury of their own personal transport and pollute the planet, while the rest of the world doesn't have enough to eat. Examine the moral issues surrounding car ownership.

ICT

Investigate advertising on the Internet. In many ways this is different to other kinds of advertising and less well regulated, e.g. unwanted 'pop-up' advertisements, advertisements that change your homepage or add an unwanted bookmark, advertisements that come in unwanted 'junk' emails.

European dimension

'German cars are best'. Examine the myth and the reality behind this statement.

UNIT 12: THE NEWSPAPER PROJECT

RESOURCES: Photocopiable resources in unit and a selection of tabloid and broadsheet newspapers

BOARD: AQA coursework (A), prereleased news item (B); Edexcel unprepared (A), coursework (B); OCR unit 1; WJEC paper 2

RANGE: Media

AO	TEACHING SEQUENCE	RESOURCES	OUTCOMES
A02 **i–v**	Explore the differences between tabloid and broadsheet newspapers (This introductory lesson may be omitted if time is limited)	107, 'Tabloid and Broadsheet 1: Overview' A selection of tabloid and broadsheet newspapers	Notes on differences between tabloid and broadsheet newspapers Discussion of notes Understanding of main differences
A02 **i–iii**	Explore how a specific news item is treated in tabloid and broadsheet newspapers, focusing on content	108, 'Tabloid and Broadsheet 2: Content Analysis' 110, 'Tough on Crime?', 111, 'Alarm over huge rise in street crime and thefts' *or* own selection of articles	Notes on content Essay on the content of one of the articles *or* A comparison of the two articles
A02v	Explore how a specific news item is treated in tabloid and broadsheet newspapers, focusing on stylistic features	109, 'Tabloid and Broadsheet 2: Stylistic Features' 110, 'Tough on Crime?', 111, 'Alarm over huge rise in street crime and thefts' *or* own selection of articles.	Notes on stylistic features Essay on the stylistic features of one of the articles *or* A comparison of the two articles
A02 **i–v**	Answer comprehension questions on one of the newspaper articles	112, 'Questions on the Articles'	Answers to questions on an article
Various	Students choose one written assignment and one other General Assignment	113, 'General Assignments'	Written assignment Any other assignment

Introduction

This unit helps students to understand the differences between tabloid and broadsheet newspapers and to respond to examinations and coursework tasks based on newspaper articles. Two sample newspaper articles are included, one from the *Daily Mirror* and one from the *Independent*. These make a useful starting point as questions and tasks on the articles have been included in the resources. However, with something as ephemeral as news media, it is important to work with current examples.

Notes on the Resources

107. TABLOID AND BROADSHEET 1: OVERVIEW

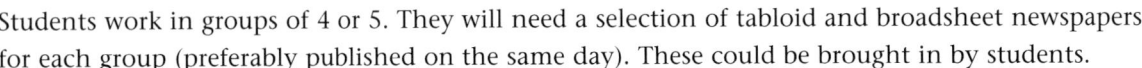

AIM: understand the differences between tabloid and broadsheet newspapers

Students work in groups of 4 or 5. They will need a selection of tabloid and broadsheet newspapers for each group (preferably published on the same day). These could be brought in by students.

Begin by explaining the difference between a tabloid and a broadsheet newspaper: the words 'tabloid' and 'broadsheet' refer to the size of the newspaper. Tabloid is a non-metric size of paper, which is approximately A3 size. Broadsheet is twice the size. However, the difference is more than just one of size: broadsheet newspapers are regarded as being more 'serious'. They contain a higher proportion of text to photographs and articles tend to be longer and more analytical. Examples of broadsheet newspapers are the *Guardian*, *Independent*, *Telegraph* and *The Times*. The language of the tabloids is simpler and is often more sensationalised. Examples of tabloid newspapers are the *Express*, *Mail*, *Mirror*, *Star* and *The Sun*.

Continue by explaining the differences in the front page between a tabloid and a broadsheet style. Nothing gives a stronger indication of editorial policy and target audience than the news story which is chosen for the main headline and the front page. For example, on 12 July 2002, the *Daily Mirror* headline was 'Tough on crime? They'd laugh if it didn't hurt so much'. This introduced an extended report on the government's latest crime statistics. For the same day, the *Independent* headline was 'Another black day for the markets: £45bn off shares'.

List the main news stories

Make a list of the main news stories and the column inches given to each one. This can be done by simply measuring the columns with a ruler. Comparison between lists made from different newspapers will give an idea of their editorial priorities.

What is the editorial about? What is the editorial point of view?

The editorial in the *Independent* (above) covered three topics: the Interbrew case, proposed increases in student fees, and the crash of the HMS *Nottingham*. These are arguably all topics that would interest the middle classes. The increase in crime – which was given a very high profile in the *Mirror* of the same date – was not mentioned in the editorial or on any of the additional two and a half pages of opinion.

How many pages are given to non-news items, e.g. sport, finance, horoscopes?

(List the topics of non-news items)

This can be estimated quickly, or it can be analysed in detail by drawing up a table like the following and measuring the column inches. Where appropriate, notes should be added, e.g. what kind of job advertisements? The type of non-news item included will indicate the readership of the newspaper. For example, business and financial pages are more likely to be found in broadsheet newspapers.

NON-NEWS ITEMS	TABLOID	BROADSHEET
agony column		
business/finance		
horoscopes		
job advertisements		
letters		
opinion		
reviews		
sport		
TV guide		
women's features		
other		

How much space (%) is given to advertising?

An interesting study could be made of the advertisments alone. How much space (as an approximate percentage) is given to advertising. This should be related to the price of the nespaper. Also, the subject matter of the advertisments will reveal much about the readership of the paper. For example, is it a car advertisement for a compact family saloon or an executive car?

108. TABLOID AND BROADSHEET 2: CONTENT ANALYSIS

AIM: be able to make comparisons between the content of articles on the same topic in tabloid and broadsheet newspapers

The resource sheet can be used to compare two articles on the same topic in any tabloid and broadsheet newspaper, or to analyse the content of any newspaper article. These articles can be selected from the newspapers brought in by students (see Resource 107). Alternatively, use Resource 110, 'Tough on crime?' and Resource 111, 'Alarm over huge rise in street crime and thefts'. Note that the resource sheet only provides enough space for short articles. When working on longer articles, students should follow the headings on the sheet, but write on separate pieces of paper.

Main points in article

Underline the main points and then copy them onto the resource sheet or a separate piece of paper. This exercise can be taken a step further by asking students to rewrite the points as a paragraph of continuous prose, making whatever changes are necessary to make the paragraph read well.

Point of view

All newspapers have an editorial point of view in that they take a particular stance on current issues. Sometimes this is associated with a political party: usually it is generally 'left-wing' or 'right-wing' in varying degrees. Newspaper articles are similar. The journalist will express his or her views (which will, of course, be in line with editorial policy). They will argue for one side of an issue even if in the process they explore the arguments on both sides.

Bias

All newspaper articles are biased in the sense that they argue for one side of an issue, but it is heavy bias that the reader needs to be aware of – in other words, the *unfair* presentation of one side of an issue. Watch out for the following:

- emotional arguments
- too many opinions and too few facts or reasoned arguments
- character assassination
- ridicule
- misrepresentation of facts.

Fact and opinion

Students work through an article, underlining facts in one colour and opinion in another. Toolkit Resource 18, 'Fact and Opinion', will help students to do this, and will also help them to identify another important category – reasoned argument. Some of the most telling examples of each should be noted on the resource sheet.

Reader response

Newspaper articles are written to shape opinion. Students should now consider the article as a whole, including stylistic features, and ask themselves what is the likely effect on the reader. What does the author want them to think or to do? How has the author tried to influence the readers' opinions?

Discussion

When the notes on content have been completed, students should compare the content of the two articles by discussing the notes in small groups of 4 or 5.

Writing

GCSE questions are sometimes based on a newspaper article. There are usually one or more questions about the content of the article, and a separate question on the impact of layout features. To prepare for this, students should use their notes as the basis for an essay on the content of one of the articles, or write a comparison of the two.

109. TABLOID AND BROADSHEET 3: STYLISTIC FEATURES

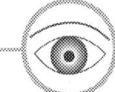

AIM: be able to make comparisons between the stylistic features of articles on the same topic in tabloid and broadsheet newspapers

The resource sheet can be used to compare two articles (articles are called 'stories' in the trade) on the same topic in any tabloid and broadsheet newspaper, or to analyse the stylistic features in any newspaper. Note that GCSE questions often ask students to comment on these features (see current specifications and sample papers for details).

Headline, subheads and bylines

Write the headlines, subheads (or subheadings) and bylines in the appropriate boxes.

Length of article

State the length of the article. Giving the number of words is the most accurate way to do this, but is time consuming. Column inches can be calculated quickly by measuring each column. However, this is less accurate as it does not allow for column width or font size.

Photos and captions

Comment briefly on the subject of each photograph and note down the caption. Estimate the percentage of space taken by photographs.

Other layout features

Look at the design of the whole page and how the different elements are put together to achieve different degrees of emphasis. Note the effect of the following features:

TYPEFACES OR FONTS:

Note that most newspapers use plain serif font for most body copy. Sans serif is sometimes used for contrast. Headline typefaces vary, but are always easy to read. Some key terms relating to typefaces are:

UPPER CASE, lower case, **bold**, *italic*, underlined, `serif`, sans serif, 'ɹǝʌǝɹ'.

LISTS AND TABLES:

In addition to photographs, the following features are often used to present information more clearly or in a more interesting way: lists, bullet points, graphs, tables.

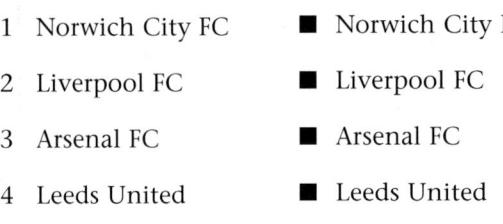

1	Norwich City FC
2	Liverpool FC
3	Arsenal FC
4	Leeds United

■ Norwich City FC
■ Liverpool FC
■ Arsenal FC
■ Leeds United

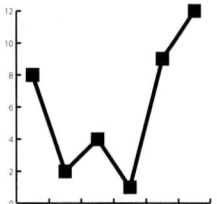

Player	Goals
Owen	9
Cole	6
Smith	8
Henry	3

Words of two or more syllables

This is an indication of the readability level of the text. Generally, the readability level of broadsheet newspapers is higher than that of the tabloids. Work out a percentage by counting the number of words with two or more syllables in the first 100 words. Give some examples.

Emotive and 'journalistic' language

Emotive and journalistic language are used to make an article sound more exciting. Generally, the tabloids use this kind of language more often whereas the style of the broadsheets is lower key and more serious.

Comparison

When the table is complete, ask students to compare the use of stylistic features and write a paragraph in which they describe the differences between tabloid and broadsheet newspapers using the information in the table as an example.

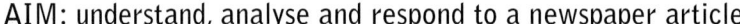

110. 'TOUGH ON CRIME?'

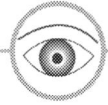 

AIM: understand, analyse and respond to a newspaper article

Front-page headline: 'Tough on crime? They'd laugh if it didn't hurt so much'. No text, but nine colour photographs of victims of crime showing facial injuries. This was followed by a ten-page special report on crime. The sample on Resource 109 is adapted from the first page of text from the special report.

This article can be used with Resources 107, 108 and 109 as a supplement, or an alternative to working on current newspaper articles. It can also be compared with the report on crime statistics in the *Independent* of the same date (see Resource 111).

Finally, the article can be turned into a formal exercise for GCSE coursework or examination practice (check latest specifications) by using the article with Resource 112, 'Questions on the Articles'. This provides questions on the article and a linked directed-writing task.

111. 'ALARM OVER HUGE RISE IN STREET CRIME AND THEFTS'

AIM: understand, analyse and respond to a newspaper article

Front-page headline: 'Another black day for the markets: £45bn off shares'. The article on crime is on page 4 and takes up half a page, reflecting the different priorities of *Independent* readers.

This article can be used with Resources 107, 108 and 109 as a supplement, or an alternative to working on current newspaper articles. It can also be compared with the report on crime in the *Daily Mirror* of the same date (see Resource 110).

Finally, the article can be turned into a formal exercise for GCSE coursework or examination practice (check latest specifications) by using the article with Resource 113, 'Questions on the Articles'. This provides questions on the article and a linked directed-writing task.

112. QUESTIONS ON THE ARTICLES

AIM: understand, analyse and respond to a newspaper article; compare newspaper articles; develop vocabulary

The main questions are similar to those found in the new specification examination papers, i.e. there are usually one or two broad questions rather than several more specific ones. This makes it particularly important that students make full use of any guidance notes given. Students will also find it helpful to have a mental checklist of things to write about. For example:

- the points made in the article
- the balance of fact and opinion
- the types of arguments used
- the use of language, particularly emotional or journalistic language
- the impact of layout features, particularly photos and captions, different typefaces, lists, bullet points, graphs, tables, etc.

The vocabulary and questions on fact and opinion and types of argument can be used to build up students' skills in these areas although they are unlikely to be found in this form on examination papers.

113. GENERAL ASSIGNMENTS

AIM: write in a specified form for a specified audience and purpose

The written tasks are similar to the 'directed writing' type of task found on several examination papers. They are also eminently suitable for coursework. The advantage of linking this kind of task to a text is that students are given a starting point and – depending on the task – a model for writing. Students should choose one written assignment and one other assignment. Foundation-tier students will find Toolkit Resource 17, 'Forms of Writing', helpful for some of the written assignments.

107. TABLOID AND BROADSHEET 1: OVERVIEW

OVERVIEW	TABLOID	BROADSHEET
LIST THE MAIN NEWS STORIES (and the column inches given to each one)		
WHAT IS THE EDITORIAL ABOUT? WHAT IS THE EDITORIAL POINT OF VIEW?		
HOW MANY PAGES ARE GIVEN TO NON-NEWS ITEMS, e.g. SPORT, FINANCE, HOROSCOPES? (List the topics of non-news items)		
HOW MUCH SPACE (%) IS GIVEN TO ADVERTISING? (What kinds of products are advertised?)		

108. TABLOID AND BROADSHEET 2: CONTENT ANALYSIS

CONTENT ANALYIS	TABLOID	BROADSHEET
MAIN POINTS IN ARTICLE		
POINT OF VIEW/BIAS		
FACT AND OPINION		
READER RESPONSE		

109. TABLOID AND BROADSHEET 3: STYLISTIC FEATURES

STYLISTIC FEATURES	TABLOID	BROADSHEET
HEADLINE, SUBHEADS AND BYLINES		
LENGTH OF ARTICLE (in words or column inches)		
PHOTOS AND CAPTIONS (and percentage of space taken)		
OTHER LAYOUT FEATURES (e.g. typefaces, lists, bullet points, graphs, tables)		
WORDS OF THREE OR MORE SYLLABLES (give percentage and some examples)		
EMOTIVE AND 'JOURNALISTIC' LANGUAGE (give examples)		

110. 'TOUGH ON CRIME?'

'I'm concerned at

By BOB ROBERTS
Political Correspondent

ROBBERIES have soared 28 per cent in a year, shock new figures out yesterday showed.

Police chiefs blame drug addicts and school tearaways for much of the alarming increase in street crime.

Home Secretary David Blunkett said: 'I am concerned about the significant rise that we have seen in robbery offences. That is why we have given such high priority to the fight against street crime since March this year. This is now starting to have an impact.'

The figures come months after Tony Blair promised the Commons that street crime will be under control by the end of September.

Opposition politicians said that after five years of Labour and 57 law-and-order initiatives from Mr Blunkett, gangs and hoodlums were in control of the streets.

Overall, recorded crime in England and Wales jumped by seven per cent last year.

Ministers claimed five per cent of the rise was down to a new method of recording which means that more minor offences, including low-level criminal damage and assaults, are now put down as crimes.

The annual figures show that 5.52 million crimes were recorded by police in the 12 months to April 2002 – 356,239 more than the previous year. There were 121,375 robberies.

More than 80 per cent took place in 10 police force areas covering the big cities across England.

All violent crime – murder, assaults, sex offences and wounding – rose by 11 per cent to a total of 812,954 incidents.

Murders were up four per cent, attempted murders 21 per cent, assaults 11 per cent and racially-aggravated assaults 10 per cent.

Drug offences rose seven per cent to more than 121,000.

- ## Violent crime up 11%
- ## Rapes increase by 14%
- ## Robberies rise by 28%

POLICE should use special attack dogs and plastic bullets when threatened by the most dangerous thugs, it was urged yesterday.

The dogs would seize criminals instead of just cornering them and barking.

And the bullets would cut deaths among villains shot by officers in fear of their lives.

The double measure was urged by the Police Complaints Authority, which is investigating four fatal shootings by police last year and three non-fatal ones.

A year ago Merseyside Police shot dead schizophrenic Andrew Kernan for allegedly refusing to drop a large samurai sword.

The force already had attack dogs among its 38 alsatians, but they arrived too late.

PERCENTAGE RISE IN CRIME	
Violent crime rose 11% to more than 812,000 incidents	

Crime	Increase
Murder	4%
Attempted murder	21%
Common assault	11%
Race attacks	10%
Robbery	28%
Sexual offences	11%
Reports of rapes of women	14%
Rapes of men	11%
Aggravated house burglary	14%

110. 'TOUGH ON CRIME?'

continued

rise in robberies . . .'

FRANK Whiteley, spokesman for the Association of Chief Police Officers, said there were four key factors behind the increase in street crime:

• **MORE** crack and heroin addicts on the streets.

• **THE** large numbers of youngsters expelled and playing truant from school.

• **SWITCH** from burglaries and car crime to more profitable crimes.

• **THE** simplicity of stealing and re-selling mobile phones.

Mr Whiteley, Deputy Chief Constable of Northamptonshire, called for more drug rehabilitation work, help to get children back into schools and improvements in mobile phone technology.

Senior Government officials said the real rise in overall crime was only two per cent.

A police source said: 'Under the new rules minor offences are recorded as crimes as soon as someone reports them.

'Previously they would not be recorded until we were satisfied that a crime had been committed.

'We're talking about minor things such as having a wing mirror broken off your car, a drunken brawl or someone putting a brick through a window.'

But Tory home affairs spokesman Oliver Letwin said: 'No amount of statistical manipulation can conceal what everyone in our inner city estates knows – that it is the gangs and the drug dealers rather than the forces of law and order who are in charge.'

Paul Cavadino, head of crime reduction charity Nacro, said the figures must be kept in perspective.

He said: 'Today there is a one in four chance of being a victim of some form of crime, the same as 20 years ago. Levels of crime are stable following a prolonged downward trend.'

AROUND 90 per cent of burglaries, phone and car thefts, shop robberies and muggings are committed by criminals who need money for drugs.

A senior detective with West Midlands force said, unlike people who commit offences because they are drunk, most of these crimes are carried out by people who haven't taken drugs at the time.

He said: 'They are in full control of themselves, they are just carrying out the crime to pay for the drugs they crave.

'There is a subtle difference. Alcohol and violence are inextricably linked.

'People get drunk and fight, they beat up their wives, or smash up a restaurant.'

● **Racial attacks up 10%**

● **House burglary up 7%**

● **5.52M recorded crimes**

TOP 10 ROBBERY HOT SPOTS

82% of robberies take place in just 10 police force areas. The top 10 and the number of robberies in each area last year were:

London's Met	53,547
West Midlands	13,322
Greater Manchester	11,027
West Yorkshire	5,674
Avon and Somerset	4,889
Merseyside	3,155
Thames Valley	2,894
Nottinghamshire	2,726
South Yorkshire	1,952
Lancashire	1,608

HALF of all street robberies take place in just 20 local council inner-city areas.

Birmingham had the highest number last year with 7,915, followed by Lambeth, South London, with 6,465.

But in terms of the number of offences per 1,000 people, Lambeth topped the robbery league table at 23 per cent, compared to Birmingham's 7.8 per cent.

Last year there were 61,735 robberies in the 20 areas out of 121,375 in England and Wales. Fourteen of the areas are in London.

The others are Birmingham, Manchester, Bristol, Leeds, Liverpool and Nottingham.

But Home Office statistics chief Professor Paul Wiles said robbery accounts for just two per cent of all crime.

Daily Mirror, 12 July 2002

111. 'ALARM OVER HUGE RISE IN STREET CRIME AND THEFTS'

CRIME *Figures indicate overall level is stable but increase in muggings . . .*

Alarm over huge rise in street crime and thefts

BY JASON BENNETTO
Crime Correspondent

MUGGINGS AND robberies have risen by 28 per cent in the past year despite overall crime levels staying stable, official figures revealed yesterday.

Two surveys published by the Home Office – one from the police and one of the public – reveal how crime in Britain is changing, with some offences soaring and others falling.

Burglaries have increased for the first time since 1993 but there have been welcome drops in violent and sexual offences.

The total number of crimes recorded by the police has jumped by 7 per cent to 5.52 million, but new methods of counting mean that the real rise is only 2 per cent, according to the Home Office.

The *British Crime Survey*, a separate study of 33,000 members of the public, which is considered more accurate shows that crime fell by 2 per cent in the 12 months to April, to just under 13 million.

The Home Office said the figures showed that the overall rate had stabilised after five years of falling crime. However, the Conservatives accused the Government of 'statistical manipulation'.

While the publication of two sets of conflicting reports is confusing, the overall figures reveal encouraging trends for the Government and police – but also an alarming rise in robberies being committed, largely, by drug addicts and youngsters stealing mobile phones.

Robbery was up 28 per cent to more than 121,000 incidents. This included a 31 per cent rise in robbery of personal property. Some 82 per cent of all robberies took place in just 10 police force areas, although this type of offence still accounts for only 2 per cent of all crime.

The Prime Minister has pledged to bring street crime under control by September after initiating a 'cross-Government' action plan.

The Home Office said that initiatives run by the Metropolitan Police, which has to deal with 44 per cent of the country's robberies, were starting to have an impact on the crime spree. The 2 per cent rise in overall recorded crime is the second increase in the total number of offences in the past seven years. Under the new counting system, crimes such as vandalism and minor assaults, which used to go unrecorded, are now included.

Using the adjusted figures, recorded offences involving violence dropped by about 5 per cent. Murders were up 4 per cent, attempted murders up 21 per cent. The total number of sexual offences declined by about 8 per cent under the adjusted system. This includes, however, a 14 per cent rise in reported rapes of women and an 11 per cent rise in reported rapes of men.

Burglary was up by about 5 per cent. There were also slight rises in vehicle offences. The second report, the *British Crime Survey*, showed that crime was down 22 per cent since 1997 and by 14 per cent in the past two years.

David Blunkett, the Home Secretary, said: 'The statistics indicate the overall crime levels were stable last year. The crimes that affect most people, burglary and vehicle crime, remain at the lower levels seen after the significant reductions in recent years.

'While most crime continues to fall or remain at lower levels, I am concerned about the significant rise that we have seen in robbery offences.'

Oliver Letwin, the shadow Home Secretary, said: 'No amount of statistical manipulation can conceal what everyone on the estates in our inner cities already knows – that it is the gangs and the drug dealers rather than the forces of law and order that are in charge.'

Simon Hughes, the Liberal Democrat home affairs spokesman, said: 'Levels of crime may be stable but they are still far too high. Only sensible, long-term policies will bring further reductions.'

CRIME LEAGUE TABLE

	No. of robberies recorded	Offences per 1,000 pop.
Birmingham	7,915	7.8
Lambeth	6,465	23.4
Manchester	4,751	10.8
Bristol	4,074	10.0
Leeds	3,307	4.6
Southwark	3,086	12.9
Hackney	3,009	14.8
Westminster	2,763	11.3
Haringey	2,626	11.7
Camden	2,439	12.0
Newham	2,400	10.0
Brent	2,359	9.3
Ealing	2,264	7.3
Waltham Forest	2,154	9.8
Tower Hamlets	2,117	11.3
Croydon	2,095	6.2
Liverpool	2,013	4.4
Nottingham	1,984	7.0
Lewisham	1,966	8.0
Wandsworth	1,948	7.2

111. 'ALARM OVER HUGE RISE IN STREET CRIME AND THEFTS'

continued

> *… threatens Prime Minister's pledge to curb menace of street attacks*

The figures only show a state of confusion

ON A FIRST reading of the Home Office's latest crime figures, it would appear that the old adage of lies, damn lies and statistics is alive and kicking.

Police recorded a rise in reported crime of 7 per cent, but the Home Office's chief statistician says it is actually 2 per cent. Meanwhile, a separate survey of 33,000 householders has found that while the police recorded 5.5 million crimes, there were actually twice as many committed in England and Wales.

Professors Paul Wiles, the director of the Home Office's research, development and statistics department, conceded yesterday that we have no idea how many crimes are committed.

Today sees the first publication of both the police's recorded crime figures and the *British Crime Survey*.

The way police compile their figures is changing. In future a wider variety of offences will be recorded. Most notably, low-level crimes such as drunken brawls and vandalism are to be included in the official statistics. Nine police forces are already using the new National Crime Recording Standard. The effect of the changes for the year up to April 2002 is that about 250,000 crimes that would not have been previously recorded now appear in the statistics, accounting for a 5 per cent rise in crime, according to the Home Office experts. When all 43 forces adopt the system, recorded offences could rise by 20 per cent. But Professor Wiles stresses: 'It does not mean there is an increase in crime, it means the police are recording more of the crime.'

These anomalies are seen most starkly with violent crime. The new figures show that these offences rose by 11 per cent to 812,000 incidents. But when the extra cases are stripped out, this becomes a 5 per cent drop.

Even when these changes are taken into account, however, a worrying trend is a small rise in burglaries and car crime, which could herald a new spree of lawlessness.

The *British Crime Survey*, covering 33,000 adults, is considered more accurate than the police figures because it includes crimes that are not reported to the authorities. (Many people will not go to the police because they believe nothing can be done, do not intend to make an insurance claim or have something to hide).

The survey estimates that in 2002–02 there were 991,000 break-ins in England and Wales, but only 60 per cent, about 600,000, were reported.

The survey has big gaps – it does not include offences by under-16s, commercial crimes or sexual offences – but it provides a more accurate insight into crime trends. It shows that while crime rose steadily from 1981 to 1995, since then it has fallen by 22 per cent and has been stable in the past year.

JASON BENNETTO
The Independent, 12 July 2002

112. QUESTIONS ON THE ARTICLES

'Tough on crime?' (pp. 193, 194)

Give the meaning of the following words and phrases as they are used in the article:

◆ *law-and-order initiatives* (col. 1, para. 5)

◆ *low-level criminal damage* (col. 1, para. 7)

◆ *racially aggravated assaults* (col. 1, para. 11)

◆ *rehabilitation* (p. 194, col. 1, para. 2)

◆ *statistical manipulation* (col. 1, para. 7)

◆ *the figures must be kept in perspective* (col. 1, para. 8).

How does Bob Roberts express concern about the rise in crime? In your answer, you should write about:

◆ the content of the article

◆ use of language

◆ the way the page is laid out, especially the use of photographs, charts, lists, text boxes, typefaces, etc.

Analyse the balance of fact, opinion and reasoned argument in the article (use Toolkit Resource 18, 'Fact and Opinion', to help you).

Analyse the arguments presented in the article (use Toolkit Resource 10, 'Types of Argument', to help you).

'Alarm over huge rise in street crime and thefts' (pp. 195, 196)

Give the meaning of the following words and phrases as they are used in the article:

◆ *the overall rate had stabilised* (col. 1, para. 6)

◆ *the old adage of lies, damn lies and statistics is alive and kicking* (p. 196, col. 1, para. 1)

◆ *conceded* (col. 1, para. 3)

◆ *anomalies* (col. 2, para. 2).

How does Jason Bennetto try to explain a confusing set of crime figures? In your answer, you should consider

◆ his use of language

◆ the two parts of his article

◆ the use of different typefaces to create different emphases

◆ the photograph and the table.

Analyse the balance of fact, opinion and the arguments presented in the article.

Compare 'Tough on crime?' and 'Alarm over huge rise in street crime and thefts'. In your answer, you should discuss:

◆ fact, opinion and reasoned argument

◆ emotional impact

◆ balance

◆ the way the articles are laid out.

113. GENERAL ASSIGNMENTS

Speaking and listening

Discuss and or debate the following, using information from the articles as part of your argument.

◆ Capital punishment should be reintroduced as a deterrent.

◆ New York-style zero-tolerance policing should be introduced in the UK.

◆ Prisons should emphasise reform and rehabilitation – not punishment.

◆ We need more police on the beat.

◆ The general public should be allowed to carry weapons, as in the US.

Reading

Read a range of current local and national newspapers and make a collection of clippings about crime. Use the information as part of your evidence base for discussion, debate and writing.

Writing

Foundation tier

Extract the key information from the articles and use it to design a poster on crime.

Write about crime in your own area. You may refer to your own experiences, those of friends and relatives and any information from local newspapers. Using the articles and your own knowledge and imagination, write a series of diary entries by a young person living in a crime-ridden inner city estate.

Higher tier

Write a letter to your MP in which you express your concern about the level of crime and suggest some solutions. You can refer to the information in the articles as well as to your own experiences.

Write a two-part essay about the 2002 crime statistics. In the first part you should present the facts only; in the second part you should express your opinion.

Write a letter to the editor of the *Independent* asking why such an important report received such a small amount of coverage on page 4 of the newspaper.

The wider curriculum

In a geography lesson, explore the regional characteristics of crime. In a history lesson, explore changing patterns of crime throughout the centuries.

Spiritual, moral, ethical, social and cultural issues

How would a religious approach to crime differ from the way we approach crime today? Consider, for example, the teachings of Christianity and Islam.

Some communities are relatively crime-free and some countries have higher rates of crime than others. What are the social and cultural featuress that cause these differences?

European dimension

Recently, following an appeal to the European Court of Human Rights, it was ruled that prisoners cannot be made to serve extra time as a punishment. What are the implications of this judgment for the prison service? Do you think it is right that a remote committee of bureaucrats can make a decision affecting people they do not know?